THE
HEART OF
EVANGELISM

THE HEART OF EVANGELISM

JERRAM BARRS

:: CROSSWAY WHEATON, ILLINOIS

Library of Congress Cataloging-in-Publication Data
Barrs, Jerram.
 The heart of evangelism / Jerram Barrs.
  p. cm.
 ISBN 13: 978-1-58134-715-9 (trade pbk. : alk. paper)
 ISBN 10: 1-58134-715-4
 1. Evangelistic work—Biblical teaching. 2. Bible. N.T.—Criticism, interpretation, etc. I. Title.
BS2545.E82 B37 2001
269'.2—dc21
          2001002975

CH		19	18	17	16	15	14	13	12	11	10
18	17	16	15	14	13	12	11	10	9	8	7	6

To my wife, Vicki,
whom I adore and who has been my companion,
friend, lover, wife, mother to our sons,
partner in the Gospel, and my joint heir
of the grace of life for more than thirty years.

And to the Lord,
King of earth and heaven,
who is not ashamed to call me "friend."

I dedicate this book to you two,
the seal upon my heart and the sealer of my heart,
that it might be pleasing to you, not because of my worth,
nor because of the worth of this book,
but because you love me.

CONTENTS

INTRODUCTION

This book is the fruit of more than thirty years of reflection on what the New Testament teaches us about evangelism; and it is the fruit of more than thirty years of desiring to practice in some poor way what I have learned from that study. One of the concerns that has spurred me on has been my observation that many Christians are afraid of sermons and seminars on the topic of evangelism. They are afraid because so often they have been made to feel guilty and inadequate about their involvement in making the Gospel known. All too frequently this has not been a Spirit-induced sense of guilt and inadequacy that has led consequently to a deeper trust in God, to a growing gratitude for His love, or to transformation in the patterns of one's life. Rather this has been a humanly induced sense of guilt and inadequacy that has been paralyzing and that has driven an even deeper wedge between Christians and unbelievers. I long to see believers set free from this feeling of frustration and failure. In place of this I pray that the Lord will help believers realize that evangelism should be an encouraging and even exciting subject to think about and to put into practice.

What I have sought to do in this book is to examine once again what Jesus and His apostles teach us about evangelism, and also to look at the way they practiced evangelism so that we might learn both from their instruction and from their example. The hope inspiring all my teaching and writing on this subject is that we might recover the New Testament pattern of evangelism.

The first section of the book is a study of two of the occasions on which Jesus gave the Great Commission to His disciples. We also look at the Day of Pentecost when the Holy Spirit was poured out on the church to empower her for her task of witness to Christ. We will reflect on the different horizons for mission that Christ gave His apostles and consider how we might apply those horizons to our own context today. We will turn from this to see how the command of Jesus to go out into the unbelieving world with the truth about Him is a command for the whole church all through its history, a command for each particular congregation, and a command for every individual believer. The latter part of Section One asks what this commission will mean for our prayers and for our daily lives at home, in the workplace, and out in the wider society.

Section Two turns from our responsibility to reach out with the truth to think instead about the work of God as He draws people to faith in Christ. God is the Great Evangelist! He is the One who saves, and He is the One who calls us to serve Him in His work of bringing men, women, and children to faith in His Son. We often forget this aspect of evangelism, mistakenly thinking that it is all up to us. Such a feeling can breed inadequacy, hopelessness, and even despair about the task of evangelism—that is, if we are honest about our weaknesses, failings, and poor efforts. Or it can breed arrogance if we foolishly believe that we are good evangelists!

In contrast to ourselves, we will see how patient and gracious God is. He labors, often for many years, to woo people and to win them to begin to love Jesus. In these chapters we will consider some of the infinite variety of means that God uses to touch people and to kindle the flame of faith in their hearts. In reflecting on these means we will study a number of biblical stories and some contemporary ones that teach us about the saving work of God in the lives of individuals.

In Section Three we will examine some of the barriers that stand in the way of Christians being faithful to the calling to make the Gospel known. We will look first at the barriers within ourselves—fear, anxiety, guilt, and overcommitment, and especially at the problem of the internal Pharisee we all carry inside us. Second, we will look at barriers between the church and the world:

- The loss of conviction about the truth of the Gospel.
- The unhappy consequences of the sacred/secular division.
- The failure to use language that is understood by non-Christians.
- The wall we erect between "us" (the Christians) and "them" (the unbelievers).

We will study this last problem in some detail, for I am convinced that it is often the primary reason why so many of us and so many of our churches are uninterested and ineffective in evangelism. An "us versus them" mentality can produce fear of the world, a condemning, even hateful attitude toward "sinners," a desire to retreat into the safe haven of our Christian institutions, and an insistence on personal separation from "sinners." If we do not know non-Christians in any personal depth, it is evident that the only evangelism that can take place is technique-based raids from behind the wall of the church into the "enemy-occupied territory" of the world.

This is certainly not the kind of evangelism we read about in the New Testament. Consider the life and ministry of Jesus! But it is frequently what has replaced the pattern of evangelism that we find in the pages of the Gospels and the book of Acts. If I have a passion, it is that we Christians will learn to see the "glory and honor" (Psalm 8:5) of the unbelieving men and women around us and will delight in getting to know them and building friendships with them. As a seminary professor this is my prayer and longing for each of my students—that as they go out into ministry, they will be excited about committing themselves to a lifelong intention to be persons who, like Jesus, are welcomed gladly by the "sinners" around them.

From this barrier of "us versus them" we will turn to sketch briefly the barriers between the world and the church. Or to put it another way, to identify some of the characteristics of our postmodern culture that make communicating the Gospel a particular challenge today.

In Section Four, the final section of the book, we will look in detail at seven principles of communication that characterize the evangelistic ministry of the apostle Paul. These are respect, building bridges, understanding those to whom we go, using the right language, reasoned persuasion, clarifying the truth, and challenging the heart and mind.

These seven principles are drawn from a careful study of the messages given by Paul in three different settings, set down for us by Luke in the book of Acts. One of these messages is presented to Jews and God-fearing Gentiles in a synagogue, one to uneducated pagans in Lystra, and one to educated pagans gathered on Mars Hill in Athens. We will see how these principles govern Paul's practice of evangelism, and we will then apply them to our own differing situations today. Our study of the pattern of Paul is supplemented by reflection on several examples of evangelism in the ministry of Jesus.

Each of these principles arises from Paul's commitment to be "all things to all men so that by all possible means I might save some" (1 Corinthians 9:22). Paul respected those he met—Jews and Gentiles, men and women, God-fearers and pagans, slaves and those who were free— for he saw that behind all their problems, all their unbelief, and all their sin they were persons made in the image of God. Paul built bridges, for he knew he would always find traces of the image of God that he could affirm in people's lives, as well as elements of God's truth that he could commend in the thinking of those he met. Paul could do this, for he believed that all people are constrained by God's revelation of Himself in their own inner being and in the world in which they are set. Paul committed himself to understanding those to whom he desired to proclaim the Gospel, for he knew that only by understanding them could he, like Jesus, be able to communicate the truth to them in ways that would touch their hearts and minds. Paul worked hard at using the language of his hearers, rather than always using the language of his own biblical heritage, because he was eager for those listening to grasp the meaning of his message in words familiar to them.

Paul sought to persuade them of the truth of the Christian faith because he knew that it was true and that the whole world was full of testimony to that truth. He was eager to clarify the particular aspects of the truth that those he met needed to hear. Paul desired them to come to a right understanding of the nature of God, of themselves, of the world in which they lived, and of the saving work of God to deliver them from the coming judgment. Paul labored hard to challenge his hearers at those very points where their hearts were captive to the worship of idols and other gods and at those places where their minds were subject to false thinking about the human condition. Paul knew that everyone he met needed to turn from these things to the living God and to His Son Jesus, that they might be saved. In the same way, we have to challenge our contemporaries at the very points where they are bound by idolatry and by the faulty thinking of our culture.

It is my prayer that this book will be used by the Lord to kindle in you a desire to learn from this reflection on New Testament evangelism. I pray that you will be eager to shape your life according to the pattern of Paul, that God might be pleased to save some through you.

MISSION TO
THE WORLD

1

SENT TO ALL NATIONS

In the four Gospels and in the first chapter of Acts we have the privilege of listening in to Jesus' conversations with various people. We are in effect eavesdropping on God! The last three of these conversations that are recorded for us in the New Testament have to do with Jesus' task for His disciples after His return to reign at the Father's side. Christians often refer to this task assigned by Jesus to His disciples as the Great Commission. It was given in the days before our Savior's ascension into heaven, several weeks after the Resurrection.

Despite ongoing doubts among His disciples, being hard-hearted and slow to believe, just as you and I are, most of them were now thoroughly persuaded that Jesus was indeed risen from the dead, and so their faith that He was the Christ, the true Son of God, was firmly established. Now they were ready to get their marching orders, ready to hear from His lips what work it was that He wanted them to do. He gave this Great Commission on several occasions and in various forms so they would have no uncertainty about their calling.

We will look first at the account we find at the end of Matthew's Gospel (28:18-20). Jesus appeared to His disciples on a mountain in Galilee. They were back on home ground since so many of them came from the region around Lake Galilee. He gave them a command, and along with His command He added some words of encouragement.

> "All authority in heaven and earth has been given to me.
> Therefore go and make disciples of all nations, baptizing them
> in the name of the Father and of the Son and of the Holy Spirit,

*and teaching them to obey everything I have commanded you.
And surely I will be with you always, to the very end of the age."*

GO AND MAKE DISCIPLES!

He commanded them to "go and make disciples of all nations." We are so familiar with these words that we don't stop to think how challenging they must have been to those who heard them from Jesus' lips. This little group of eleven ordinary people were to go to all the nations of the earth and turn their hearers into disciples of Jesus like themselves! They were having a hard time believing in Him even though they had been with Him for three years and had lived through all the extraordinary events of His ministry and, in particular, of these past few weeks with His death and resurrection. Yet this little group who were so slow to believe were to convert the nations of the earth!

Most of them had probably not traveled beyond their own little patch of the world, the small kingdoms and provinces along either bank of the Jordan River and across Israel to the Mediterranean Sea. They would have heard from travelers about other parts of the vast Roman Empire that stretched right across north Africa, way up into northern and western Europe, up into Asia Minor (present-day Turkey and Armenia), and over eastward to the borders of Persia (present-day Iran). But they would have no personal knowledge of these faraway places or of the unknown countries and nations beyond these that they perhaps had heard described.

Yet these ignorant, unschooled men—these eleven—were to go and teach the nations to obey everything Jesus had taught them, and to baptize many in these nations into their newfound faith as they became followers of Jesus. Think of the challenge this commission still is to us today, and we take it for granted that we are part of a worldwide church numbering untold millions of followers of Jesus. Then try and imagine how the apostles must have felt!

THE AUTHORITY OF CHRIST

But Jesus also gave them some comforting words (they needed them!). He told them, "All authority in heaven and on earth has been given to me." He rules the unseen world of the spirits. He triumphs over the demons. He defeats the false gods of the nations and breaks their power so that His disciples are able to go out into the world with confidence. They will know, as they proclaim the Gospel, that Jesus has the name that is above every name in the heavens, above every power of darkness, above every spiritual force of wickedness. These men already knew that in the Roman Empire and beyond, people worshiped many different gods. They were being sent out into a pagan world where most of the people they would try to reach would be under the influence of spirits and false gods. They had experienced firsthand the power of the hosts of Satan as those enemies tested them and sought the death of Jesus. But Jesus assured them that just as He had conquered Satan by His death on the cross and made that adversary's plans of no effect, so he would rule the heavenly powers for them as they went into the pagan world.

RULER OF THE NATIONS

Jesus also encouraged them by saying that all power has been granted to Him over this earth. Jesus would rule the nations for their sake as they traveled to them. He would open doors around the world to places that seemed inaccessible. He is the Lord above every lord, the King above every king. Even Caesar, the emperor of an area so vast it was unimaginable to them, would be subject to Jesus. This was the first of His comforting words to the disciples as He gave them their "impossible" calling.

It is the same for us. All the powers of the nations, all the unseen powers of darkness, are in subjugation to Christ. There is indeed only one superpower today, and it is not the United States or its President. It is the Lord Jesus Christ. He rules the nations for the sake of His church, for the sake of the Gospel going out to those nations.

THE PRESENCE OF JESUS

Jesus had some additional encouraging words for them. The first were about power. The second were personal. Jesus promised that He Himself would be with them. Wherever they would go, however hard the road, however challenging the situation, however unwelcoming the people, whatever their feeling of weakness, He would be beside them providing comfort, encouragement, and strength, just as He had been for the past three years of their lives. They would never again be alone. This is His promise to us too, to accompany us always along whatever path into the world He calls us to travel.

2

THE POWER OF THE SPIRIT

Our second example of the Great Commission Jesus gave His disciples is found in Acts 1 and was spoken to them immediately before the Ascension. He had previously urged them to wait in Jerusalem until the Holy Spirit came to baptize them with His presence. The Spirit was the gift that His Father had promised Him for His disciples. On the night before He died, and on many earlier occasions, Jesus had spoken about this gift of the Spirit that they would receive. Now, He said, that gift would soon be coming, a gift they would receive on the Day of Pentecost, but that we today receive when we first come to faith in Jesus Christ (see Romans 8:9; 1 Corinthians 12:12-13; Ephesians 1:13-14).

The disciples were still waiting for this gift when they saw Jesus for the last time. They asked Him one final question: "Lord, are you at this time going to restore the kingdom to Israel?" (Acts 1:6). They were not thinking about the task Jesus had set before them on several occasions. They did not at this moment want to remember His words to them that they must preach the Gospel to all the nations before the end would come.

They wanted to know *when* the kingdom would come, and they wanted it to come *now*. They wanted to hear about His plans to drive the Romans out of the Promised Land and begin His victorious reign as Messiah. They recalled clearly enough that He would rule the nations, and they wanted Him to start right away and set them on thrones ruling beside Him. He had power over all things; He could surely exercise it for Himself, for them, and for His people Israel! But Jesus replied to them in a very different way than they expected.

UNAVAILABLE KNOWLEDGE

They would not be told when the kingdom will come, when Israel will be restored, when the Second Coming in glory will be. This knowledge was not available to the apostles, nor is it available to us! They undoubtedly were speculating among themselves about just when Jesus Christ would use His power to reign over the nations. Christians love to speculate about the end of the age and make predictions and plans for it, just as many have been doing in our time in the transition from the second to the third millennium A.D. Jesus has said that it is not ours to know; indeed He said that it is not His to know either (Matthew 24:36). Not even Jesus, the Son of God, knows when He will come! We may pray for His coming. We should long for it. But we cannot know when it will be.

AVAILABLE POWER

"If you want power," Jesus said to them in effect, "you will have it. When the Spirit is given to you, power will be yours. But it will not be power to restore Israel and to destroy the enemies of the kingdom. It will not even be the knowledge of when these things will take place. It will be power to witness about Me and the truth of the message I have given you to spread around the world." The church has power today. You and I have power today. But this power is very different than the power we may desire. We want power to see the kingdom coming, power for the healing of our loved ones, power for getting our way personally, or power for having a "Christian nation once again," power for America in the world.

We all have our own agendas for Jesus, just as the apostles had one for Him. He, however, has an agenda for us. His agenda is power for us to be living, speaking testimonies for Him to an unbelieving world, power to love our enemies, power to bless those who curse us, power to forgive as He forgives us, power to love one another. This is the coming of the kingdom that He has in mind for us now. The other kind of power will come later; but this is the power He exercised in His death on the cross, and it is the power He gives us. There is no other power for the church or for the Christian now.

The disciples would be given this power of the Spirit to witness to the world. What did this mean for them, and what does it mean for us?

On an earlier occasion Jesus had promised that the Spirit would be a witness to Him.

> *"When the Counselor comes, whom I will send to you from the Father, the Spirit of truth who goes out from the Father, he will testify about me; but you also must testify, for you have been with me from the beginning."*
>
> —JOHN 15:26-27

As the apostles went out into the world, they could have the confidence that whenever they talked about Christ, the Spirit would be witnessing to Christ along with their testimony. The same is true for us. We are never alone when we seek to communicate the truth about Jesus.

Later on that evening, during those final hours before His betrayal, Jesus told His disciples more about the work that the Spirit would do. His task would be to work in the hearts of men and women, convicting them of guilt and of righteousness and of judgment (John 16:8ff.). We sometimes think it is our responsibility to convict people of sin, our task to make them feel their guilt. But Jesus teaches us that this is the Spirit's work, that He is able to touch the hearts of unbelievers (and of believers, too, of course) in a way that we never can.

We have confidence, then, that the Spirit is witnessing to the hearts and minds of people alongside us. (Perhaps it would be more appropriate to say that we are witnessing alongside the Spirit as He works within unbelievers' minds and hearts. He calls us to help Him, rather than us calling Him to help us!) Does He assist us in our task of evangelism in other ways too? Does He give us power to be Christ's witnesses?

Jesus promised that the Spirit will aid our memories, so that we are able to recall the words of Scripture that we have heard and read (John 14:26). He will also guide us into the truth and enable us to speak the truth (John 16:13), for the Scripture promises us that if we lack wisdom, we can ask for it and God will give it to us generously and without finding fault with us (James 1:5). In addition, Jesus told His disciples there would be occasions when they would be called before kings and governors or would be arrested and put on trial for their faith. He encouraged them not to worry ahead of time about what they should say, for the Holy Spirit would give them the words to speak (Mark 13:9-11).

Though Jesus was speaking to His disciples about arrest and trial as consequences of persecution, there is a wider application of His promise. Whenever we are called to bear witness to Jesus we are on trial for our faith, our faith in Christ is on trial, and Christ Himself is on trial; so we can ask for the Spirit's help with the expectation that it is His delight to answer such prayers.

As well as helping us know what to say, the Spirit will also help us to speak clearly and graciously if we ask Him. The apostle Paul asked for prayer that God would help him speak clearly (Colossians 4:4), and we may make the same prayer. In addition Paul asked people to pray that he would be given courage (Ephesians 6:19-20). All of us also need courage, and we may be assured that the Spirit will be pleased to help us. He, the Spirit, is our counselor, our guide, the One called alongside us to help us in our every need. So we may go to Him asking for His assistance in every possible way whenever we want to share the truth of the Gospel.

There is one further way in which the Lord helps us, and that is by opening doors for us to share the Gospel (Colossians 4:3). We follow One who rules the nations, but He also rules over our own personal lives and over the events that take place from day to day. Even the hairs of our heads are numbered by Him; every detail, no matter how insignificant, is within His fatherly care. So we can ask that He will provide opportunities for us to share what we have come to believe. As He goes before us and prepares our way, He calls us to follow His lead and make the most of the opportunities and the open doors that He gives us (Colossians 4:3-6).

What more do we need? Christ is ruling the nations for us (consider the present possibilities for proclaiming the Gospel in what was the Communist bloc). The Father is watching over our lives personally, providing opportunities and open doors. The Spirit is working both in us and in those to whom we are called. With such promises of help, why do we all find evangelism burdensome, difficult, or sometimes even impossible? We will try to answer this question in a later chapter, but for now we return to the Great Commission as it is found in Acts 1.

3

HORIZONS FOR OUR MISSION

THE FINAL COMMISSION (ACTS 1:6-11)

On previous occasions when Jesus commissioned His disciples He had promised help and power for the task of witness, in addition to sending them to the nations. On this final reminder of their calling, Jesus reaffirmed to His disciples the worldwide extent of the Commission. Just before His ascension, He spelled out for them several horizons for the unfolding of their missionary endeavors:

- Jerusalem.
- Judea.
- Samaria.
- The ends of the earth.

As we read the book of Acts we can see that Luke shows how the mission to these four horizons began to be fulfilled in the years following Pentecost. (See, for example, Acts 2:5; 6:7; 8:2-5; 11:19-21; 28:30-31.) Because the Great Commission is for the whole church of Christ and not just for the apostles, it is an appropriate application to conclude that the church in every age is called to a similar range of horizons. However, as we will see a bit later, we may express this calling as five horizons of mission rather than four. These horizons provide a challenge and a measuring stick for the faithfulness of each of our churches to Jesus' commission.

OUR JERUSALEM

Our Jerusalem, we may say in application, is the city in which we live, work, study, and raise our families, whether it is small or great. Jerusalem, for me personally and for the church in which I serve, is St. Louis City and County. What is your Jerusalem? What are you doing and what is your church doing to draw people from your locality to Jesus?

OUR JUDEA

Our Judea, we may say, is the country to which we belong, whether by birth, adoption, or immigration. For me, though I am British by birth, my Judea is the United States, for this is now my home. Are we planting churches and sending out missionaries into every part of this nation (for example, into the schools, the colleges, the military, the business world, the prisons, as well as into our cities, suburbs, and rural communities)?

OUR SAMARIA

Our Samaria is those people among us and alongside us who are different from us. Samaria was right next to Judea, and its people, despite their historical ties to the Jews, were racially, culturally, and religiously so different that there was deep hostility between the two. We need to ask ourselves, "What is our Samaria?" Are we reaching across the racial, cultural, and religious barriers that exist in our society with the Gospel of Jesus Christ made known in our lives and in our words of reconciliation? What barriers are you reaching across with the love of Christ? What is your church doing to build bridges to its Samaria?

THE ENDS OF THE EARTH

Whom are we sending to the nations of the earth, especially to those places and peoples where there are no believers or very few? In Isaiah 49:5-7 we find one of the most beautiful statements found in any part of Scripture.

> And now the Lord says . . .
> "It is too small a thing for you to be my servant
> to restore the tribes of Jacob

and bring back those of Israel I have kept.
I will also make you a light for the Gentiles,
that you may bring my salvation to the ends of the earth."

God tells His Son, the Messiah, that it was too small a thing for Him, the Lord and Father, to send His Servant, Christ, into the world just to reach His people Israel and to redeem them. Rather than saving just one people, He desired His salvation to reach to the ends of the earth. In the same way, it should be "too small" for us just to reach out to our own people, for God calls us to have a worldwide concern. What is your part and what is your church's part in taking the Gospel to the nations?

THE FIFTH HORIZON

I would like to also mention a fifth horizon—the original, literal "Jerusalem, and . . . Judea." God has not forgotten the people of Israel, and neither should any Christian believer. The Jewish people are God's olive tree into which we are grafted if we are Gentiles. Paul writes of the people of Israel:

Theirs is the adoption as sons; theirs the divine glory, the covenants, the receiving of the law, the temple worship and the promises. Theirs are the patriarchs, and from them is traced the human ancestry of Christ, who is God over all, forever praised!
—ROMANS 9:4-5

We should love the Jewish people for the sake of their heritage, which we have been privileged to receive through Jesus Christ. We should pray for them and long to see them come to know their Messiah. The apostle Paul expressed this same calling in other words. He said in the first chapter of his letter to the Christians in Rome (1:16):

I am not ashamed of the gospel, because it is the power of God for the salvation of everyone who believes: first for the Jew, then for the Gentile.

There is indeed a priority for the Jews as a nation in God's work in history, and so in a sense the Gospel is always for the Jew "first," for the Jews were the people whom God chose to be His vehicle of blessing to the whole world. Initially, from the time of Abraham, through their obedience in living and making known to the nations the truth God entrusted to them; then, after more than 2,000 years, by their being the people through whom the Messiah, Jesus, was born into this world for the saving of all peoples.

In addition to recognizing this special place in God's plan for the world, the apostle Paul also had a deep passion to communicate to his fellow Israelites because they were his own people. He wrote that he could wish himself accursed for their sake:

> *I speak the truth in Christ—I am not lying, my conscience confirms it in the Holy Spirit—I have great sorrow and unceasing anguish in my heart. For I could wish that I myself were cursed and cut off from Christ for the sake of my brothers, those of my own race, the people of Israel.*
> —ROMANS 9:1-4

Moses expressed his love for his people in this same way after they had created the golden calf and then fell down in worship before it:

> *"Oh, what a great sin these people have committed! They have made themselves gods of gold. But now, please forgive their sin—but if not, then blot me out of the book you have written."*
> —EXODUS 32:31-32

Moses and Paul were ready to be forsaken by God for the sake of their people. They, of course, were not good enough or powerful enough to do this for the people they loved so deeply. But Christ *was* good enough and powerful enough to be accursed for them and for us. He not only declared that His love was even greater than the love of Moses or Paul—He died to demonstrate the reality of this great love. Indeed, He died to become a curse for us, to bear the fair justice of His Father that sentences us to eternal separation from God. The contemporary English hymn writer Graham Kendrick has captured this love of Christ for us in a song:

Such love, pure as the whitest snow,
Such love weeps for the shame I know,
Such love paying the debt I owe,
O Jesus such love!

Such love springs from eternity,
Such love streaming through history,
Such love fountain of life to me,
O Jesus such love!

We cannot take upon ourselves the sins of others or bear their sin's curse and the judgment it brings upon them. But our heart attitude can be the same as that of Moses and Paul, and of the Lord whose self-sacrificing love they imitated. We are to love those who are our own people to such a degree that we would wish ourselves cut off from our Father's fellowship if it would save them from His just judgment. Those believers who have family members or others they care for deeply will understand this depth of feeling very well. How we long to see those we treasure come to know the Lord!

Whether we are black, white, Hispanic, Asian, or Native American, whatever our national and ethnic background, we should have "such love" as we long to make God's truth known to our brothers and sisters. In addition, we are called to love and reach out to the Jews and to all other peoples across the world.

This brief reflection on the love that Paul, Moses, and, above all, Jesus had for people reminds us that the primary motivation for outreach is love. First, it is to be love for the Lord who loved us with "such love." Only His love for us will change our cold hearts and enable us to be willing to obey His command to reach our Jerusalem, Judea, Samaria, and all nations (including Israel) with the Gospel. Second, it is to be love for those around us in family, neighborhood, community, city, nation, and the world, whether they are like us or whether they are different from us. Again, it is only His love, poured into our hearts by the Spirit He gives us, that will empower us with the first fruits of "such love."

4

How Clear Was Jesus?

We have been considering the horizons Jesus gave for the missionary outreach of the disciples, and also the help He promised to give them, both through the Spirit and through His rule over the nations and over their personal lives. So far we have seen that Jesus' command is universal in its scope. Was Jesus really so clear about this? Or are we perhaps reading too much back into the Great Commission? Did the disciples understand what we have assumed the texts to mean?

It was the Eleven, the apostles, who first heard Jesus charge them with the Great Commission. This was Jesus' last command to them; so they were left in no doubt that this going "to all the world" with the Gospel was the passion of His heart for their years of ministry. He laid out a plan for them, beginning at home in Jerusalem, then going out to Judea, Samaria, and the nations. This was a plan that, if they understood its scope, would clearly take more than their lifetime to fulfill.

APOSTOLIC TESTIMONY

It is evident from their writing that they did understand the long-term nature of this commission. Consider, for example, the words of Paul in Romans 15:16, 20-21. (Paul was given this same worldwide task by Jesus when he was confronted, converted, and called to be an apostle on the Damascus Road—Acts 26:12-18.)

> [I was called] to be a minister of Christ Jesus to the Gentiles
> with the priestly duty of proclaiming the gospel of God, so that

the Gentiles might become an offering acceptable to God. . . .
It has always been my ambition to preach the gospel where
Christ was not known, so that I would not be building on some-
one else's foundation. Rather, as it is written: "Those who were
not told about him will see, and those who have not heard will
understand."

From this example of Paul's sense of calling, it is apparent that the apostles clearly understood that Christ was sending them into the whole world with the Gospel. He desired them to go to those who had never heard the good news about His salvation so that they too might believe in Him and enter the kingdom.

THE DEMONSTRATION OF PENTECOST

On the Day of Pentecost the apostles and the small group of believers with them were given a dramatic illustration by Jesus of what He had planned for them, and in this way His spoken command was underlined, so to speak, by a historical event. The Feast of Pentecost (the fiftieth day after the Sabbath of Passover week) was also called the Feast of Weeks, the Feast of Harvest, and the Day of Firstfruits (Exodus 23:16: Leviticus 23:15-16; Numbers 28:26; Deuteronomy 16:10).

The Father sent the Spirit onto the disciples, just as Jesus had promised, His presence manifested in wind, fire, and tongues. Wind represents the creative power of the Spirit who can give life where there is not yet life (as in Genesis 1 at Creation), or even where there is death (as in the Valley of Dry Bones of Ezekiel 37). Fire represents the holiness of the Spirit, who will burn away the dross of sin and uncleanness in a new believer's heart and bring purity and righteousness in their place. The gift of tongues represents the diversity of languages in the human race and the Spirit's intent to reach all nations.

Jesus demonstrated His promised rule over the nations and over His people's lives in the events of Pentecost. Luke tells us that there were people, both Jews and Gentiles, "from every nation under heaven" (Acts 2:5). Pentecost teaches the disciples (and us) several lessons.

The New Humanity

At Babel God had separated the human race into nations by dividing the languages in order to limit the abuse of power by sinful rulers and to limit the hubris of humanity in its desire to live without God. Pentecost created a new humanity no longer separated by sin or by language divisions, but rather united by Christ and by love for one another through the Spirit of love poured into human hearts. The Spirit enabled those present to understand each other across the barrier of language. While today we are not usually granted the gift of tongues (instantaneous ability to speak in or to comprehend a previously unknown language) in order to understand the words of other believers when we travel, yet a Christian does experience a wonderful unity despite the divisions of language. We are truly part of a new race, a race that is to transcend the bitter hostilities that tear people apart.

All the Languages of the World

The diversity of languages represented there in Jerusalem at Pentecost was the firstfruits of the harvest of languages that Christ will gather from every part of this world. In the kingdom to come there will be people who have come to believe in Christ representing every language group. Pentecost demonstrates that Christ wants His disciples to go to people of every language with the Gospel and that He is able to gift those He calls so they can understand and communicate in the languages of the people to whom they go. I am not suggesting here that every missionary is promised the ability to speak new languages instantaneously, but God does desire that His people go to all language groups, and He does indeed give His people language gifts for the tasks to which He calls them.

Every Corner of the Globe

There was also a diversity of people geographically there in Jerusalem to hear the apostles preach the good news about Jesus. If we look carefully at Luke's list of some of the places from which those at Pentecost had come, we see that it includes people from every point of the compass who had converged on Jerusalem for the Feast: Pontus and

Cappadocia to the north; Mesopotamia, Parthia, and Media to the northeast; Elam to the east; Arabia to the southeast; Judea to the south; Egypt to the southwest; Crete to the west; Rome, Asia, Phrygia, and Pamphylia to the northwest. Some of these places, like Pontus, are near to Jerusalem, relatively speaking; some, like Rome, are much farther away. Luke clearly wants us to understand, and teaches us that Jesus wanted the church to understand, that the Gospel is for every corner of this earth. Jesus had earlier told His disciples:

> *"People will come from east and west and north and south, and will take their place at the feast in the kingdom of God."*
> —LUKE 13:29

Every Race

Another way to express this diversity would be to look at Luke's list and see there people who are descended from the three racial groups represented by the sons of Noah: Hamites from North Africa; Shemites from the Middle East; Japhethites from Europe. The Gospel of Christ is for all races, and all ethnic and racial divisions are to be transcended by the unity we have in Christ.

Every Kind of People from Every Sort of Place

We can add that Luke includes peoples from within the Roman Empire and peoples from beyond its borders, such as the Parthians and Elamites. He includes people from great cities like Rome, the capital of the vast empire, and from the deserts of Arabia; people from great empires and their provinces and from islands in the ocean. He includes both Jews, the inheritors of the covenant, and Gentiles. In other words, Luke covers every possible way he can think of to show the universal scope of the Great Commission. With this extraordinary demonstration on the Day of Pentecost, Jesus showed His disciples that the Gospel is intended for all peoples. The apostles understood this, as we see from the way Luke presents his account of Pentecost to us, and as we see elsewhere in the New Testament (for example, in the writings of John). When John looked into heaven, he heard the "new song" of the elders and living creatures before the throne of Christ:

> *"You are worthy to take the scroll*
> *and to open its seals,*
> *because you were slain,*
> *and with your blood you purchased men for God*
> *from every tribe and language*
> *   and people and nation."*
>
> —REVELATION 5:9

5

"WHOM SHALL I SEND? AND WHO WILL GO FOR ME?"

So far in our study we have assumed that the Great Commission applies to us as well as to the apostles to whom it was originally given. Is this an appropriate assumption, or are we demanding of the church today something that was intended for the apostles only? Who is Jesus' command for? We need to consider this question carefully.

It was, as we have seen, for the Eleven, to whom it was first given, and in addition for the apostle Paul. He describes himself as one "abnormally born" (1 Corinthians 15:8), for he was called by Jesus, in a post-ascension resurrection appearance, to serve as the Apostle to the Gentiles.

It is evident too as we read the pages of the New Testament that the new church as a whole understood that it was called to participate in the mission to the world. They saw clearly that it was not only the apostles who were sent by Christ, but *all* believers. To demonstrate this we need only look at the way Luke describes the spread of the Gospel beyond Jerusalem. The apostles heard the horizons of their mission from Jesus, but they must have very soon taught the whole church this calling.

In the book of Acts, chapter 7, we read about the martyrdom of Stephen, resulting from his fearless proclamation of the Gospel to the Sanhedrin, the highest religious authority of the Jewish people (the people in Jerusalem being the first horizon of the apostles' mission). Stephen, of course, was not himself an apostle, but he was in fact one of the first deacons appointed to oversee the distribution of food to needy widows in the church of Jerusalem. At the beginning of chapter 8 we learn that Paul (at that time still known as Saul) was present at that martyrdom, giving approval to the killing of Stephen. Then Luke describes what happened after Stephen's death:

> On that day a great persecution broke out against the church at Jerusalem, and all except the apostles were scattered throughout Judea and Samaria. . . . Those who had been scattered preached the word wherever they went. Philip went down to a city in Samaria and proclaimed the Christ there.
>
> —ACTS 8:1-5

Notice how Luke draws our attention to the way the second and third horizons of the mission were reached first by believers other than the apostles. The apostles did not start missionary endeavors to Judea and Samaria themselves in obedience to Christ's command, nor did they formulate a plan to send others out to fulfill the Commission. Rather God, in His sovereign rule over the life of the church, used even the tragedy of persecution to bring about the spread of the Gospel. God also teaches us in this passage that the Great Commission is the responsibility of the whole church; he does this by showing how the ordinary men and women of the Jerusalem church first spread the Gospel in Judea and Samaria. One of these "evangelists" was another of the early deacons, Philip, and God used his witness powerfully both in Samaria and then in the conversion of the Ethiopian eunuch (Acts 8:5-25, 26-40).

Later in his history, after telling of Peter's first visit to a Gentile home (Acts 10), Luke shows how the Gospel began to spread into the pagan Gentile world.

> Now those who had been scattered by the persecution in connection with Stephen traveled as far as Phoenicia, Cyprus and Antioch, telling the message only to Jews. Some of them, however, men from Cyprus and Cyrene, went to Antioch and began to speak to Greeks also, telling them the good news about the Lord Jesus. The Lord's hand was with them, and a great number of people believed and turned to the Lord.
>
> —ACTS 11:19-21

Once again, it was not the founders of the church, the ones who heard Jesus' command to go the nations, but new believers who reached out to this fourth horizon of the Great Commission. Luke carefully draws our attention to the identity of these first evangelists to the Gentiles. It was not the apostles who began a sustained mission to Gentiles. Nor was it even believers from the Jerusalem church, who were daily hearing the teaching of the apostles, who were obedient to this command of Christ. Rather, it was believers from Cyprus (an island in the Mediterranean Sea) and Cyrene (a city and province on the north coast of Africa) who were the first to reach out to Gentiles in any systematic way. This new commitment took place not in Jerusalem, the mother church, but in the city of Antioch in northern Syria.

It is to this church in Antioch that Barnabas (one of the first members of the Jerusalem church, Acts 4:36-37) went to help with the teaching, and from there Barnabas journeyed to find the recently converted Saul to ask him to join him in ministry in the church of Antioch (Acts 11:22-26). Francis Schaeffer used to say that the church of Antioch was his favorite church in the New Testament because of its commitment to overcome cultural and racial barriers. At the beginning of Acts 13 we read about the leaders of the church in Antioch. There were two from Africa, Simeon and Lucius, at least one of whom, Simeon, was black. Two were Jewish, Manaen ("brought up with Herod the tetrarch") and Saul, a Jew with a Pharisee's training and also with Roman citizenship. It was this church in Antioch from which the first missionaries, Paul and Barnabas, were sent, and thus missions, as we think of them today, began and became a part of the life of the church from that day to this (Acts 13:1-4ff.).

From this brief study of a few passages in Acts it is clear that the apostles and the whole church understood that the command to reach out with the Gospel was not for the apostles only but was for the entire church of that day. It was also a command not only for that day, but for every day in the life of the generations of believers to come. If we think of Jesus' words to the apostles, this is obvious. He told them that when they went out to obey the Great Commission, He would be with them until the close of the age. Jesus' words of encouragement that He would rule heaven and earth on behalf of His disciples and His promise of His help and presence were not meant for a few brief years until the apos-

tles died, but for the whole of this age. In fact, on another occasion Jesus
had told the disciples that the end of this age would only come when the
Gospel had been preached to all the nations (Matthew 24:14). Jesus
knew, the apostles knew, and the early church knew that the proclamation of the Gospel is a calling for the whole of this present age, however
long that will be.

If this is a calling for the whole church of Jesus Christ at every time
during this age, then it is also a calling for every church. We might today,
by the term *church*, be referring to the denomination of which we are a
part or the particular congregation of which we are members. The New
Testament uses *church* in a whole range of ways. *Church* may refer to
the whole church of Jesus Christ through all of time (Ephesians 5:25—
"Christ loved the church and gave himself for her"). *Church* may refer
to the church throughout the world, without being specific about a particular place (Acts 15:22; 1 Corinthians 10:32; 15:9—"I persecuted the
church of God"). *Church* may refer to the church—that is, all the
churches—in a geographical area (1 Corinthians 16:19—"the churches
in the province of Asia send you greetings"). *Church* may refer to the
church in a city, which may include several churches (Acts 20:17—"Paul
sent to Ephesus for the elders of the church"). Or *church* may refer to a
particular local congregation of believers (Romans 16:3-4—"Greet
Priscilla and Aquila . . . Greet also the church that meets at their house").
However we use the term *church* today, whether to refer to a denomination, to the churches in a city, state, or nation, or to a particular congregation, it should be clear to us that it is the responsibility of every
church to be obedient to the Great Commission.

It would be good for each of our congregations to check our commitment to mission against the commission given by Jesus. His charge
to the church to go to "Jerusalem . . . Judea and Samaria, and to the ends
of the earth" is His charge to your church and my church. What are we
doing as a church to reach the five horizons of our own locality, our own
nation, those different from us who live alongside us, the nations, and
the Jewish people? This challenge can produce an appropriate vision
statement for every church's missions board or missions committee.

Whoever is in leadership in any Christian church has an obligation
to call that church to be obedient to Jesus Christ and to commit itself to
being a mission-supporting and mission-sending church. This is true

whatever form of government a church has, whether its leadership is its pastor, a group of elders, a board of deacons, a church council, trustees, the congregation, or whatever other form of leadership there may be. A church cannot pretend to be faithful to its Lord unless it is making a serious commitment to try to be obedient to the Great Commission. Even if the leadership of the church does not take Jesus' command seriously, the Great Commission is still the responsibility of any church member who loves Christ and who wishes to serve Him as He asks. Such a member would have the obligation to begin to pray for, to encourage, and to challenge the leadership of that church to follow its Master's last will and testament for His people.

If we examine the practice of the apostle Paul we will find that whenever he planted a new church he encouraged that church to pray about mission (Ephesians 6:19-20; Colossians 4:2-4). He also urged each church to support mission financially (Philippians 4:14-19) and to become involved directly in the missionary task by sending its own members to learn mission on the job with Paul (Acts 16:1-5; 20:1-4). Stephen Neill has written about this missionary zeal of the whole first-century church:

> We know a great deal more about Paul than we know about anyone else. He tends to dominate the scene, and we are inclined to think of him as the typical missionary. In point of fact the picture is far more complex than that. We have to think of a great many full-time missionaries moving rapidly in many directions, and also of that mass of unprofessional missionaries . . . through whose witness churches were coming into being all over the place, unorganized, independent, yet acutely aware of their status as the new Israel and of their fellowship with all other believers in the world. (*A History of Christian Missions*, The Pelican History of the Church, Volume 6 [Harmondsworth: Penguin, 1964], p. 29)

Each church that desires to follow the Lord's command and the command and practice of the apostles needs to ask itself the following questions:

Is mission a priority for our church? What is our commitment to mission with regard to each of the five horizons of mission?

Where does the money go? What proportion of our annual budget is going to the proclamation of the Gospel? Sadly, many churches spend almost all their members' offerings on their own buildings and ministry. It is not wrong or unbiblical to build large buildings; nor is it wrong to use vast amounts of money on the immediate ministry of a local church. However, if these things are done to the virtual exclusion or minimization of giving to the other horizons of mission or of giving to ministries of mercy, there is a problem. If this is the situation in our church, then we are failing to listen to the clear commandments of Christ to spread the Gospel throughout the world and to be generous to the needy, both those close at hand and those farther away. Though the New Testament does not give us a figure or a percentage, I would suggest that giving a mere tithe of our church's budget to the horizons of mission is not adequate to meet the spirit of the Bible's emphasis on the importance of mission.

What about our prayers? Are we praying for mission as Paul commanded the churches? Returning to the five horizons of mission, are we praying for individuals or ministries that are committed to reaching each of these horizons? It would be a practical and helpful goal for a church missions committee to ensure that it is in contact with people involved in each of these five horizons. This contact would involve soliciting prayer letters from those laboring in different fields, and it would require bringing to every congregation information about what the Father is accomplishing through particular missionaries and ministries as He helps His church to be obedient to the command of Jesus.

Are we sending anyone? Who are we sending from our own church to join the task force that the Spirit is calling into the world of unbelief? We may and should be supporting by prayer and finances individuals and ministries from other congregations whose needs and work the Lord brings to our attention. But in addition, whenever the Scriptures are clearly and faithfully taught, we may be sure that the Spirit will use the Word to call people from our own congregation to the task of taking the gospel to "Jerusalem . . . Judea and Samaria, and to the ends of the earth." So whom shall we send from our own church? If no one is being called by the Spirit from our own body, we can be sure that we are not teaching the Word of God faithfully.

6

WHAT ABOUT ME?

Every church is called to mission to the world. But what about the individual members of each church? Do all believers have a part to play in the drama of the Gospel growing and spreading across the world, and if they do have a part, what is that part?

Simply by being a member of the church of Jesus Christ each Christian has a responsibility to be involved in the missionary call of the whole church. We should all be praying, all giving, all sending. What my church is called to do, I am called to do or support in some way. In addition, we have already seen that it was not only the apostles, the teachers, and the leaders of the church but also the deacons and members of the churches who were involved in going out from Jerusalem to reach Judea, Samaria, and the Gentiles. It was that great crowd of ordinary witnesses to Christ who were responsible, under God's hand, for planting many of the churches that came into existence during those early years after Christ ascended and gave His Spirit to His people for the task of proclaiming the truth about Him.

There are two particular passages in which the apostles call all believers to be involved in the work of evangelism. These two New Testament texts will be foundation stones for much of our reflection in the rest of this book. We quote first a passage from Paul (Colossians 4:5-6), and then one from Peter (1 Peter 3:15-16).

> *Be wise in the way you act toward outsiders; make the most of every opportunity. Let your conversation be always full of*

grace, seasoned with salt, so that you may know how to answer everyone.

In your hearts set apart Christ as Lord. Always be prepared to give an answer to everyone who asks you to give the reason for the hope that you have. But do this with gentleness and respect, keeping a clear conscience, so that those who speak maliciously against your good behavior in Christ may be ashamed of their slander.

The words of the Lord through His apostles are clear. Evangelism is not simply the task of church leaders, pastors, and evangelists who are especially called and gifted. (Though the New Testament does recognize the particular responsibility of leaders and pastors in this task and teaches us that God does indeed gift some for this work with special abilities; see, for example, Ephesians 4:7-12; 2 Timothy 4:1-5.) But it is not only the teachers and evangelists who have this task set before them; rather, every believer is called to be ready "to give the reason for the hope that you have" and to "make the most of every opportunity."

Peter uses the word *apologia*, which can be translated "answer," "defense," or "reasoned account." It is the word from which we derive the word *apologetics*, the name for courses at seminaries and elsewhere on presenting and defending the Gospel. In the New Testament the word *apologia* is most often used in legal contexts, for it is a word of the courtroom. For example, Luke describes the apostle Paul as making his defense (*apologia*) of his faith in Christ, of himself, and of the truth of the Gospel whenever he is on trial (see Acts 22:1; 24:10; 26:1-2). The related Greek words translated "witness," "testimony," and "testify" are also courtroom terms that we find repeatedly in legal contexts in the New Testament.

An "apology" or "defense" of my faith is always personal as well as reasonable because it is *my* faith. Christ is my only hope in this life and in the life to come; so I will gladly give an answer for those who ask me the reason for "the hope that [I] have." My personal testimony is also always to be a reasoned and reasonable testimony, one that could stand up to close examination in a court of law. I have trusted in Christ because He is absolutely trustworthy. I have every reason to believe the truthfulness of His promises. All the evidence in the world points to the truthfulness of the Bible and the trustworthiness of Christ. There are in the end no evidences and no arguments that can stand against Christ or against His word, for He is the Truth, and His Word is truth.

Of course, not every Christian finds himself or herself constantly on trial for his or her faith, though we know that at any moment somewhere in the world there are Christians who are literally on trial for what they believe, just as the apostle Paul was. Yet Peter uses this legal word, "defense" or "answer," for believers in the ordinary circumstances of their daily lives, and not just for courtrooms. In the same way, the legal language of "witness" is used for the believer in the context of everyday life. In the letter to the Philippians we find a passage that is helpful to us as we reflect on this issue. Paul is, in fact, in prison when he writes these words.

> *Now I want you to know, brothers, that what has happened to me has really served to advance the gospel. As a result, it has become clear throughout the whole palace guard and to everyone else that I am in chains for Christ. Because of my chains, most of the brothers in the Lord have been encouraged to speak the word of God more courageously and fearlessly. It is true that some preach Christ out of envy and rivalry, but others out of goodwill. The latter do so in love, knowing that I am put here for the defense of the gospel.*
>
> —1:12-16

Again in this passage Paul uses the language of "defense" though he is not at every moment actually on trial. Wherever he is, whatever he is doing, Paul regards himself as on trial and his faith in Christ as on trial. Wherever he is, whatever he is doing, Paul regards himself as put there for "the defense of the gospel."

This is how we are to think about our own lives. We are always on trial for Christ; our faith is always on trial. In our homes before our children and spouses; in our schools and colleges before our teachers, students, friends, and classmates; in our workplaces before our colleagues, bosses, employees, and customers; when we are playing or relaxing;

whatever we are engaged in, wherever we find ourselves, we are put there by God for "the defense of the gospel."

This is underlined by some further words of Paul found in Philippians 1:7. We know from the context that he is writing about his concern for the Philippians:

> It is right for me to feel this way about all of you, since I have you in my heart; for whether I am in chains or defending and confirming the gospel, all of you share in God's grace with me.

Whether he is in prison or out in the world, whether he is in the courtroom on trial or free and facing no charges, Paul always considers himself as responsible to be "defending and confirming" the Gospel. This is true not only when he is preaching or witnessing but in all his words and in all his life.

This means, of course, that for us too it is not simply our specific attempts to witness that are important "for the defense of the gospel." It is my whole life, everything I say and do, that makes a credible defense. That is why Paul urges the Colossians to "be wise in the way [they] act toward outsiders" and to "let [their] conversation be always full of grace, seasoned with salt." In the context of 1 Peter 3, Peter describes the Christians as maliciously criticized by unbelievers and maligned for their faith. Even so, he says, prove that the criticisms of your life are unjust by your "good behavior." Even so, he says, speak with "gentleness and respect" to those who are attacking you. Why? Because you and I, our faith, and Christ Himself are on trial before the world.

As Francis Schaeffer used to say often: "We live before a watching world." It is incumbent, then, on us to remember that our behavior, our words, our manner of speech, and our attitudes of heart are always being judged by non-Christians. Unbelievers are drawing conclusions about Christ and about the truth of Christianity from everything we say and do.

7

WHERE DO WE BEGIN?

All believers are called by the Lord to "make the most of every opportunity" (Colossians 4:5) and on every occasion to be "prepared to give an answer to everyone who asks you to give the reason for the hope that you have" (1 Peter 3:15). Most of us feel quite unprepared for this task. Indeed, if we are honest with ourselves, we feel thoroughly inadequate! However, be encouraged, for this is the appropriate way to feel! The truth is that we *are* unprepared and inadequate when it comes to doing evangelism; furthermore, we are all incapable of converting anyone.

The apostle Paul teaches us how we are to think about those who are involved in the work of evangelism, including himself, perhaps the greatest evangelist ever apart from Christ Himself:

> *What, after all, is Apollos? And what is Paul? Only servants, through whom you came to believe—as the Lord has assigned to each his task. I planted the seed, Apollos watered it, but God made it grow. So neither he who plants nor he who waters is anything, but only God, who makes things grow. The man who plants and the man who waters have one purpose, and each will be rewarded according to his own labor. For we are God's fellow workers; you are God's field, God's building.*
> —1 CORINTHIANS 3:5-9

Paul, in these words, reminds us to be properly humble about the part we play in bringing someone to faith in Christ. In comparison to what God does in saving someone, what we do, even what the great apostle did, is nothing. Paul does not mean that what we do is literally worth nothing, for he carefully adds that "we are God's fellow workers" and that God has indeed assigned to each of us a task in the work of someone's conversion. Later on in this same context Paul describes himself as an "expert builder" (v. 10), and he expands on his statement, saying that God will reward us for the part we play in helping others come to the knowledge of Christ (vv. 10-14).

This recognition that "unless God builds the house" all our labors are in vain (Psalm 127:1) is the right place to start. In seeing this we will ask, "Where do we begin in our calling to be evangelists?" We begin with a proper sense of humility about our role and about our fitness for the task ahead, and that humility should lead us to prayer.

PRAYER

Recognizing our dependence on the Lord to bring people to faith in Christ, what should be the focus of our prayers? God has placed each of us in a "family" of those we love and those who love us—both actual family members and also the "family" of our close friends, the people whose lives have become closely intertwined with ours. Our first and perfectly appropriate desire will be to pray for these people whom we already love.

In every part of Scripture it is evident to us, even with the most cursory reading, that God delights in extending His kingdom through families. Children are brought up in "the training and instruction of the Lord" by their parents (Ephesians 6:4; cf. Deuteronomy 4:1-14; 6:1-25; 2 Timothy 1:5). Husbands become believers through their wives (1 Peter 3:1-4); adults are led to the Lord through children (2 Kings 5); households of people, including near family members, servants, masters, soldiers, relatives, and close friends, come to the Lord together and through each other's influence (Acts 10).

God has set us in "families," and He gladly uses these most natural pathways for the extension of His kingdom. So we begin with prayer for those we live with and those we love. These, above all, should be the people for whom we care so deeply that we pray for them. "I have great sorrow and unceasing anguish in my heart. For I could wish that I were cursed and cut off from Christ for the sake of my brothers" (Romans

9:1-3). (Or parents, children, sisters, cousins, uncles, aunts, close friends—fill in the blank with the names of those you love who do not know Christ, just as Paul did for his fellow Israelites.)

Sometimes Christians care so much about family and friends that they start questioning God about the fairness of His judgment against those who do not know Christ. It is better to struggle with these questions and doubts than to wall ourselves off from such difficulties. The only alternative to painful struggles is either breaking off close ties with those who are not Christians or refusing to get close to anyone who is not a believer because of the emotional ties that come and the questions that arise with those ties. Jesus cares so deeply for the lost that He weeps over them (Matthew 23:37-39). He loves so passionately that He cried out for the forgiveness of those who crucified Him and mocked Him as He died (Luke 23:34). The Father grieves so sorrowfully for those who turn away from Him that He gave His Son over to death for them.

God does not desire that we "just be happy" or that we become unconcerned about the judgment that will come upon those who do not know His Son. He does not want us to wall ourselves off from the pain of knowing and loving people who are unbelievers. He would rather that we care so deeply for people that we agonize over the prospect of their condemnation. He is big enough and strong enough to cope with our doubts and questions about the justice of His judgment. Real prayer, passionate prayer, sorrowing prayer should arise from our hearts for those we love and for those with whose lives we are bound together in the web of daily existence.

Our next circle of prayer will be for those whom God providentially places in our lives at work, at school or college, in our leisure activities, in our neighborhoods. Each of us has a wider community like this, a wider circle of acquaintances, workmates, classmates, and neighbors. God rules over our lives individually for the sake of the Gospel as well as ruling over the nations. Consequently the people we meet during the course of our regular daily activities are not there by chance. These are the men and women, boys and girls for whom God desires that we feel a sense of responsibility and for whom we are to pray.

We sometimes start praying for the whole world "out there," the millions of unbelievers in countries faraway whom we will never meet. This can be overwhelming to us, an impossible mountain to climb. Our minds try to pray for nameless faces, countless numbers of them. Thus we become discouraged easily. This does not mean we shouldn't pray for the whole world, but that we ourselves are not big enough to cope with the whole world. But God *is* big enough to cope with the whole world, for He is infinite in His knowledge, His power, and His love.

We are finite, very limited in our knowledge, power, and love. But God sets us in particular places, in contexts of work, study, and play where we meet a limited number of people. He wants us to pray for them, for our relationships with them, for the impact of our lives on them, and for their salvation. He can handle the big picture; He wants us to concentrate on our small part of the vast landscape that He is painting.

I am not suggesting that we should only pray for those we know. Of course it is right and good to pray for people on the other side of the world whom we will never meet. But even in these cases most of our prayer will be for missionaries we support who are meeting these people who are unknown to us. In this stage of our study, however, we are reflecting on our personal responsibility to be evangelists. In this context we may be sure that God calls us to pray for particular people, the particular people that He brings into our lives when we open ourselves to Him to be of service as He builds His kingdom.

8

FOR WHAT ARE WE
TO PRAY?

The Lord encourages us to bring Him our requests as we seek to make the Gospel known to those around us. But for what exactly are we to pray as we bring our loved ones, family members, friends, workmates, classmates, neighbors, and acquaintances before the Lord?

THE WORK OF THE SPIRIT IN OUR FRIENDS

We pray, first, for the work of the Spirit in the hearts and minds of those around us. We know that He can reach the parts of them, the inner workings of their minds and hearts, that we cannot reach. He can soften the hard heart, bend the stubborn will, open the closed mind, challenge the long-held prejudices, and heal the painful memories that are inaccessible to us. Paul writes:

> God, who said, "Let light shine out of darkness," made his light shine in our hearts to give us the light of the knowledge of the glory of God in the face of Christ.
>
> —2 CORINTHIANS 4:6

And Jesus encourages us with these words:

> "No man can come to me unless the Father who sent me draws him."
>
> —JOHN 6:44

When we long to see someone come to Christ, the most important thing we can do is to pray for that person, asking God to do what we cannot.

OPEN DOORS FOR THE GOSPEL

We are to pray for open doors in our relationships so we will have opportunities to make the Gospel known. This is how Paul asked believers to pray for him:

> *Pray for us, too, that God will open a door for our message, so that we may proclaim the mystery of Christ.*
> —COLOSSIANS 4:3

Christ has promised us that He is ruling the nations and our own personal lives for the sake of the Gospel. So we can have confidence that He will answer our prayers when we ask Him to open doors as we build relationships with people. We do not need to try to force the Gospel on family members, friends, and acquaintances who are not yet ready to listen. The Lord will open doors in His time. And when He does provide the opportunity for us to share some aspect of the truth with a friend or family member, we should make the most of that opportunity.

I have a friend for whom I have been praying for many years. He has not been open to hearing the Gospel, yet he knows very well where I stand as a Christian. I have prayed for an open door in God's time. After a long time, when a close relative of his died, he called and asked me to take the funeral service. This was an open door indeed! Apart from my friend himself there were many other relatives and elderly friends of the deceased who had never before heard a clear exposition of the Gospel.

We may sometimes think that God is very slow to answer our prayers or even doubt that He will answer them at all. We may wonder if the heavens are closed to us and if He is even listening to our cries on behalf of those we love. But the apostle Peter reminds us:

> *Do not forget this one thing, dear friends: With the Lord a day is like a thousand years, and a thousand years are like a day. The*

*Lord is not slow in keeping his promise, as some understand
slowness. He is patient with you, not wanting anyone to perish,
but everyone to come to repentance.*

—2 PETER 3:8-9

Peter is writing about the return of Christ here, but the principle
taught in this passage applies. God is eager to save people, and we must
persevere when our hopes, dreams, and prayers are slow in being fulfilled, for He is faithful and will answer our longings more fully than
we could ever imagine. So keep praying for those friends and relatives
and for open doors! God will give the opportunity to share the truth in
His time, and when He does you will know that His time is the best
time.

PRAYER FOR YOURSELF FOR COURAGE

Pray for yourself in all your relationships. Paul asked the believers to
pray for him (Ephesians 6:19-20), that he would have courage to make
the Gospel known when he was given the opportunity.

*Pray also for me, that whenever I open my mouth, words may
be given me so that I will fearlessly make known the mystery of
the gospel, for which I am an ambassador in chains. Pray that
I may declare it fearlessly, as I should.*

We can sometimes make the mistake of thinking that Paul was
always naturally courageous and fearless, that he never struggled, like
we all do, with problems of timidity, discouragement, fear of people, and
hesitation in boldly speaking about Jesus. His words to the Ephesians
make it evident that Paul was just like us. He needed God's help just as
much as you and I do. He was sometimes afraid, just as you and I are
sometimes afraid. He sometimes wrestled with the effort of getting into
a conversation with people, feeling tired, knowing that the other person
was demanding and would take hours of his time, just as you and I wrestle with these kind of problems. He was not a superman or "Super
Christian," always eager to witness without hesitation or ambivalence.
He needed prayer for courage. So do I. So do you. Be glad you can be

honest with the Lord and with fellow believers. It does not help anyone to pretend that you are always a bold and ready witness, and such pretense certainly does not please God. He is delighted when we acknowledge our weaknesses to Him.

PRAYER FOR CLARITY

Paul also struggled with being clear in his presentation of the Gospel and requested prayer in this area too (Colossians 4:4). After asking the believers to pray for open doors for him, he added: "Pray that I may proclaim it clearly, as I should."

Paul found it difficult to be always clear. He was not always the best communicator; he knew he needed prayer and did not hesitate to ask for it.

In the passage quoted in the previous section we notice that, as well as asking for courage, Paul wanted God to give him the "words" to say when he was witnessing (Ephesians 6:19). Not one of us knows exactly what to say to our family members and friends. Not one of us is clear enough when we try to make the Gospel known. We confuse people; we make straightforward issues obscure; we give simplistic answers to tough questions. We need help in what to say and how to say it!

Even Jesus tells us that the words He spoke and the manner in which He said them were given to Him by the Father:

> "I did not speak of my own accord, but the Father who sent me commanded me what to say and how to say it. I know that his command leads to eternal life. So whatever I say is just what the Father told me to say."
>
> —JOHN 12:49-50

Jesus, who was perfect, depended on His Father for the words he spoke. There is a beautiful statement in Isaiah 50:4, in one of the Servant Songs, the poems about the Messiah:

> The Sovereign LORD has given me an instructed tongue, to know the word that sustains the weary. He wakens me morning by morning, wakens my ear to listen like one being taught.

This is how Jesus lived. He did not presume that He would always know what to say. (Yes, He was and is the Son of God, equal with the Father; but in His incarnation He deliberately did not use all His powers and rights as God.) He did not try to get everything figured out ahead of time so that He had learned the right words to say before He even met a particular person. He prayed day by day that the Father would teach Him what to say and how to say it; and when the time came, the Father indeed taught him. It is to be the same with you and with me. We need to acknowledge that we do not know what to say, that we are unclear and confused, that we do not say things the way we should. If we confess our sins and shortcomings in the area of witness, just as in any other area of our lives, Jesus promises not only to forgive our failures and inadequacies but to come to our aid and to teach us what to say and how to say it.

9

AFTER PRAYER,
WHAT COMES NEXT?

Prayer is our most important calling. As the Scripture says:

> *Unless the LORD builds the house, its builders labor in vain.*
> —PSALM 127:1

So we pray because we have His encouragement to pray and because we know that prayer is a necessity, for without God's work there will be no expansion of the kingdom. But what does the Lord want me to do about evangelism in addition to trusting Him for all that I cannot accomplish? He desires that I live in a way that will make the Gospel attractive to all around me.

LIVING FAITHFULLY

Jesus stated it very simply and directly for us in the Sermon on the Mount in two powerful images, images that are to shape the way we Christians are to think about our calling in the world:

> *"You are the salt of the earth. But if the salt loses its saltiness, how can it be made salty again? It is no longer good for anything, except to be thrown out and trampled by men. You are the light of the world. A city on a hill cannot be hidden. Neither do people light a lamp and put it under a bowl. Instead they put*

it on its stand, and it gives light to everyone in the house. In the
same way, let your light shine before men, that they may see
your good deeds and praise your Father in heaven."
—MATTHEW 5:13-16

If we reflect a little on these two images of salt and light, it is evident how closely our putting Jesus' words into practice is related to the task of evangelism. Jesus teaches us that if we live in obedience to God's commandments, loving Him and loving our fellow men and women, then people will see the beauty of our lives, the acts of kindness, the daily life of integrity and faithfulness, and their response will be to glorify God. The attitudes of unbelievers toward God are changed by genuine righteousness in the lives of believers. Conversely, if we live in a way that dishonors God and Christian truth, if we are hypocrites who say one thing and live another, then unbelievers will reject us, and they will also reject the Gospel. They will throw it out and "trample" it underfoot.

Jesus also challenges us in these words to live our lives in the world, where unbelievers can see how we live. He does not want Christians to retreat from the world and from non-Christians; he wants us to live "before men." Many of us are tempted to hide our light, to make ourselves secure and comfortable by surrounding ourselves with Christian friends and "Christian culture." But this is clearly not what Jesus has in mind for us. His two images, "salt" and "light," demand a life that is to be lived in the world and applied to the world, out in the darkness where there is no light, out where the savoring salt is needed to make the food tasty. These images and Jesus' use of them require Christians to be in the world, and not simply in the church. They require us to be with non-Christians, and not simply with fellow believers. Faithful, biblical evangelism cannot take place unless Christians take these words of Jesus to heart.

The apostles returned to this theme repeatedly, for they were aware, as was Jesus, how tempting it is for believers either to copy the world and be indistinguishable from it or to retreat from it for safety and be ineffective in it. Peter writes in 1 Peter 2:12:

Live such good lives among the pagans that, though they accuse
you of doing wrong, they may see your good deeds and glorify
God on the day he visits us.

Christians will be accused of doing wrong, just as unbelievers criticized Jesus in His day. This is a given in this world, but we are to make
sure that the criticism is undeserved. Think of the damage done to the
Gospel by every scandal in which a minister is accused of adultery or a
prominent Christian businessman is shown to be dishonest in his business dealings. An unbelieving friend said to me one day, "Jerram, why
are so many of the Christian businessmen in this city so lacking in
integrity in their business practices?" I will never forget those words, for
this non-Christian is honored for his integrity by the business community,
and he is right to ask such a question. It has challenged me to try to live
before him in such a way that he will see genuine virtue in my life and
will one day praise God as the source and measure of all true goodness.

Later in his letter (1 Peter 3:1-4) Peter adds advice for Christian
women who are married to non-Christians (in the previous section Peter
has written of Jesus who lived in subjection to his heavenly Father):

Wives, in the same way be submissive to your husbands so that,
if any of them do not believe the word, they may be won over
without words by the behavior of their wives, when they see the
purity and reverence of your lives. Your beauty should not come
from outward adornment, such as braided hair and the wear-
ing of gold jewelry and fine clothes. Instead, it should be that of
your inner self, the unfading beauty of a gentle and quiet spirit,
which is of great worth in God's sight.

When we are married to someone who is not a believer or are living with a family member who is not a Christian, the kind of life we live
becomes especially important. A husband or wife, a parent or child, a
brother or sister who sees us every day is aware of exactly what it is like
to live with us. Someone living so close to us will take no notice of any
attempts to tell them about Christ if our lives are not demonstrating the
truth of the message we claim to believe. Why should they pay any attention to a word that claims to bring forgiveness and new life to people if

they see no evidence that we are living a new life and if they see no indication that we are becoming forgiving, forbearing people ourselves?

Peter teaches us that our lives are more important than our words, not because our words are intrinsically unimportant, but because words without life are empty. Indeed, they are worse than empty; they are hypocritical and actually turn people away from Christ. The apostle John, writing about our care for one another as Christians, has this same emphasis on the importance of the unity of word and life:

> *If anyone has material possessions and sees his brother in need but has no pity on him, how can the love of God be in him? Dear children, let us not love with words or tongue but with actions and in truth.*
>
> —1 JOHN 3:17-18

Evangelism that is only with "words or tongue" causes the non-Christian to ask, "How can the love of Christ, of which this Christian speaks, be true when their life shows no evidence of love?" In the course of my ministry I have met many people who have turned away from Christianity because of the ugly lives of those who claimed to be Christians but did not live out that claim. I remember a teenager whose father was a pastor and had constantly spoken to his son about the Gospel and yet at the same time had been repeatedly unkind to his wife in the way he spoke to her and in his actions. Eventually it came out that the father was having regular affairs with women in his congregation. The son remembered the behavior of his father far more than he remembered his father's words about Christ; and when he did remember his father's words about Christ, they only served to make him more bitter and cynical, both about his father's hypocrisy and about the Gospel.

10

LIVING FAITHFULLY IN THE WORKPLACE

The front lines of evangelism in any moment of history will be, first, the family and then the workplace. For most adult believers (unless our immediate family members are non-Christians), the context in which we are most likely to meet unbelievers is our place of employment. There day after day, for eight or nine hours or even longer, we will be working under, over, or alongside people who do not know Christ. (For those who are younger, the most likely context to be among non-Christians will be when they are with other children and young people, their friends and neighbors where they live, and those they meet as they attend school. This will even be true for those who attend Christian schools, for not all of the children present will be committed to the Gospel in their hearts.)

This was as true in the New Testament period as it is now. There, of course, the social context was different, as many people working in the pagan Greek and Roman world were slaves. In many of the New Testament letters the apostles addressed Christians living and working within the context of slavery. Masters who had become Christians were commanded to recognize the humanity of their slaves and to treat them with justice and fairness (Colossians 4:1). They were to remember that they had a Master too, to whom one day they would have to give an account of the way they had treated those under them (Ephesians 6:9).

Both these texts call masters to recognize that they are accountable to God in this life, and they will stand before Him on the Day of

Judgment alongside their slaves, not as superiors, but as equals. God hears every cry from those who are treated unjustly, and He will give appropriate payback to those who have mistreated, not paid fairly, or brutalized their workers (James 5:1-6). There is a wonderful passage in the book of Job (31:13-15) that summarizes this teaching:

> *If I have denied justice to my menservants and maidservants*
> *when they had a grievance against me,*
> *what will I do when God confronts me?*
> *What will I answer when called to account?*
> *Did not he who made me in the womb make them?*
> *Did not the same One form us both within our mothers?*

In his brief letter to Philemon Paul wrote to a man who had been converted and who was the master of a runaway slave. That slave, Onesimus, had become a Christian through Paul's ministry in Rome, the capital city of the empire, where he had gone to escape. He was now going back to his former master carrying a letter from the apostle Paul (actually several letters, as he took with him also the letters to the Ephesian, Colossian, and possibly Philippian churches as well).

In the letter to Philemon we get clear insight into the teaching of the apostle as it touched the issue of slavery. Paul describes Onesimus as "my son" (v. 10) and tells Philemon to welcome back the runaway slave as a brother in Christ (v. 16); to treat him not as a slave, but as if he were the apostle Paul himself (v. 17). We must assume that this is what happened, for how would this letter have survived if it had not reached its destination and been obeyed? Wherever masters were converted and listened obediently to this kind of teaching (a teaching that we find everywhere in the New Testament), there must have been a profound transformation of the institution of slavery. This transformation would have ultimately led to slavery's abolition, at first in individual homes and then, as the salt and light worked its way into the surrounding culture, affecting the society's institutions and laws.

To those in servitude the apostles encouraged faithfulness and diligence (Ephesians 6:5-8; Colossians 3:22-25). Parts of the Colossians passage (3:23-25) apply to every Christian working at any job in any context. They provide for us a "workers' mandate":

Whatever you do, work at it with all your heart, as working for the Lord, not for men, since you know that you will receive an inheritance from the Lord as a reward. It is the Lord Christ you are serving.

Too often we think of work for the church as "sacred" work that really matters to God and all other work as "secular" work that is not as significant to Him. Nothing could be more in disagreement with these words of Paul or with the general teaching of Scripture. God's Word knows nothing about a sacred/secular dichotomy, though this kind of teaching has become very widespread. Some well-known Christian leaders have publicly called believers to "leave their secular jobs, become full-time evangelists, and do something truly significant for the kingdom of God." This appears to have a kind of wisdom, and some feel compelled to leave their jobs and go into "ministry." However, there is nothing in the Bible to support such teaching. The Holy Spirit does not need the help of this kind of pressuring of people with unbiblical ideas when He decides to call those He wants to serve Him as ministers of the Word.

A further problem of such teaching is that it devalues the work that most Christians are doing and makes them feel like second-class citizens in the kingdom. Many Christians, by this false teaching, are made to feel that their work is only valuable for one of the following three reasons:

- They are commanded by God to support themselves and their families; so this makes their work important.
- They are able to give a tithe of their earnings to support the "really" important work of spreading the Gospel, and this financial support of "ministry" makes their own work significant.
- They might have opportunities for witness at work, and so their work has spiritual value for this reason.

There is an element of truth in each of these three points. God does call us to provide for ourselves and for our families (2 Thessalonians 3:6-12; 1 Timothy 5:8). He does call us to give of our earnings to support the ministry of the Word and also to help those who are in need (1 Corinthians 9:14; Galatians 6:6; Ephesians 4:28). He does challenge us to take advantage of every opportunity to bear witness to Christ.

However, none of these three important points touches the fundamental reason why our work is valuable to the Lord.

God has created us to work as those who are made in His image. Work in itself is significant. That is why Paul says what he does in Colossians 3. Whatever we do, we are working for the Lord. It is the way we do what we do, whether plowing a field, programming a computer, preparing a meal, or preaching the Word, that is of concern to the Lord. Jesus Himself spent most of his adult life as a carpenter. Are we to think that the Son of God was in some way a second-class citizen in the kingdom until He began His public ministry? Are we to think that He was doing only "secular" work until He started teaching? These questions about the Perfect Man demonstrate the folly of the sacred/secular division and the falsity of this teaching that has done such enormous damage to the people of God.

God wants people to be farmers, schoolteachers, nurses, janitors, lawyers, homemakers, doctors, tradesmen, accountants, etc. He delights in raising up people to serve Him in every job. We are to regard every kind of work as a sacred calling, and we are to teach all of God's people to work as those who are working for the Lord. As we do this spiritual and blessed daily labor, we are given the added blessing and possibility of being living testimonies to the power of the Gospel by the way we work. Paul writes in Titus 2:10 that Christians in all work situations are to "show that they can be fully trusted, so that in every way they will make the teaching about God our Savior attractive."

When this is the reality, when we are making the teaching of God our Savior "attractive" by the way we work, work surely will be the front line of evangelism. Unbelievers will see that their Christian employees, bosses, and workmates have honesty, integrity, faithfulness, diligence, a servant's heart, concern for their fellow employees, and a cheerful spirit. Such obedience to God's Word will open many doors for the Good News. But even if our obedience does not open doors, we will be glad to do these things anyway, for such service is pleasing to God. For this we were created, for this we have been redeemed, that our lives might be a constant praise to Him in all we do.

11

A LIFE OF LOVE

Integrity, diligence, fidelity, purity—these are watchwords for us as we seek to bear witness to the truth of the Gospel in our homes and in our workplaces. Jesus lived out these moral qualities in His daily life. In addition, He taught His disciples a "new command" and embodied it to perfection:

> "A new command I give you: Love one another. As I have loved you, so you must love one another. By this all men will know that you are my disciples, if you love one another."
> —JOHN 13:34-35

Was the command to "love one another" truly a "new" commandment? The Old Testament Law could be summarized by the two commandments "Love God" and "Love your neighbor." So on the surface it seems that Jesus' commandment was an old commandment. But if we look a little deeper we will see that what was new was not the command to love, but the command to love as Jesus had loved His disciples. What was new was the manner in which Jesus fulfilled the command. No one had ever loved as He loved. He gave Himself up to death not for the righteous or for the good, but for the sinful, for the disobedient. He gave Himself up to death not for His friends or for those who loved Him, but for those who denied and forsook Him, for His enemies, for those who hated Him. This was new. Nothing like it had been seen in the history of the world.

This is the "new command" that He gives to us who believe in Him and who desire to follow Him. We are to love one another, and all people, with the same kind of self-sacrificing love that Jesus demonstrated on the cross. We are not to love only Christians, for Jesus did not love only those who already believed in Him but also those who were still full of doubts and unbelief and turned away from Him. Just as Jesus did, we are to love without regard for the righteousness or goodness of those we seek to love. We are to love whether people love us or not. This kind of love is the mark of the Christian, Jesus teaches us. This is how people will know that we are the disciples of Jesus Christ. This is the kind of love that we are to live every day in our families and in our places of employment. We are to love one another as Jesus loved us—husbands and wives, parents and children, bosses and workers. Of course, we never do this perfectly; but to the extent that there is a reality of this kind of love in our lives, there will be a compelling testimony to the love of Christ.

Are we to love only our submissive children and reject those who are rebellious? This is not how Jesus has loved us. Are we only to love our children when they are obedient or good and have nothing to do with them when they are disobedient and unloving to us? This is not the way Jesus loves us. Every believer knows that Christ is full of patience, kindness, forbearance, forgiveness, and grace toward us over and over again. We are all coldhearted, slow to love Him, reluctant to obey Him, unwilling to change, struggling to obey; and yet He continues to love us. This is how He calls us to treat our own children, our spouses, and other people in our homes, in our churches, in our workplaces, and out in the world. This is the new commandment that is to govern our lives.

Later on that same night before he died, Jesus added these words about the power of love when He was praying for His disciples:

> "My prayer is not for them alone. I pray also for those who will believe in me through their message, that all of them may be one, Father, just as you are in me and I am in you. May they also be in us so that the world may believe that you have sent me. . . . May they be brought to complete unity to let the world know that you sent me and have loved them even as you have loved me."
>
> —JOHN 17:20-23

How will people know that we are followers of Jesus Christ? How will people believe that the Father sent the Son? How will the world know that Christ has come from the Father and has loved us so fully in His death on the cross? Jesus tells us that unbelievers will know these things and will come to faith when they see the reality of His love lived out by us.

But what are the contexts in which our love will be seen? Much of the love we pour out to one another will be evident in our homes as we love our wives, our husbands, our children, our parents, our brothers and sisters with the love Christ has shown for us. This is the setting in which many first experience the love of Christ and come to faith in Him. In almost any church that has been in existence for twenty years or more, many of the members will be children or spouses who have come to their Christian commitment through the family.

Sometimes (just as in the story Jesus told about the prodigal son) a child or young person raised in a Christian family turns away from God. Whether this turning away lasts for a few months or for many years, when there is an eventual return to the Father, it is so often the reality of love experienced in the home and never forgotten that is the means the Father uses to draw the rebellious one back to Himself.

This reality of the extension of the kingdom through the family seems so straightforward that we often forget its importance. Yet God has indeed made His promises to us about loving our families, praying for them, and raising them in the knowledge of the truth and in the reverent fear of the Lord. Where this becomes more difficult for us is in the broken situations that are the reality for so many people who are becoming Christians in this generation. One third of all children in the USA are being raised in single-parent families. In the great majority of such situations the father has left a mother and children. Any church that is being obedient to the Lord's command to love widows and orphans and others in need of help will find that it will have a growing number of single-parent households represented in its congregation.

Divorce and all the troubles that result from it will be another reality with which churches will have to deal. Yet, in these broken contexts the Lord calls us to show the same kind of self-giving love. Will we love, in the way that Christ commands, the new husband or wife that our parent marries, whether the second marriage comes about through the tragedy of early death or through the pain of divorce? Will we love, in the way that Christ commands, the children of our spouse's previous marriage whether these children are two years old or twenty-two? Will we love, in the way that Christ commands, these new brothers and sisters with whom we have no blood relationship? Will we love a new father, mother, son, or sibling whether he or she loves Christ or not, whether he or she loves us or not, whether he or she is kind and good or not?

Imagine yourself in the following situation. You and your wife decide to take your father into your home as he is not doing well in an extended care facility where he went to recover from major surgery. His health has so deteriorated that he is actually close to death; so in effect you save his life. But he is not at all easy to live with! He is critical of everyone—your family in your home as well as any visitors who drop in to see you. You have saved his life, but he seems to take delight in making your lives miserable!

Or put yourself in the following scenario. Your father marries again after your mother's death. On the wedding day your new stepmother gets drunk and flirts with your husband. From that day on your father's life becomes increasingly difficult. All the special pleasures in his life are now denied him because his new wife says they interfere with his devoting every moment of his waking life to satisfying her desires. Relationships with you and his other children and grandchildren become more and more difficult because of the stepmother's insecure and jealous nature.

Or consider how you might cope with a difficult marriage situation. Your friend has a husband who typifies some of the worst aspects of male chauvinism. He always has to have his own way and the last word in every conversation. If a drawer or a cupboard is not tidy enough to meet his exacting standards, he simply empties it onto the floor, leaving his wife to find it and "measure up." He is also passionately opposed to her Christian convictions and forbids her to have any Christian friends anywhere nearby when he is around.

These three "imagined scenarios" are all real situations. Christians all over the world find themselves in just such troubled and "impossible" relationships every moment of every day. What are we to do when we find ourselves in such problematic life settings? How should we advise friends who have to endure this kind of life? Some might say, "Pray that the rascal will die!" Others might encourage the unhappy spouse to get a divorce or to insist that the difficult and self-centered relative be put in a nursing home. "Why put up with such an 'impossible' person when you have an easy solution at hand?" they might say. Yet, as C. S. Lewis pointed out in one of his essays, we have no absolute right to happiness. For the Christian one's own personal happiness can never be the deciding factor in such troubled life settings. We must rather ask what pleases the Lord. He urges us to endure difficulty, looking to His Son who "endured such opposition from sinful men" (Hebrews 12:3). Or as Peter puts it: "If you suffer for doing good and you endure it, this is commendable before God. To this you were called, because Christ suffered for you, leaving you an example, that you should follow in His steps" (1 Peter 2:20-21). He calls on us to love the unlovely person, just as we have been loved by Him despite our lack of loveliness. It is in such difficult situations that we often see God most powerfully at work, drawing people to Himself through a life of self-sacrifice lived out by His children. He does not promise us an easy life; but He does promise His help, and He delights in saving "impossible" people.

12

An Open Home

Whether we find ourselves in extreme settings or in what we hope will be more normal ones, all of us are called to follow Christ by committing ourselves to a life of service and love. Apart from our immediate families, who will see this love? This is an important question, and often the answer is, "No one outside the family will see this love." This, however, is not a biblical answer. Scripture calls every Christian to "practice hospitality" (Romans 12:13; Hebrews 13:2; 1 Peter 4:9). The call to be hospitable is not an option for the Christian or a helpful suggestion off the apostle's cuff. It is not an option or a suggestion but a command, just as much as "You shall not commit adultery." All believers in a position of leadership in the church, whether men or women, are required to be examples of showing hospitality, just as they are required to be examples of fidelity in marriage or of honesty (1 Timothy 3:2; 5:10). But it is not only leaders who are to be hospitable but all believers. When we are hospitable, many others in addition to our family members will have the opportunity to see our love at work.

Who should be the recipients of this hospitality? Well, of course it is appropriate to be hospitable to our wider families, to our friends in the church, to those we already love. When writing about widows Paul emphasizes their responsibility to their wider family and to the church (and their family's responsibility to them):

> If a widow has children or grandchildren, these should learn
> first of all to put their religion into practice by caring for their
> own family and so repaying their parents and grandparents, for

this is pleasing to God. . . . [A widow is to be] well-known for
her good deeds, such as bringing up children, showing hospi-
tality, washing the feet of the saints, helping those in trouble and
devoting herself to all kinds of good deeds.

—1 TIMOTHY 5:4, 10

This passage and many others like it make it clear that we are called
by God to be hospitable to immediate families and to our wider families
and to members of our churches. But God's Word asks for even more than
this. The letter to the Hebrews calls us to be hospitable to "strangers"
(Hebrews 13:2), and this is in fact the literal meaning of the Greek word
for *hospitality*—"loving strangers." Jesus put it even more bluntly:

"When you give a luncheon or dinner, do not invite your
friends, your brothers or relatives, or your rich neighbors; if
you do, they may invite you back and so you will be repaid. But
when you give a banquet, invite the poor, the crippled, the lame,
the blind, and you will be blessed. Although they cannot repay
you, you will be repaid at the resurrection of the righteous."

—LUKE 14:12-14

Genuine, biblical hospitality is not having a few church friends over
to show off our new house or our new sofa set or our cooking skills and
being upset if they don't invite us back! Scriptural hospitality is inviting
people over who need our love, who need a meal, who are unlikely ever
to repay us with a return invitation. Consider adopting a widow or wid-
ower, a single-parent family, a college student away from home, an inter-
national student, someone struggling with psychological difficulties. Don't
ask yourself if these people will ever invite you back. Don't ask if they are
Christian believers. Don't even ask if they are nice people. Hospitality
might mean asking a person in need to come and live with you and your
family for a while. Three examples will help us see what this might mean.

A PREGNANT TEENAGER

A young woman (Eva) had become pregnant. The boyfriend (Steve) was
pressuring her to have an abortion. Eva needed time to reflect on what

she ought to do, as well as needing care and love during her pregnancy. She was invited to live with a family and stayed with them for about six months, until the baby was to be born. She decided not to have an abortion and later chose to keep her little girl rather than putting her up for adoption. This time with a Christian family was of crucial importance in Eva's life and in the life of little Beth, her daughter. It was a challenging time for the family to have someone extra to love and care for, but by doing so they were showing the love of Christ. It was challenging in other ways as well. Steve was so angry about Eva being encouraged to keep "her" baby rather than have "it" aborted that he came around with a gun one day, threatening to shoot the father of the family who had taken Eva in. That was frightening for the wife who was home with three little children! I know, however, that this family never regretted their decision to open their home to Eva.

STRUGGLING WITH DEPRESSION

A young man (John), turned down by the woman he loved, had become severely depressed. He was for a short time beginning to be suicidal, and in his depression he was in danger of making foolish decisions about his future. A family invited him to come and live with them while he worked through this tough stretch in his life. John spent six months with them, six of the happiest months of his life until that time. He wasn't always the easiest member of the family. He liked the wife's cooking so much that he would take extra-large helpings of food without considering who still had not been served. He seemed to have no sense of the couple's need for privacy; to get any time alone they had to ask friends to invite him out for a meal. He felt so at home that he would wander around the house half-naked. When the husband was away for two weeks on business, the couple was concerned about what the mailman and milkman might think coming to the house every day (this was in England) and seeing a man other than the husband half-dressed early each morning. They asked some neighbors to have John stay with them for those two weeks to give the wife some relief as she looked after the children by herself and to preserve propriety before the watching world. The first morning in the neighbor's home John came running down the stairs at breakfast time (fully dressed). When they asked where he was going, he replied, "They will be expecting me for breakfast at home!"

Such a story has its amusing side (long afterwards!) as well as being an illustration of the challenges of opening one's home. Again, however, while it was at times very hard having this young man stay with them, the family looks back on that period and on their relationship with John with happy memories, with love for him, and with gratitude to the Lord.

There are other ways of being hospitable to someone in need besides having the person come to live with you. Consider the option mentioned earlier of adopting a widow or some other person or persons who need family support. A single person or single persons sharing a house or apartment can do this too, of course.

AN ELDERLY WIDOW

A family adopted an elderly widow whom we will call Mary. Mary has no surviving family of her own to help look after her. The family invited Mary to share all birthdays with them and also all other special occasions and holiday seasons—Christmas, Thanksgiving, Easter, Independence Day. Whenever there is a reason for a family celebration, Mary is there for meals and festivities, and often on Sundays after church and at other times too. Sometimes the family takes meals to Mary—for example, when they make a family favorite for breakfast (cinnamon rolls or coffee cake). Parents and children regularly visit her and help with chores around her house and garden. The wife often takes Mary shopping with her or does Mary's shopping for her if she is unable to come. If there are family visits to the theater or concerts, Mary is always invited.

Mary truly became another member of the family, while also being able to maintain her independence. It was a relationship that gave joy to everyone involved. This taught the children in the most practical way possible that they were not the only people deserving attention, that Christian faith is to be put into practice, and that the words they heard from Scripture (for example, James 1:27—"Religion that God our Father accepts as pure and faultless is this: to look after orphans and widows in their distress . . .") are not empty words that are read but then ignored, but are words of life to be respected and obeyed. They learned that there is great joy in being doers of the Word and not simply hearers of it.

If your children are at a school with kids from unbelieving families, encourage them to make friends with them, to love them, to invite them into your home. If they go to a Christian school or are homeschooled, encourage them to get to know the kids in the neighborhood, to make friends with them, to love them, to invite them into your home. You cannot teach children to keep apart from unbelievers until they are twenty-one and then teach them to suddenly change the habit of a lifetime and start loving non-Christians. There is not one set of commandments for believers who are six, or twelve, or sixteen and another set of commandments for believers who are twenty-one and over. All of God's children, of whatever age, are called to be like Him.

> *A father to the fatherless, a defender of widows,*
> *is God in his holy dwelling.*
> *God sets the lonely in families,*
> *he leads forth the prisoners with singing.*
> —PSALM 68:5-6

Many of the opportunities my wife and I have been given to share the truth of the Gospel with people have come in the context of being hospitable to the friends of our children. This kind of hospitality has to be extended not just once or twice, but repeatedly over the years. There are young men and women in their middle twenties who have become our friends and visit us who have been coming into our home for ten years or more. Some of these young people are from broken homes, from homes where there is little love, from situations of drug abuse or severe sexual sins or even serious crime. Did we worry about our children getting to know children from such contexts? Of course we did. But we prayed and continue to pray. We talked to our own children carefully about the temptations and challenges they faced and continue to face, just as we face them. We sought to love and continue to try to love these young men and women. We have prayed and continue to pray for open doors to make the truth known to them. God answers those prayers in His own time. Your children will themselves be given opportunities to share what they believe and to discuss the Christian faith with their friends. These discussions may well lead to your being able to help with questions that your children find difficult to answer.

Other open doors will arise at weddings and other occasions. Your sons' and daughters' friends will come to their weddings, and there some of them will hear the Christian faith clearly and succinctly, perhaps for the first time in their lives. Be glad for such friends for your children. Do not be afraid. God is able to care for His children and to make them a blessing to other people, even if at times they have to struggle through some deep waters during the voyage of their faith.

No matter how tough it is sometimes to obey God's call to be hospitable, God is no one's debtor. He opens, and will open forever, the windows of heaven to pour out His blessing on any attempt of ours to be faithful to His calling. Is it easy to do this? Is it always comfortable? Are the people one invites pleasant company on every occasion? No, no, and no! God, however, always gives His help to those who ask Him to come to their aid when they find it hard to follow His calling. He promises to welcome us into His eternal dwelling. He is going to be hospitable to us forever. We are called to imitate Him for this short time that we are here in this world of broken and needy people.

13

THE NEW COMMUNITY

We have been thinking about the home as the place in which Jesus' "new command" (John 13:34-35) is to be lived out. The home, however, is not the only context where Christian love is to be on display. Any non-Christian who comes into our churches or into any community of Christians ought to be able to clearly see the practice of self-sacrificing love in the lives of those whom God calls to Himself. This love should be expressed in two ways—by the way we love one another as believers and by the way we love the stranger who comes into our churches.

Because we are all such broken people, damaged by our own sin and by the sin of others, we are to be realistic about each other. We know that those with whom we live and work and worship are going to be sinners just like ourselves. The love Christ has for us is a patient, forbearing, and forgiving love. In any group of Christians this must be at the heart of all our relationships. We will not expect each other to be perfect; we will be ready to overlook weaknesses and faults; we will be eager to forgive, knowing that we too need forgiveness. The apostle Paul writes about such love in 1 Corinthians 13:4-5:

> *Love is patient, love is kind. It does not envy, it does not boast, it is not proud. It is not rude, it is not self-seeking, it is not easily angered, it keeps no record of wrongs.*

Imagine a Christian school, college, seminary, mission agency, or church where this is a reality—not fully realized, of course, for this is only realized fully in Christ Himself and in the age to come, but at least the firstfruits of it. Francis Schaeffer used to speak of the need for "substantial healing" of our relationships in the present age or of "supernaturally restored relationships." Our communities, he said, are to be "pilot lights" revealing to the world what is possible through Christ and what will come to full realization in the age to come, when we see Christ clearly and become fully like Him.

This is the pattern of life to which we are called. This is the vision that we are to hold before us. To the extent that we live this way we will indeed give light to the world and cause people to give glory to God. When people see such love, the Spirit will lead them to believe that the Father loves us and has sent His Son into the world for the salvation of sinners. I regularly tell our seminary students that if I happen to visit the church in which one of them serves, I will not ask first, "Is this man a good preacher?" Rather, first of all I will ask the secretaries, office staff, janitors, and cleaners what it is like to work for this pastor. I will ask, "What kind of a man is he? Is he a servant? Is he demanding and harsh, or is he patient, kind, and forbearing as a man in authority?" One of our graduates may preach great sermons, but if he is a pain to work for, then you know he will cause major problems in any congregation. Leaders in the church are required by Scripture to set an example in the areas of love, kindness, gentleness, patience, and forbearance before they are appointed to preach, teach, and rule. If we obediently require these attitudes and character traits of our leaders, what will our "new community" look like?

THE POWER OF FRIENDSHIP

George and Amelia started attending church about a year after they had moved into the area for a new job. They had several children, the youngest being a son, Peter, who was eight at the time. When asked by Joe, "What was your first contact with the church?" Amelia mentioned that at Peter's new school several children from the church had befriended him. These new friendships eased his transition into a new school and new area and led to his being invited to a couple of birthday parties. George and Amelia, in the process of taking him to and fetching him from these parties, had the opportunity to meet some of the other parents. These casual meetings led to their learning about the church and coming to the Sunday morning service.

When questioned further about why they were coming George replied, "We have lived in several different countries, and we have moved around this country as my job has changed. But we have never met a group of people like this before, people who have been so open, so warm and friendly to us and to our children. We don't know what you've got, but we want to be part of it." You can imagine how encouraged Joe was. He thought in his heart, *The Lord is helping us do something right!* This is the way all our churches ought to be—showing an evident love for one another that attracts people, an openness and warmth to those who are not yet part of the fellowship.

THE POWER OF HUMILITY

Along with warmth and openness, love must express itself in humility toward one another if genuine unity is to be realized, the kind of unity that will attract people to the Gospel. Humility is perhaps the central Christian virtue—humility before God and humility before each other. We sometimes misunderstand what humility is and see it as a sense of our own worthlessness, a recognition that we are of no value and that nothing in our personality or accomplishments is of any use to God or anyone else. If we think of humility this way, we will try to work ourselves into a state of self-hatred. But this is not what God desires, and it is ultimately deeply dishonoring to Him. The Scripture calls us to love our neighbor *as we love ourselves.* To be made in the image of God means that we are *crowned with glory and honor* by God Himself. To deny our worth is to make God a liar. Sin does not obliterate our human glory, though sin most certainly defaces the likeness to God. In addition, God has set His love on us in His Son, and this means that we are of infinite value to Him.

So what is true humility if it is not despising oneself? Consider the words of Paul in Philippians 2:1-8. In this passage Paul describes true humility, the humility of Jesus Christ, and commends Christ to us as the model for our own humility.

If you have any encouragement from being united with Christ,
if any comfort from his love, if any fellowship with the Spirit,
if any tenderness and compassion, then make my joy complete

*by being like-minded, having the same love, being one in spirit
and purpose. Do nothing out of selfish ambition or vain con-
ceit, but in humility consider others better than yourselves.
Each of you should look not only to your own interests, but
also to the interests of others. Your attitude should be the same
as that of Christ Jesus.*

—vv. 1-5

Paul then describes how Christ humbled Himself in His incarnation,
in His life of service, and in His death on the cross. Christ's humility is
the heart of the Gospel of God's love, and humility is to be the heart of
any community, whether it is the little community of the family or the
larger community of a church or of a Christian institution such as a
school or any other ministry.

Imagine a community where those working together think more
highly of each other than they do of themselves. What a spirit of mutual
honor and of serving one another there would be! What delight in
another person's gifts and accomplishments! What pleasure in being
together! What unity! The years I have taught at Covenant Seminary
have been like this. It has been an honor to work with my colleagues.
They are genuinely humble men, men who think more highly of one
another than of themselves. They are men who delight in giving honor
to one another and seeing others honored; men who gladly praise one
another to their students; men who would never miss a faculty meeting
because of the spirit of unity and the pleasure of being together. I do not
recall one unpleasant faculty meeting in twelve years, one incident of
hearing a colleague criticized by another, one example of jealousy, envy,
or malice. Working together has been a joy for us, a gift of God we do
not take lightly, a gift we pray that He will continue to give us. It has
been a remarkable fruit of the Gospel and a blessing from the Lord, evident to any visitor to the campus, whether believer or unbeliever.

THE POWER OF CARING

Supernaturally restored relationships flowing out of hearts that are
humble before God and before one another—this is love. Such love
will express itself in service, in practical acts of kindness. It cannot

remain at the level of warm thoughts or even of gentle words but must find ways to put itself into action. The apostle John writes about this in 1 John 3:16-18:

> *This is how we know what love is: Jesus Christ laid down his life for us. And we ought to lay down our lives for our brothers. If anyone has material possessions and sees his brother in need but has no pity on him, how can the love of God be in him? Dear children, let us not love with words or tongue but with actions and in truth.*

Two years ago my wife, Vicki, had to deal with colon cancer—first major surgery, then six months of chemotherapy that made her very ill. If I had been asked to express beforehand what manner of love should be shown to a family going through such an experience, I would not have set the bar as high as the care that has been shown to us. It would take a book to detail all the love poured out on us by family, friends, and our church and seminary community, and perhaps one day I will write that book. But a few examples will suffice to make the point.

Three of my colleagues' wives came twice each month all through the chemotherapy to wash our floors and bathrooms and clean the house. They did this labor cheerfully and gladly. When I thanked one she said, "It is an honor," and her words were obviously sincere. For months we received meals from friends, church, faculty, administration, and student families. So many meals came that we could not eat them all and had to store some of them in the freezer. These were meals prepared with care; meals accompanied with cards, decorations, and flowers; meals that were sometimes simple and sometimes as elaborate as a full Thanksgiving meal (though it was not Thanksgiving when it came, but just an ordinary day).

In the hospital Vicki received so many flowers, about thirty bouquets, that the hospital turned a room for two into a room for one much of the week of her stay. Doctors, nurses, orderlies, and visitors to other patients would come into her room to admire the flowers, drawn by the fragrance and abundance. The flowers continued coming all through the chemotherapy in such numbers that the deliveryman became familiar with our home and started commenting on the love

shown us each time he came. Vicki and I received so many cards, letters, E-mails, phone calls, words of encouragement, assurances of
prayer and care, visits, and practical expressions of love that we were
truly upheld with the sense of support.

I will never forget the five hours that she was in surgery. My pastor,
a colleague at the Schaeffer Institute, the president and dean of the seminary, and another pastor and personal friend all came to be with me
during that time, to pray, to encourage, to support by their presence and
love. These are a few highlights of the love shown to us during that time.
For now, only God knows the eternal consequences in people's lives of
this extraordinary outpouring; but the day will come when we will see
what He has accomplished through this. I have no doubt that there will
be people in the kingdom because of the love shown to us during that
year of severe suffering.

THE KINDNESS AND PERSEVERANCE OF GOD

14

IS GOD RELUCTANT?

One of the most common objections non-Christians raise against the Christian faith is the reality of God's judgment. This "problem" is also one of the most frequent matters of concern, doubt, and struggle for believers as well as unbelievers. We might ask, "Why are not more people Christians? Where is God? What is He doing? Why are so many people judged by Him? What about those who have never heard the Gospel? Doesn't God care about people? Is He truly a God of love? Is He fair and just in His judgment?" The impression we sometimes give with such questions is that *we* care more about people than God does, that we would do anything to make sure lost people are saved, whereas God is too laid-back about the whole problem of the destiny of unbelievers. It is as if we think we are eager to save people, but God is reluctant. But is it true that God is the one who is reluctant to reach people with the good news of Christ's salvation?

If we were to study the history of mission throughout the past twenty centuries, we would soon discover that the church has always been strangely reluctant to go out into the world with the Gospel. This is true as we read the book of Acts in the New Testament; and it has been true of every period of church history since that time. If we turn our attention to our own congregations today, we will discover the same reluctance. Very few of our churches take a truly active role in reaching out with the Gospel; and even the churches that are most active in mission are cool-hearted and lukewarm in their zeal at best. If we gaze honestly into our own individual hearts, we find a similar reluctance. We may protest about God's fairness and lack of eagerness to save, but what are *we* doing? How much self-sacrificing love, how much time and energy, how much true zeal do we pour into the effort to help unbelievers come to know the truth about Jesus Christ?

If, in contrast, we turn our attention to God and ask, "What does He do to save people? What effort, what zeal, what love does He expend on this task?" we find a very different answer than the one we find to our questions about ourselves, our churches, or the history of God's people.

So how has God loved people? What does He do to save them and us? We can give several answers to this question about how God has demonstrated His love and His determination to save.

We read in Scripture that God has loved us and planned for our salvation from the foundation of the world and even before that time (Revelation 13:8; 17:8). We know that God promised from the Fall that he would send His Son into the world to die for us (Genesis 3:15). The Old Testament is filled with prophecies made by God's people as they paid attention to what the Holy Spirit revealed to them about the coming of Christ. We ought to read the history of the human race from the time of Adam and Eve's rebellion up until the incarnation of Jesus as the history of God's preparing a people among whom and from whom His Son would be born. When we read the Gospels we read of God's demonstration of His love to us in the life, the ministry, and supremely the death of Christ.

And yet, as we consider these matters we have to acknowledge that all this by itself will not bring about the salvation of one individual. This may seem like a blasphemous thing to say, for of course it is true that Christ's death is sufficient to atone for the sins of the whole world. It is the manifestation above all other manifestations of the love of God for sinners. It is the means by which we are made acceptable to God; and without that work of Christ on our behalf no one would be saved. But still it is true that because of the hardness of our human hearts, the objective fact of Christ's death by itself will not save us.

Christ's death on the cross as an event in history has to be brought to our attention and applied to our hearts by the work of God. This is why the Holy Spirit is sent into the world to draw our hearts and minds to Christ and all He has done for us. Jesus acknowledged, "No one can come to me unless the Father who sent me draws him" (John 6:44).

Jesus said that both He and His Father have been working ever since the Fall (John 5:17)—working to save, working to draw people to faith. And this is hard work.

Paul compares this work of kindling faith in the hearts of sinners to the original work of creating the universe:

> For God, who said, "Let light shine out of darkness," made his light shine in our hearts to give us the light of the knowledge of the glory of God in the face of Christ.
> —2 CORINTHIANS 4:6

It is probably appropriate to say that in a sense it is a harder work for God to kindle faith in Christ in a hard heart than it was for Him to create the physical universe. It is harder because we are not sticks and stones or other physical objects that do not resist the voice of God. Rather we, as God's image-bearers, have a mind and will of our own; and as rebels against God we have a mind and will that have turned away from Him, a mind and will that distort His image rather than displaying it faithfully.

We need to reflect, then, on what God does to save us individually, on how He draws people to faith in Jesus Christ, and then to ask again whether we believe that God is reluctant. A few scriptural examples should help us understand that God is not a reluctant evangelist, even if you and I are!

THE ETHIOPIAN EUNUCH (ACTS 8:26-40)

The setting for this story is that Philip was in Samaria proclaiming the Gospel among the Samaritan people. The Jerusalem church had not planned a series of outreach events in Samaria. Rather, the believers had gone to Samaria as a result of the persecution of the church in Jerusalem, a persecution led by Saul following the stoning of Stephen (Acts 8:1-4).

God had brought His reluctant evangelists to witness to the Samaritans, and there in Samaria an angel of the Lord called Philip to go to a particular place on the road that crosses the southern desert between Jerusalem and Gaza. Once Philip was near that road, the Holy Spirit told him to approach a particular chariot traveling back to Ethiopia from Jerusalem. This was indeed a divine appointment! When Philip came near the chariot, he heard the man in it reading from the Scriptures and, emboldened by this open door, engaged the man in conversation. Following a discussion about the meaning of Isaiah 53, the Ethiopian eunuch came to faith and was baptized by Philip. The eunuch went on his way rejoicing in his newfound faith, and Philip was taken away suddenly by the Holy Spirit to continue the work of evangelism elsewhere.

As we read this story we are struck by the way God intervened directly to bring this man to salvation. Luke's account is about God's miraculous work in reaching this man. Philip was not the initiator of this evangelistic encounter. God was. We learn from Luke's narration about how God ruled over the circumstances of two lives to bring the Ethiopian to faith in Christ. Our hearts magnify the Lord's saving work in drawing this man to himself. We do not read this story and think, "Wasn't Philip a wonderful, clever, and bold evangelist!" Rather, we praise God. This is as it ought to be whenever we hear of a believer leading someone to faith, for then, in just the same way as in this Bible story, God is bringing two people together. We need to learn to see God's work rather than thinking how courageous, intelligent, clear-speaking, and good we are as evangelists. I am not saying the human role is unimportant, for Philip needed to be obedient to the Spirit's call; he needed to talk to the Ethiopian and to make the Scriptures clear to him. Yet, because of the way the story is told, we know that God is the One who is most to be praised when we read of this man's conversion. *May this be our daily experience, O Lord! May we worship You!*

What we should also notice about this story is that there was a history behind the Ethiopian's coming to faith. There are two indications of this history in Luke's account. The first is his telling us that the Ethiopian had been up to Jerusalem to worship God at the temple (v. 27). This man was not a typical pagan; rather, God had already been at work in his life, perhaps for many years. We are not told in the text, but we would like to ask and one day will be able to ask, "How had an

Ethiopian from faraway Africa become a worshiper of the one true God, the God of Israel?"

We know that there had been Ethiopian believers for many centuries before this man became a Christian. Moses' wife was an Ethiopian (a Cushite). Psalm 87 speaks of those from Cush of whom it would be said that they were "born in Zion" (v. 4) and that their names were recorded in God's "register of the peoples" (v. 6). In the days of Solomon it is probable that people from Ethiopia traveled to Jerusalem because they had heard of the king's wisdom, for we are told that people from all over the world came to Jerusalem to learn from him. During the time that Jeremiah prophesied, one of the remnant of faithful believers was an Ethiopian, Ebed-Melech, and he was in fact the one man who had compassion on Jeremiah when he was thrown into the muddy cistern and left there to die (Jeremiah 38—39). Jeremiah himself is said to have died in southern Egypt or northern Ethiopia when he was taken against his will with the rebellious people left in the land after the Babylonians had conquered Judah and exiled a large part of the population.

We know, then, that there were Ethiopians who were worshipers of God long before the New Testament period. It is quite possible that the Ethiopian court official of whom we read in Acts 8 was a descendant of one of these; but we will find out for sure when we get to see him face to face someday.

There is a second indication in Luke's account as to the history of God's work in the eunuch's life. Luke records the fact that the court official from Ethiopia was reading the Old Testament, and not just any portion of the Old Testament but one of the most beautiful and powerful of all the messianic prophecies. He was reading the song about the Suffering Servant who died for the sins of His people. This song, one of the most familiar passages of Scripture to Christians all through the ages, is found in Isaiah 53. The Ethiopian treasurer was reading about the suffering of Christ, and he wanted to know who it is that the prophet was describing. What an open door, and Philip began at that passage and then explained the good news about Jesus!

We may be sure that it was not by chance that the Ethiopian was reading this Scripture. Again we would like to ask, "Why were you reading this passage of the Old Testament as you rode home in your chariot from Jerusalem? Had someone encouraged you to read it, someone you met while you were visiting in Jerusalem? Or was it simply the Holy Spirit urging your heart to read these words and wonder about them?" And again Luke does not answer this question for us, so we will have to be patient and wait until we get to meet this "black diamond" in God's kingdom and can ask him for ourselves.

But the important point is, not only was God not reluctant regarding this man's salvation—He was actively seeking out his soul and bringing him to salvation and new life in the Lord Jesus Christ!

15

A RELUCTANT EVANGELIST

In thinking about the salvation of the Ethiopian eunuch we saw how God brought this man and Philip together. We marveled at the way God had been preparing the Ethiopian's life and heart, readying him for his encounter with Philip. The important point here is that this man had a history before Philip witnessed to him on the desert road. God had already been at work in his life long before Philip was able to reap his harvest, a harvest that God had been preparing for just this occasion.

This reality of a history is true every time we see someone come to faith in Christ. Invariably God has been at work for a long time, drawing a person to Christ before a believer has the privilege of being a midwife at a new birth. When we recognize this truth of God's long, hard labor each time He saves someone, we should be able to have a more accurate perception of our part in the process of conversion. We are not to think, "I am the man!" when we call someone to repentance or lead them in a prayer of faith for the first time.

We turn now to another story in Acts that underlines for us the contrast between God's eagerness to save and the reluctance of the evangelist.

CORNELIUS THE CENTURION (ACTS 9:43—10:48)

Jesus had commanded His disciples to take the Gospel to their fellow Jews, to the Samaritans, and to the Gentiles. As we read the early chapters of Acts we find the apostles obeying the first part of this command, proclaiming Christ with boldness to their fellow Jews in Jerusalem, sometimes even at the cost of their own comfort, safety, and, in Stephen's case, life itself. Yet they made no effort to go beyond their own people and reach out to non-Jews. In our previous chapter we saw how God miraculously intervened in Philip's life to bring him to his first Gentile. Now, in Acts chapter 10, we read about what it took to get Peter, the leader of the apostles, to the point in his life where he was prepared to share the Gospel with a Gentile. Throughout Acts 10 Luke draws our attention to the work of God as he brought Peter to the home of Cornelius.

A PROVIDENTIAL PLACE TO STAY

We find Peter, in God's providence, staying at the home of Simon, a tanner (9:43). Simon the tanner worked at curing and preparing animal skins so they could be used for clothing, rugs, wall hangings, and tents. This work was considered unclean by the Pharisees and teachers of the Law, for Simon's profession required him to handle the skins of animals that were unclean according to the Law of Moses. Peter was staying in a home where all around him were reminders of the clean/unclean distinction that God had given to His people with the primary purpose of making them a nation that was set apart. Israel was set apart from the nations around it in every aspect of its life, not only in its commitment to serve God and in its public worship, but even in the kind of food the people were allowed to eat.

God had given these laws to teach His people that they were to be different from the pagan nations, that they were to be devoted to Him, that they were to be holy in all of their life. But by the New Testament period these laws had been expanded and applied to every conceivable situation so that Jews were required by their religious leaders to keep themselves totally apart from "unclean" Samaritan and Gentile "sinners."

In the home of Simon the tanner by God's providential guidance, Peter was being asked by God to think about what it means to be separate from the Gentile nations. Christ had on many occasions told Peter and his fellow apostles to go to the Samaritans and Gentiles. Christ had shown by His own example that He desired to reach out to Samaritans and Gentiles. We see this again and again in the Gospels. We even see Jesus explicitly teaching His disciples that it is not the food we eat that makes us unclean; rather, it is the evil thoughts that arise in our hearts that make us unclean (Mark 7:1-23). That passage adds the comment

(v. 19), "In saying this, Jesus declared all foods 'clean.'" Peter had heard this teaching from Jesus' own mouth, and now God had set him in a situation where he ought to be thinking about why he was reluctant to obey Jesus' command to go to the Gentiles.

A Vision of an Angel

God now gave a vision of an angel to Cornelius, telling him to send men to Joppa to the house of Simon the tanner (the angel even gave the house location) so they could bring Simon Peter back with them. Cornelius was not a typical pagan of the time, nor was he a typical centurion in the Roman army. He and all his family are described by Luke (10:2) as "devout and God-fearing. He gave generously to those in need and prayed to God regularly." He worshiped at the local synagogue, though as a Gentile he would never be invited to eat in the home of a Jew, nor would a Jew dine at his table. Yet, it is not possible to imagine an easier Gentile for Peter's first baby steps toward reaching out to the Gentiles. God was moving Peter from where he was in his attitudes toward non-Israelites and gently leading him to where he ought to be, to where he should have been long before.

A Vision of Animals

While the men from Cornelius were on their way, Peter was up on the tanner's roof praying. As he prayed, it is probable that he was kneeling among animal skins, some clean and some unclean, spread out to dry on the flat roof. God showed Peter a vision that explicitly included unclean animals, and God told him to get up, kill, and eat. Peter, as usual, was slow to respond to the Lord's command or even to understand its meaning. His response, also as usual, was to protest at what the Lord wanted him to do: "Surely not, Lord! I have never eaten anything impure or unclean" (10:14). God replied to Peter that he should "not call anything impure or unclean that God has made clean" (v. 15).

Jesus, as we saw earlier, had already declared all foods clean, but Peter, as usual, had not understood Him at the time. To make sure that on this occasion Peter understood, the Lord gave Peter the same instructions three times. Then the vision of animals was taken back up to heaven, and Peter was left to ponder its meaning.

A WORD FROM THE SPIRIT

While Peter was still reflecting on the vision, the men from Cornelius arrived, inquiring if Peter was at the tanner's house. The Holy Spirit told Peter that some men had arrived looking for him: "So get up and go downstairs. Do not hesitate to go with them, for I have sent them" (v. 19). The Lord assured Peter that these men had come for him in obedience to God's command. Peter was left in no doubt that God was going before him on this journey! He was being led by the hand every step of the way.

AN INVITATION FROM THE GENTILES

When Peter went down to meet the men, he asked why they had come looking for him, and they delivered Cornelius' invitation to him. Their reply was very carefully worded in order to assure Peter that it would be right and good for him to go with them. First, they told Peter that Cornelius, from whom they had come, was a righteous and God-fearing man. Second, they referred to the reputation Cornelius enjoyed among the Jews in Caesarea—he was highly respected by them all, and everyone knew that he was a friend of the Jews and of the synagogue. Third, they recounted for Peter the command of the angel of God to bring Peter to Cornelius' house so they "could hear what you have to say" (v. 22). Peter was told that he had a message for these Gentiles that God wanted him to deliver. As we consider this invitation, we see again how clear and unequivocal are Peter's directions from the Lord.

AN EXPECTANT CROWD

When Peter arrived in Caesarea at Cornelius' house, he found a large gathering of people waiting for his arrival and for the message he brought from God. Cornelius' whole household was there, and in addition he had invited his relatives and close friends. So there was a crowd of Gentiles eager to hear from Peter. Before this assembly Cornelius, a man of authority, power, and dignity, fell in reverence at Peter's feet, for he knew that Peter was God's ambassador bringing God's Word to him. After making Cornelius stand, for he, Peter, was only a man, Peter went into the house with Cornelius to find the large and expectant group assembled there. His words to them were extraordinary in their lack of graciousness, in their insensitivity, and in the way they revealed Peter's continuing failure to understand why God wanted him there.

Try to imagine yourself as one of those assembled to listen to Peter, one who has interrupted the busy schedule of your day to make time to hear this man. You have been told that the man arriving is a messenger from God. Your highly respected centurion, friend, and relative has been visited by a fearful angel of God and was commanded to bring this man so you could hear from him God's true and sure word. But these are the first words you hear from him:

> *"You are well aware that it is against our law for a Jew to associate with a Gentile or visit him. But God has shown me that I should not call any man impure or unclean. So when I was sent for, I came without raising any objection. May I ask why you sent for me?"*

—vv. 28-29

How do you think you might have responded to being greeted like this?

Peter, in effect, told these Gentiles gathered to hear him that if it had been up to him he would not have come there. He was a Jew who did not associate with Gentiles or even visit them, and he suggested that was God's Law, for Jews equated "our law" and "God's law." (We should note that actually God had not forbidden His people to eat with or to visit Gentiles.) Until very recently, Peter informed them, he had thought of Gentiles as impure and unclean, but now God had shown him that was wrong. So he had no objection (at last!), and here he was. But he still did not know why he was there and what he was supposed to do and say.

A REQUEST FROM CORNELIUS

Cornelius then recounted for Peter his encounter with the angel. Cornelius carefully mentioned everything he could that would help Peter

to know that God had brought this occasion about. Cornelius was praying—clearly a customary activity for him. An angel appeared to him and
commended him for his gifts to the poor and for his prayers, for God
had taken note of both. The angel commanded him to send for Peter,
and he was thankful that Peter had come. Peter's words lacked grace,
but Cornelius' words were humble and respectful. Cornelius ended his
account by reminding Peter that they were all assembled "in the presence of God to listen to everything the Lord has commanded you to tell
us" (v. 33).

There is some irony in these words, not from Cornelius, but from
Luke in telling this story. What the Lord had commanded Peter to tell
these Gentiles was the Gospel, the command of the Great Commission.
Peter had received no other command from the Lord but this. The providential place to stay, the angel appearing to Cornelius, the vision on the
rooftop, the direction from the Holy Spirit, the invitation of the
Gentiles—each step on Peter's path that we have examined points to and
reinforces Jesus' command to take the Gospel to the Gentiles.

A RELUCTANT EVANGELIST FINALLY GETS IT

After Cornelius' reminder of the Lord's command and the Lord's presence, Peter at last understood why he was there:

> *"I now realize how true it is that God does not show favoritism,
> but accepts men from every nation who fear him and do what
> is right."*

—vv. 34-35

Then Peter proclaimed the Gospel of Christ, and the Gentiles immediately responded. Peter did not have to issue an invitation, for while he
was still speaking, the Holy Spirit was poured out on the Gentiles and
they began to speak in tongues, just as the apostles themselves had on
the Day of Pentecost. God wanted to make it abundantly clear to Peter,
and to the other Jews who had come with him, that He accepted these
new believers in Christ, even though they were Gentiles, even though
they were not circumcised, even though they did not observe the food
laws. God accepted and forgave them in Christ. God gave them His

Spirit fully, just as He had given the Spirit to the leaders of the Jewish church. The Jewish believers who were present were astonished by what happened, for they had thought in their hearts, "Even if God lets a Gentile into the kingdom, surely such a man will be a second-class member!" But, no, for "the gift of the Spirit had been poured out even on the Gentiles" (v. 45).

A CRITICAL FOLLOW-UP

After the news spread to the churches that Peter had visited in a Gentile's home, had eaten with uncircumcised men, and had baptized Gentiles, he was roundly criticized by his fellow believers (Acts 11:1-18). He was not the only reluctant evangelist! Peter recounted all the events that led him to Cornelius' home and what transpired there, and we can see the wisdom of God in giving Peter so many and such clear signals of His guidance along the way. Peter finished his account with these startling words:

> "So if God gave them the same gift as he gave us, who believed in the Lord Jesus Christ, who was I to think that I could oppose God?"
>
> —ACTS 11:17

The criticism was silenced (for a time), and they praised God:

> "So then, God has granted even the Gentiles repentance unto life."
>
> — v. 18

As we look back at this retelling of the conversion of Cornelius, his household, his friends, and his relatives, what is so remarkable to us is the trouble to which God will go to get the Gospel to people He longs to save. God is the eager evangelist! Peter, those around him, you and I are the reluctant evangelists. The Father, the Son, and the Spirit are always working to seek and save those who are lost. We, like Peter, reluctant, unwilling, protesting, are dragged into serving God in the work that He calls us to do.

16

The Importance of
Our History

In the story of Cornelius, just as with the Ethiopian, it is evident that the Gospel did not come to his house out of the blue or with no preparation. God was not only hard at work during the few days recorded in Acts 10, the days in which he brought the reluctant Peter to Cornelius' home. God had been working in Cornelius' heart for many years, speaking to him through the words he heard read from the Old Testament Sabbath by Sabbath in the synagogue in Caesarea; drawing him to Himself in Cornelius' own reading and prayers; moving his heart to compassion for the poor. When Cornelius came to faith in Christ, it was the culmination of God's calling him to Himself.

So it is with every conversion. Each new birth is the result of a process of delivery, sometimes short and sometimes long (only God knows just how long), sometimes painful and sometimes pleasant for the one being delivered, but always a challenging process for God in a sense because of the hardness of the human heart. But there is always a history of God's work in the heart and mind of the person he is saving.

The Conversion of Saul (Acts 8:1; 9:1-30; 22:2-16; 26:4-18)

The account of the conversion of Saul of Tarsus is perhaps the most dramatic salvation story in the New Testament. Saul was, according to his own description in Philippians 3:4-6, a man who lived at the very heart of Judaism:

. . . a Hebrew of Hebrews; in regard to the law, a Pharisee; as for zeal, persecuting the church; as for legalistic righteousness, faultless.

—vv. 5-6

Elsewhere (Acts 26:5) he describes himself as living "according to the strictest sect of our [the Pharisees'] religion." Saul was present at the death of Stephen, the earliest Christian martyr. He was the leader of the first severe persecution of the young church in Jerusalem. What did it take to save this man? Is it likely that the Christians were praying for his conversion? Do we pray today for those who persecute the church or whom we regard as bitter enemies of the Gospel? Certainly when Saul did come to faith, the Christians were still afraid of him and did not believe that he was truly a disciple of Christ (Acts 9:26).

Who, then, reached out to Saul? It is clear that he did not become a Christian through any human evangelist, reluctant or otherwise. Christ Himself appeared to Saul, and He appeared not to a man who was seeking Him, but to a man who was journeying to Damascus seeking to expand the persecution he had begun in Jerusalem. Christ made a post-ascension resurrection appearance to Saul, for He desired to call this man to Himself and then to appoint him to be one of His apostles, an apostle who would go to the Gentiles and make the Gospel of Christ known to them.

"Why Saul?" we might want to ask. Our answers will be speculative, but we can suggest two reasons. First, Saul had been on the very inside of Judaism, and once he had understood where it was mistaken in its interpretation of the Old Testament Law, there was no one better fitted to set aside its burden of legalism and to joyfully reach out to the Gentiles. He knew that Christ had redeemed him from the slavery of thinking that observing this endless code of laws would make him right before God.

Second, Saul stands as a reminder to the church in every age that we ought never to give up on people, that enmity to Christ, to the Gospel, and to the church does not necessarily mean a person is beyond reach. We are encouraged by the example of Saul's conversion not to consign anyone to a list of those we think are "hopeless cases," those for whom it is no longer worth praying, or so we conclude. If Christ could save Saul, then he can save our family members who seem antagonistic, our friends who are closed, our enemies who seem to hate us and who passionately reject the Gospel. It is not appropriate for us to conclude that anyone is beyond the grace of God.

Saul's conversion was sudden and dramatic. It was completely unexpected by the Christians, even unbelievable to them. Yet, does this mean there was no history behind his coming to faith? Many years after his conversion Paul stated that there was, in fact, a history of God's working in his life before his blinding encounter with the risen Lord on the Damascus Road. Paul reported that on that occasion Jesus said to him, "Saul, Saul, why do you persecute me? It is hard for you to kick against the goads" (Acts 26:14).

What were these "goads" pricking Saul's mind and heart? The text does not tell us, but these words of Jesus to Saul indicate that the Spirit had already been at work drawing Saul to Christ before he met the Lord face to face. Was it the faithful testimony and courage of Stephen as Saul watched him being stoned to death? Was it Stephen's words of forgiveness as he died—"Lord, do not hold this sin against them" (Acts 7:60)?

Were the words or attitudes of some of the other Christian men and women whom Saul dragged off to prison "goads"? Was it his own excellent knowledge of the Scriptures and of the messianic prophecies that pointed to Jesus' life and death that was leading him step by step to doubt his passionate opposition to the Christian "heresy"? What was the Spirit using as "goads" to prick his conscience? We can ask him one day for the details; but we know now that even for Saul there was a history of God's work in saving him. This is a history that only the Lord knows fully in this life but that He will reveal one day to each one of us so that we will know as we are fully known.

THE SALVATION OF TIMOTHY

As we read in the Scriptures of different people coming to believe in Jesus, we see, whenever we are given enough detail, that every story is unique. Timothy's story, for example, is very different from Paul's. We are told (1 Timothy 1:2) that Timothy was Paul's "true son in the faith." This expression, and others like it, when they are used by the apostles seem to indicate that "my son" or "my child in the faith" was converted through the ministry of the one writing or speaking (see, for example, 3 John 4).

It seems probable that Timothy came to faith in Christ while Paul was preaching on his first missionary journey through the cities of Asia Minor (now southern Turkey). Timothy lived in the pagan city of Lystra (Acts 16:1), a city where Paul had been stoned almost to death on his first visit (Acts 14:19-20). As we read this account in Acts 14 of Paul's time in Lystra we do not read of any conversions. Rather, we see the pagans responding to a miraculous healing by wanting to offer sacrifices to Paul and Barnabas as if they were gods, and then turning against them at the instigation of hostile Jews from neighboring cities (vv. 8-20). But apparently Timothy, along with others, came to believe in Christ as a result of this roller-coaster ride in Lystra, for Paul returned a little later to strengthen the disciples and to encourage them to remain true to the faith (14:21-22).

A year or two later Paul returned to these cities of southern Galatia to teach and encourage the believers. Already by the time of this second missionary journey to the area, Timothy had grown in his newfound faith. His spiritual maturity was such that he was so highly commended by the other Christians that Paul took him along with him to be trained on the job as an evangelist, church planter, and teacher (16:1-5).

Yet Timothy too had a history. He was raised in Lystra by a Greek father and a Jewish mother (16:1). Paul tells us (2 Timothy 1:5; 3:15) that Timothy's mother Eunice and his grandmother Lois were believers and that they had taught Timothy the Scriptures from his infancy. It is in this context that Paul makes his famous statement that "all Scripture is God-breathed" and is "able to make you wise for salvation through faith in Jesus Christ" (2 Timothy 3:15-16). God had been at work in Timothy's heart and mind from his earliest childhood through his knowledge of the Scriptures and through the teaching, love, prayers, and example of his mother and grandmother. Then, when Paul came to Lystra to proclaim the Gospel, the Holy Spirit brought His work of many years to fruition.

So many of the believers we all know are like this. Someone may make a commitment to Christ in an evangelistic meeting, at a worship service, or during a one-on-one conversation. However, if we probe a little deeper into their history we will often discover that there is a Eunice or a Lois who has been at work in the new convert's life. There has been a Eunice or Lois faithfully praying for this person, living a godly example before them for years, showing the patient and forgiving love of Christ all through their life, teaching them from infancy the truths of God's Word.

I try to encourage our students at Covenant Seminary to learn to ask about people's histories, especially when they have the privilege of leading someone to faith or of seeing someone commit themselves to Christ as a result of their preaching or witness. Why is this important? We so easily take too much credit for ourselves when we see someone coming to faith. Pastors and evangelists in particular, and all of us when we see our efforts at sharing the truth of the Gospel succeeding, tend to think and to speak as if "I am the one who saved this person." We quickly become proud; we want to boast to others about our success. We often forget to praise God who is truly the One who has saved this individual. Instead, we need to learn to ask some questions: "Tell me, what has God been doing in your life? What brought you to this point today? Are there other Christians who have influenced you? Why are you here now?"

If we listen carefully to the answers, we will find that we are being taught to praise God for His faithful work in a person's life, a work that often has been going on for many years. We see how patient, long-suffering, and merciful He is as He draws someone to Himself. We also learn to value the impact of other people on the lives of those we see come to faith. Hearing of God's work and hearing how He has used others will help keep us humble before Him and before other believers and will help us to be appropriately thankful for the special part that the Lord has called us to play in a new believer's life.

17

GOD'S INFINITE VARIETY
OF MEANS I

As we begin to ask questions of those we see come to faith, we will discover how faithfully and patiently God has been working in their lives to bring them to the point of commitment. We will discover, too, that God uses an infinite variety of means to draw people to Himself. God has created each individual in His likeness, and He is a God who delights in diversity; so there is an infinite number of ways in which His image can be expressed. Consequently each one of us is unique; we will never find another person who is exactly like ourselves. This is true even for identical twins; they know very well the differences between them, even if others sometimes have a hard time telling because of the tendency to be misled by the obvious similarities.

Just as each person is unique, so the way in which God draws each person to Himself is unique. Every Christian has a different story to tell. We should each write down for ourselves an account of how God drew us to faith in Christ and perhaps encourage others in a Bible study or small group fellowship to do the same. We will be filled with wonder at the variety of means God uses to save people, and it will fill our hearts with praise.

For several years I asked our incoming students at the seminary to write down for me the record of how they became believers. I still have those papers, many hundreds of them, and it is truly inspiring to read them over and see how different each story is from all the others. God, in His mercy, respects our unique personality and history, and then His grace weaves a tapestry that reveals His kind and persevering ways as He calls us to Himself. To use Edith Schaeffer's image from her book *Affliction*, God is preparing a portrait gallery of marvelous variety that on a day to come in the future we will all enjoy viewing. To see a few of the means God uses we will consider some biblical and some contemporary examples.

NAAMAN THE SYRIAN (2 KINGS 5)

Naaman was the commanding officer of the army of the Syrians, successful in battle, a man in high standing with his king. What adds particular interest to Naaman's story is that the Syrians and Israelites were enemies at this moment of history (as at many other periods of history, right up to the present time!), and Naaman had been the leader of his army in victory against Israel. God had used Naaman as His means of judging His covenant people for their lack of faithfulness to Him. What were the means that God used to call this "great man . . . highly regarded . . . valiant soldier" (2 Kings 5:1) to faith?

Trouble

Scripture teaches us that "not many wise . . . by human standards, not many . . . influential; not many . . . of noble birth" are called into God's kingdom (1 Corinthians 1:26). One reason for this is that fame, fortune, and power can cause us to be so proud that we will not bow before God and acknowledge our need of His work in our lives. But Naaman, despite his reputation, greatness, and success, suffered from leprosy. Such an affliction can bring humility and an open heart and mind even to the mighty, and this seems to be what happened in Naaman's case. His leprosy humbled him so much that he was prepared to seek help.

A Young Witness

On one of the Syrian raiding parties into Israel a young girl was taken captive, and in the providence of God she was given as a servant to Naaman's wife. We know very little about her, though one day she will shine like a star in the kingdom. This period in Israel's history was a time of great apostasy, but it is clear that this girl was a believer and that, despite being a captive and slave in the home of the commander of her people's enemies, she took pity on her master. She pled with her mistress to have Naaman go visit the prophet Elisha so that he might be healed. She was evidently a girl of strong faith, for we are told explicitly by Christ that even though there were many lepers in Israel at that time, not one of them was healed (Luke 4:27). She had not been accustomed to seeing leprosy cleansed, but she trusted in the power of God for her master, and she had confidence that He would answer the prayers of Elisha, His prophet. And God rewarded her faith. We will find out one day whether Naaman's wife and others in that household also became believers through this young girl.

The Powerlessness of a King

Naaman, at the urging of his wife, obtained permission from his master, the king of Syria, to go to Israel to be healed. We read first an amusing description of Naaman's visit to the king of Israel, who assumed that the Syrians were trying to start a fight with him by sending a leper to him to be healed. When he read the letter from Naaman's king, we are told:

> He tore his robes and said, "Am I God? Can I kill and bring back to life? Why does this fellow send someone to me to be cured of his leprosy? See how he is trying to pick a quarrel with me!"
>
> —2 KINGS 5:7

Naaman discovered through this experience that no human being, even the most powerful, even one who serves as king among God's people, can meet the needs of an afflicted human being. Naaman learned that only God Himself can help the most desperate needs of body and spirit.

Elisha, the Man of God

Elisha heard of the despair of the king of Israel and sent a message to him that Naaman should come to him for healing. When Naaman arrived at his house, Elisha knew that this great man, in order to be saved, must humble himself further. So instead of inviting him in or coming out to honor Naaman and give him God's gift of healing immediately, Elisha simply had a messenger tell Naaman to go and wash in the Jordan River. Naaman was enraged by this and left in fury, his pride and his nationalism deeply stung (he compares, unfavorably, the River Jordan with the rivers of Syria). Naaman's servants (we will learn someday whether they were saved too) pled with him to do this little thing, this humbling thing of washing himself seven times in the Jordan. They reasoned with him that he would have done gladly "some great thing" if the prophet of God had commanded it (2 Kings 5:13).

The Power of God

Naaman listened to their entreaty and, humbled, went to the Jordan and immersed himself seven times in it. His leprosy was taken away, and the flesh that had been wasted away was restored. This was an extraordinary miracle, a miracle like the miracles done by Jesus Himself in His ministry of mercy here on earth. Naaman returned to the prophet to thank him, to offer him a gift (which Elisha refused), and to praise God: "Now I know that there is no God in all the world except in Israel" (2 Kings 5:15). In the discussion with Elisha that followed this declaration, it is clear that Naaman had come to a profound faith in the Lord, a faith that was going to bring transformation to his life from that day forward.

THE WIDOW OF ZAREPHATH (1 KINGS 17)

Our next example of the variety of means God uses is another story of a non-Israelite coming to faith. This account, as with the illustration of Naaman, is one that Jesus used to teach His fellow inhabitants of Nazareth that God cares not only for His own people, Israel, but also for the peoples of other nations (Luke 4:14-30). The setting of this story is Zarephath, a town under the rule of Sidon, a city-state way to the north of Israel on the coast of the Mediterranean (then known as the Great Sea) close to the kingdom of Tyre. Tyre and Sidon, like Syria, were major enemies of Israel through much of Israel's history.

Famine

This story took place during the reign of Ahab, one of the more wicked kings in Israel's history up to that time. Ahab's queen, Jezebel, was from Sidon (1 Kings 16:31-33), and she was even more wicked than her husband, leading him into ever greater sin. Jezebel had put many of God's prophets to death and had brought to Israel the worship of Baal. As judgment from the Lord, Elijah announced that there would be no rain "in the next few years except at my word" (1 Kings 17:1). A severe famine, not only in Israel but also in the surrounding countries, was the consequence. It was this experience of judgment and hardship that was the context of the salvation of the widow of Zarephath.

The Milk of Human Kindness

After being supplied with food by the ravens in the ravine of the Kerith for a time, Elijah was sent by God to Zarephath when the brook dried up. God had prepared the widow there to care for Elijah. Even in her desperate plight of having food only for one last meal for herself and her son, she was prepared to extend a kind and helping hand to Elijah. Human persons bear the image of God, both believers and unbelievers, and it is often this God-likeness in the human heart that is God's means of witnessing to someone.

Today many of those who come to our churches are parents knowing they need some help in raising their children in this morally challenging culture. Such parents often do not realize they are seeking the Lord and His truth, nor do they know that they are going to come to faith in Christ. But God uses that parental sense of responsibility they have toward their children as His means of reaching into their hearts and drawing them to Himself. All truth is God's truth, and all good human qualities arise from the image of God that is indelibly imprinted in our human nature.

All that is beautiful in human life comes from God and leads back to Him. So the Spirit is always witnessing to men and women through their own humanness. So it was with the widow of Zarephath. God used her kindness to Elijah, extended even though she was about to starve to death, as a bridge to bring her into the hearing of the word of truth.

The Provision of God

The widow made for Elijah a small cake of bread from the tiny store of flour and oil she had left. But God, in His great mercy, provided for her, her family, and Elijah so that her jar of flour never ran out and her jug of oil did not run dry. In Israel, Jesus tells us, there were many other widows who starved, but God fed this widow who came from a nation of pagan enemies of His people. The widow and her family saw God work through the prophet Elijah, and God used this loving provision for their needs as He called her step by step to faith.

Tragedy

Then the son of the widow became sick and died. Now she not only had no husband, but no son. She was overwhelmed with grief and bitterness of soul. Her words to Elijah were filled with anguish:

> *"What do you have against me, man of God? Did you come to remind me of my sin and kill my son?"*
> —1 KINGS 17:18

Often when disaster comes suddenly we are not only appalled by the tragedy of life, but also made acutely aware of our sinfulness. Even though we feel that the pain that strikes us is unfair, we have a sense that we cannot plead our own goodness as a reason why this sorrow should not have come. In mourning for her son the widow was also mourning the brokenness of her own life and of all life in this fallen world. The Spirit was, through this tragedy, convicting her of "guilt in regard to sin and righteousness and judgment" (John 16:8). While her cry to Elijah was full of bitterness, as were Job's or Jeremiah's complaints to the Lord, yet it was a cry for help, a longing that the pain in this world would be set right, for death to be turned to life, tears to joy.

Such a cry is more pleasing to God than passive resignation in the face of tragedy. For this truly is a broken world. The books are not balanced here in this age; the wicked flourish and the innocent (relatively speaking) suffer; hopes are rarely, if ever, fully realized. This is true for believers as well as unbelievers. As the apostle Paul says: "If only for this life we have hope in Christ, we are to be pitied more than all men" (1

Corinthians 15:19). Sorrow, even bitterness of spirit, is the right response to tragedy. God Himself weeps in anguish in the face of death (John 11:32-36). The widow's sorrow opened her heart to the truth, to the power, to the hope that God brings.

Elijah's Prayer and God's Response

Elijah was deeply moved by the widow's sorrow, and he cried out in his own grief and perplexity to the Lord:

> "O LORD *my God, have you brought tragedy also upon this widow I am staying with, by causing her son to die?"*
> —1 KINGS 17:20

Just as with Jesus at the grave of Lazarus, the Father heard the cry of His spokesman, and the boy was raised up to life. Death is our final enemy, but God has committed Himself to delivering us from this terrible consequence of our rebellion against Him. So here, as in the miracles of Jesus recorded in the Gospels, we see into the heart of God, into His love for us despite our sin, despite our unbelief, and despite our hostility to Him. God gave the boy back to his mother, and she came to faith (v. 24):

> "Now I know that you are a man of God and that the word of the LORD from your mouth is the truth."

One day we can ask her, "What happened next? What was it like to live as a believer in such a pagan context?" Our questions will be answered, for all hidden things will be made known. But in the meantime we can rejoice in the way God calls people to Himself from the most unlikely situations. God is a God of miracles, and the greatest miracle of all is the salvation of individuals, including the woman of Zarephath.

18

GOD'S INFINITE VARIETY

OF MEANS II

In the accounts of Naaman and the widow of Zarephath we see God working in the lives of two people who were not Israelites. He was prepared to go to extraordinary lengths to save these two individuals, even though they were not members of His chosen people Israel. There are many other such stories in the Old Testament—for example, the narratives about Ruth and Rahab, the one a Moabitess, the other a Canaanite. These two women became, through the providence of God, believers and also ancestors of Jesus as they married into families from whom the genealogy of Christ is traced.

We have no way of knowing the total number of these non-Israelites who came to faith, for Scripture is not exhaustive in the histories it gives us. However, we may be sure, because God has given us a number of such stories as an indication of His commitment to save the nations, that there was a multitude of people from the pagan nations whom He called to Himself. One day we will meet all of these people, both those whose names we know from the biblical text and a far greater number of those whose names and stories are not recorded in Scripture.

To speak of a far greater number is not wishful thinking, nor is it idle speculation; rather, it is an appropriate inference to draw from the teaching of Scripture. Take two similar examples. In the Old Testament we are told the stories of many Israelites who were believers, but no one would assume that those whose names and stories are recorded for us are the only people from Israel who will be in the kingdom. The stories we are told are clearly illustrative of God's work among His people, not a complete record of His work. For instance, in a time of great apostasy Elijah, who thought he was the only faithful one left, was assured by the Lord that there were 7,000 who had not become worshipers of Baal (1 Kings 19:18). We know the names of Obadiah and Nathan and a few others who were faithful, but the vast majority of these 7,000 are unknown to us.

For our second example, consider the four Gospels. The Evangelists give us many records of the works and words of Jesus, and yet John assures us that these are not complete. He writes:

Jesus did many other miraculous signs in the presence of his disciples, which are not recorded in this book. But these are written that you may believe that Jesus is the Christ, the Son of God, and that by believing you may have life in his name.

—20:30-31

John adds these words at the end of his Gospel:

Jesus did many other things as well. If every one of them were written down, I suppose that even the whole world would not have room for the books that would be written.

—21:25

We are told repeatedly in the Gospel records that Jesus healed multitudes of people, or that crowds came to listen to him in Judea, Samaria, Syria, and the Decapolis region. We are told, in detail and with names, the stories of just a few of these people. We will someday be able to meet all of them face to face who became believers and to hear their individual stories of conversion and what followed.

We may consider the work of God among non-Israelites or among His people Israel during the Old Testament period. Or we may reflect on the work of Jesus in Palestine and beyond its borders during His earthly ministry. Or we may study the work of the Spirit as He reaches out across the face of the whole earth during this age before the return of Christ. But whichever of these three stretches of time we examine, we may be confident that the stories we know are only a tiny part of God's great work of calling people from all the nations to Himself. Scripture assures us of the vastness of the number of the redeemed:

> . . . *a great multitude that no one could count, from every nation, tribe, people and language.*
>
> —REVELATION 7:9

Just as there is a vast multitude of individuals, so there is a great variety of means God uses to save those individuals. We will now consider some more of these means.

MANASSEH, A REBELLIOUS SON
(2 KINGS 21:1-18; 2 CHRONICLES 33:1-20)

Manasseh's story is sobering. He became king at the age of twelve and ruled with extraordinary wickedness. The list of his sins is shocking by any standard. He built altars to Baal and many other false gods all over the land and even within the Lord's temple. He practiced sorcery and divination, consulted mediums and evil spirits, engaged in witchcraft, sacrificed his own sons to idols, and "shed so much innocent blood that he filled Jerusalem from end to end" (2 Kings 21:16). In addition to his own indulgence in every kind of wickedness, he led the whole nation into the worship of other gods and into every kind of detestable practice so that "they did more evil than the nations the LORD had destroyed before the Israelites" (2 Chronicles 33:9). Yet this man was eventually brought to repentance! What did it take to bring him to his knees?

The Wages of Sin

Because God exists and because He is a God of order and consistency, we are living in a universe that is orderly and carefully structured according to patterns that can be observed, studied, and measured by the sciences. In the same way, because God exists and because He is a holy God, there is a moral order to the universe. God's own character defines for us what is good and what is evil. He is the measure or standard against which we can judge any behavior. He has created and He now governs the world in such a way that this distinction between good and evil is upheld. When we do good, there are good consequences (not always completely, of course, because we live in a fallen world)—a clear conscience; the respect of others; the direct effects of, for example, an act of kindness to someone in need or faithfully loving one's spouse. When we do evil, there are evil consequences (again, not always fully or immediately because of God's long-suffering)—a sense of uncleanness and a hardened conscience; the judgment of others; the direct effects of, for example, an act of brutality against an innocent child or committing adultery against one's spouse. It is a wonderful thing to be living in a moral universe like this. Imagine if good produced evil consequences, or if evil produced good consequences. Imagine a morally chaotic world in which there is no consistency or predictability about the consequences of our choices and actions.

Manasseh, like every other person who has ever disobeyed God's laws, must have experienced some of the consequences of his sin—a conscience, tender when he was crowned king at twelve, but then bearing a growing burden of guilt and becoming increasingly hardened; the lives of others damaged and destroyed by his cruelty; the loss of respect from people whose good opinion he had once valued; advisers of integrity and uprightness being replaced by untrustworthy flatterers and those greedy for power; his fear of the people he ruled whenever he appeared in public. These suggestions about the wages of Manasseh's sins are not idle speculations, for we see such consequences whenever a nation is ruled by one who becomes increasingly wicked.

The Judgment of God

God judges us partly through the wages of our sins, for, as the apostle Paul puts it in Romans 1:18-32, God's wrath is revealed against our sin by His handing us over to our sinful patterns of life and their consequences. This reaping what we have sown (Galatians 6:7) is the way God has structured the moral order of the universe. But God also intervenes directly into our lives to bring His judgment on us. In Manasseh's case this judgment came on him through the cruelty of the king of Assyria who took him captive to Babylon, led like a bull with a hook through his nose and bronze chains and shackles on his legs and arms.

The Assyrian commander who took Manasseh prisoner was both God's means of punishing Manasseh and God's means of humbling him. Those who are wicked and powerful become proud, but God is able to cast them down so that they are humbled and cry out to Him for his deliverance. God's judgment can be a kindness, just as the discipline of a willful child can be an expression of love. So it was with Manasseh.

The Prayers and Example of Godly Parents

Hezekiah was the father of Manasseh, and Hephzibah was his mother. We know that Hezekiah was a devout believer, and despite his sins and errors he is described as one who "did what was right in the eyes of the LORD, just as his father David had done" (2 Chronicles 29:2). He was a reforming king who led the people back to the worship of the Lord. He died at the relatively young age of fifty-four, leaving his twelve-year-old son to succeed him on the throne. We ought to assume, given the way Hezekiah is described by Scripture, that he prayed for his son Manasseh, taught him the true worship of God, and sought to live before him in a way that honored God and set an example of righteousness for him. When Manasseh finally was humbled in Babylon, he probably remembered the way of life and teaching of his father and mother and at last turned to the God they had trusted. And God answered their prayers for Manasseh and proved Himself to be faithful to His covenant promises to believing parents.

The Faithfulness of God

Hezekiah and Hephzibah were not perfect in their raising of Manasseh. If God's promises for our children required perfection of us, none of our children would ever be saved. Though we are believers, we are never perfect parents to our children. We do not pray for them as faithfully, consistently, or perseveringly as we should. We do not teach them the truth of God's Word as clearly, as accurately, or as regularly as we should. We do not set before them an example of ideal holiness, goodness, or purity. We do not always love them as we ought, nor do we discipline them with constancy and fairness. As in everything else in our lives, we do a far from perfect job in our parenting. But God is gracious, and He hears our irregular prayers, blesses our inconsistent efforts, uses our imperfect examples, and calls the children of believers to Himself. Their coming to faith may not be straightforward; there may be years of rebellion and apostasy; but God is faithful. The story of Manasseh should be an encouragement to every believer with a child who has turned away from the Lord for a time, even if that time extends to many years of angry rebellion and appalling disobedience. God is faithful to His promises!

19

A Personal Testimony

I became a believer during the final year of studying for a B.A. in English Language and Literature. What did God use to call me to Himself, or perhaps I should say, what were some of the means I am aware of that God used to call me to Himself? One day He will fill in all the details of each of our stories.

Loving Parents

My parents were not committed evangelical believers during my childhood, but they were wonderful parents, and they had one of the best marriages I have ever had the privilege of seeing. The memory of them is still a model to me of self-sacrificing love, gentleness, respect, and kindness to each other and to us, their children. Their moral strength, integrity, and goodness were a rock to me in the difficult years of university studies when I was being challenged by all kinds of immoral ideas and examples.

Even though they were very poor, they were extraordinarily kind, sharing the little they had with people in our village who had even less than they did. They were hospitable; despite the straitened circumstances in which we lived, people loved to come to our home because of the warm welcome they received and the evident happiness present there. They read Bible stories to us as children, prayed with us each night, took us to church, and sent us to Sunday school. They did all this even though they were not personally believers, for, as they said to me when I was about ten, they wanted us to have the opportunity of making up our own minds about Christianity. Even during the years when I decided I could not believe in God, this example and this teaching never left me entirely, for the image of God shone brightly in my mother and father.

A FAITHFUL WITNESS

Unfortunately, the church in our village was not at that time one in which the Gospel was clearly proclaimed from the pulpit. So even though I attended every Sunday all through my early childhood, I did not hear God's Word clearly preached. However, there was one faithful witness in that tiny village church, a witness who kept the truth alive in a building that had been erected for the preservation of that truth in the eighth century. This faithful witness was our Sunday school teacher who week by week each Sunday afternoon sought to teach the Bible to children who heard it clearly nowhere else. She was patient, kind, gentle, and persevering. One day we will know just how many of her charges eventually entered the kingdom. God, even in unpromising circumstances, does not let His Word return to Him empty. I turned away from what she taught, just as I turned away from the Bible stories and prayers shared with me by my parents. However, those words of prayer and of Scripture never departed entirely from my memory but were always there as a deposit to draw from when the time of drawing close to God would come.

LEWIS AND TOLKIEN

My parents, along with so much else that was good, for which I owe them eternal thanks, introduced me to the writings of C. S. Lewis and J. R. R. Tolkien. My father read the Narnia stories by Lewis and Tolkien's *The Hobbit* and *The Lord of the Rings* to us when we were children. Though I did not understand the Christian story that lies so closely beneath the surface of those books, they did create a longing for the world they represented. They spoke to me of the way the world truly is, though I knew, of course, that they were fantasy. Lewis speaks of this longing in his autobiography *Surprised by Joy*. For Lewis, this longing was created by mythology, fairy tales, and music. His longing for "a far country" was ultimately answered by his becoming a Christian.

For me Lewis's children's stories and the works of Tolkien had a similar effect. In revealing an echo of truth, they created a longing for truth and kept me turning to their books again and again. When I became a believer, I immediately understood why those books had been so precious to me. They also were part of the belt God strapped around my heart to draw me to Himself.

GOOD BOOKS

As well as the writings of Lewis and Tolkien, my parents taught me to love many other good books. They read aloud to us every night when we were home right through the years of school and up until the time we went off to college, and they encouraged us to read ourselves and to read widely and well. Everything was interesting to them. From them I gained a delight in good writing wherever it was found, whether in children's books, adult fiction, fantasy, drama, or poetry. Great literature deals with the human condition in all its sorrow and in all its joy. It asks the difficult questions that confront all human beings and sometimes answers those questions accurately. This is so whether it is a Christian or a non-Christian who is writing the book. People live in God's world whether they acknowledge Him or not, and they are made in His image whether they believe in Him or not. Therefore they are constrained by the reality around them and the reality within them to wrestle with truth.

During my teenage years it was this delight in literature that began to get me thinking about the big questions of life with which good writers are always struggling: "Where do we come from?" "Who are we, and what does it mean to be human?" "What is the purpose of life, if there is any purpose?" "What is the human dilemma?" "Where is history going, if anywhere?" "Does anything come after death?" "Does God exist, and if God is there, what is He like?"

If we consider just one example from literature, Shakespeare's *Hamlet*, we find that many of these questions are constantly in the background and often in the foreground of the play. They are at the heart of Hamlet's reflections about his own situation. This intrigued me and set me asking such questions for myself. I went off to university with a mind full of questions, eager to explore the answers that literature and my professors might give me.

THE FUTILITY OF HUMAN EXISTENCE

My idealism was soon delivered a crushing blow. I discovered that my teachers appeared to have no interest in my questions; and worse, they ignored the issues that literature raises. They seemed only to be interested in form and structure and the skills that make great writing work, and to have no passion for the content of the texts we studied. The result for me was a steep descent into despair, a conviction that there were no answers for my questions, a sense of the absurdity of human existence in general and of the futility of my own life in particular.

In this state of despair I began to read books, to watch plays and films, and to listen to music that expressed the same angst about human life that filled my own soul—books by Hardy, Sartre, Camus, and Hemingway; plays by Ibsen, Beckett, and Ionesco; films by Bergman, Antonioni, and Fellini; music by Richard Strauss, Bob Dylan, and the Rolling Stones. Already in the sixties in Britain much "intellectual" and "popular" culture had a deep vein of despair and nihilism running through it. This, too, was a path that would lead me ultimately onto the road of truth. But its effect at first was to drain my heart of all hope, though, thank God, my parents' teaching and example kept me from most of the destructive patterns of life that so many of my friends pursued. But even so I fell into a state of morbid depression, overwhelmed by the emptiness of all that I saw. This led to a longing for escape, and the only escape appeared to be death. I ordered my little affairs, caught a bus out of Manchester, and walked to Alderley Edge, a high cliff in the Cheshire hills, with the fixed intention of stepping over and ending my life.

THE GLORY OF CREATION

There, one step from eternity, I was held back by the beauty of the natural world around me. It was January, and it was cold with a harsh wind; but it was sunny, and the skies were clear and blue. The trees were bare, but they still had beauty; there were no flowers, but the grass was green and alive. Titmice and nuthatches flitted through the dark branches or patrolled the trunks for insect larvae. It was midwinter, and it was glorious. My parents, among so many other good gifts they had given, had passed on to us a love of the country landscape, a love of trees, flowers, birds, and all living things.

God used that glorious winter day and that eye for His creatures, awakened by my parents, to save me from death and to give me the hope that I must keep on searching. If there could be such beauty even in winter, surely there had to be some answer to my questions besides meaninglessness. I walked back to the bus stop and returned to the university determined to keep looking. Though I did not know it at the time, I had experienced what David describes in Psalm 19:1-6 and what Paul asserts in Romans 1:19-20:

> *What may be known about God is plain to them, because God has made it plain to them. For since the creation of the world God's invisible qualities—his eternal power and divine nature— have been clearly seen, being understood from what has been made, so that men are without excuse.*

The glory of God had been shown to me by earth and sky, and while I did not yet know it was His glory, I knew it was glorious and that there must be some reason for its glory. This sense of glory kindled hope in my heart once more.

A FRIEND IN NEED

About two weeks later I was led to a fellow student, a graduate who was working on a Ph.D. in ethics. Mike was from Saskatchewan, Canada. He was a committed Christian, and he had spent some time studying at L'Abri under Francis and Edith Schaeffer. I first met him through a mutual acquaintance, and he rapidly became one of my dearest friends, and he still is. He was kind and hospitable, always ready to invite me in for coffee or a meal. He was openhearted and seemed to spend much of his time extending a helping hand to needy students like myself. He was eager to discuss the issues that my professors had turned aside, willing to help me think my questions through, ready to sympathize with the troubling doubts that filled my heart and mind, discerning and knowledgeable about the literature, drama, films, and music that had contributed to my despair.

He used to play taped lectures by Francis Schaeffer for a small group of students and use them as a basis for a discussion of Christianity. No question was off-limits, and his patience seemed endless. Mike led me in a prayer of commitment to Christ as we knelt together on his kitchen floor about a year after we first met. He had given me, and continued to give me, a huge amount of his time, and he did so gladly and freely. I thank God for Mike Tymchak to this very day. He is "an Israelite indeed, in whom is no guile" (see John 1:47, KJV).

GOD'S WORD

Within a few days of my meeting Mike, he invited me to a Bible study in his apartment. I don't think he knew at that time just how appropriate his text was for me, but God led him to give a study on the first two chapters of the book of Ecclesiastes. He began by reading the following passage:

> *"Meaningless! Meaningless!"*
> *says the Teacher.*
> *"Utterly meaningless!*
> *Everything is meaningless."*
> —1:2

He carried on and read those first two chapters in their entirety. I was amazed. Until that moment it had never occurred to me that the Bible is a book about life, that it addresses the deep questions of the human dilemma. Just like most non-Christians in the modern western world, I had always thought of the Bible as a "religious book." By this I mean that I had thought of it as a book for people with a "religious temperament" or with a "religious background," a book to be read on "religious occasions." But I had never thought of it as a book that speaks to the questions all people have about our existence, our needs, our problems, a book that answers these questions. It was as if Ecclesiastes was written for me and was speaking directly to me.

I have since found that it is a book that speaks to many modern and particularly to postmodern people simply because it is so direct about the futility wrapped up in the human condition. It pulls no punches but rather acknowledges the sense of emptiness that pervades so much of our life in a fallen world. It offers partial healing for the wounds we feel, but this healing is not given easily or lightly, nor as if the medicine applied to us will wipe away all our tears in the present time. This sober realism in Ecclesiastes was God's means of convincing me to take His Word seriously and to begin to consider His Word as words of truth, truth that makes sense of the world in which we live, truth that fits like a glove on the hand of reality. Ecclesiastes is still my favorite book in the Bible.

FAITH FROM INFANCY

My wife's story is completely different. Vicki grew up in a home where her parents were deeply committed believers. She does not remember a time when she did not believe in Christ. For her, being a child meant being a child of God. Just as she loved her parents, so she loved her heavenly Father. Just as she trusted her parents, so she trusted Christ. She came to Him for mercy, forgiveness, and help in times of need and sorrow, just as she came to her parents. Of course, there were times of struggle, questioning, and doubt later on in her high school and college years, as there have been since that time. But this is so for all believers; we all go through testing times whatever our age. But there has been no time when she lost her faith or turned away; rather there has been an ongoing trust and commitment to obedience for all of her life as far as she can remember.

All of us know people in our churches like this, whether the particular church teaches a theology of God's covenant promises for the children of believing parents or whether it does not. My wife's church did not; it taught, in effect, that you could not really be a committed Christian unless you "made a decision" and "had a conversion experience" at some point after you had reached an "age of accountability," presumed to be at some point in the teenage years. The effect of this teaching and the constant pressure from visiting evangelists and some youth group leaders to "make sure you are really saved" or to "make a real commitment" caused a sense of insecurity and created a loss of assurance. This was confusing to her, and she made many commitments and recommitments "just to be sure"; but underneath it all she knew that she was already a believer and that Christ was her only hope, rather than depending on her repeated attempts to follow the advice of her spiritual mentors.

One lesson from her story is the importance of taking seriously the faith of little children and not despising their desire to love and serve Christ as unreal, too early, or immature. Jesus Himself dealt with a similar problem when He urged His disciples:

> *"Let the little children come to me, and do not hinder them, for the kingdom of heaven belongs to such as these."*
> —MATTHEW 19:14

We should treasure and encourage faith wherever we find it and allow God in His divine power to give the new birth whenever and to whomever it pleases Him, including little children who are born again by His Spirit. One day when Vicki stands before the Lord He can tell her the day and the hour of her new birth; but for now we do not always have the knowledge to perceive just when that new birth takes place.

My wife was raised to put her hope in Christ, but we all know that many stories are not as straightforward as hers. Some children of believers come to a very early faith before their clear memories can recall the moment. Some have a hazy memory of a period of time lasting months or years during which their faith developed and took shape. Some remember exactly the day and hour when they turned to Christ, at the age of five or ten or fifteen or at any other time in the years of their childhood and youth. For some this commitment was uncomplicated; for others it was the culmination of a time of wrestling and struggle. For some it followed a time of severe questioning and troubling doubts. For some there were conscious times of rebellion and turning away from their parents and from the Lord (like the prodigal son in Jesus' parable). For some, like Manasseh, this period of apostasy may have lasted many years and was accompanied by gross idolatry and desperate wickedness.

Just as with those who, like me, came to faith from unbelief, those who grow up in explicitly Christian homes each have their own story to tell. God respects the unique way He has made each person, and He has myriad ways of calling various individuals.

In our limited selection of examples from Scripture and from contemporary experience, we gain a glimpse of the great variety of means God uses. He speaks to some through His self-revelation in the glory of creation as we see Him made known in the physical universe around us. He draws some to Himself by His likeness manifest through our humanity. His likeness is made known in our moral nature, our desire to give and receive love, our creativity, our significance, our dominion over nature, our ability to communicate in language. All these and other human attributes that reflect God's own being—all come from Him and lead us back to Him.

He rules the affairs of nations so that He might save some—for example, Manasseh whose captivity by the Assyrians was God's means of humbling him. His providential rule over our individual lives is evident in every story as He seeks to bend stubborn wills and convince doubting minds—and this is true both in times of joy and of sorrow.

He calls out to us through the lives of believers as they provide a light radiating goodness, a light that draws us to give glory to our Father in heaven. The church, when it is at all faithful to its calling, makes known in its life the transforming power of the Gospel.

God's Word directly and as it is made known by pastors, teachers, evangelists, and others in public settings and as it is communicated by individuals one on one is a constant thread woven into His pattern of redemption.

All these, and more, the Spirit uses as He leads people to faith in Jesus Christ. His work in the heart of the unbeliever oversees and makes effective all these other means. Our understanding of evangelism must take this vast breadth of the work of God into account. It is a great encouragement to us, preventing us from having too exalted a view of our own part, and also giving us confidence in the multitude of ways that God is at work. He wants to save! He is constantly laboring to call and draw people to His Son. He knows just what is needed to save each one. Take heart!

BARRIERS IN THE WAY
OF COMMUNICATING
THE GOSPEL

20

BARRIERS WITHIN OURSELVES

Jesus and His apostles have called every one of us who knows Jesus Christ to the task of reaching out to those around us. However, if we are honest we will have to admit that the great majority of us find this calling very difficult, if not almost impossible. Faced with the challenge to make the Gospel known to people in our families, workplaces, and neighborhoods, many of us feel helpless, discouraged, and defeated. You might not feel this dejected about evangelism, but very few believers find sharing the Gospel easy or comfortable.

We may gladly support student ministries that reach into the local high school or college to make Christ known to the young people of our communities or support missionaries whom we send to the distant parts of the earth to preach the Gospel to those who have not heard of Jesus. Yet when it comes to our own responsibility we find ourselves confronted with barriers that seem insurmountable. What are some of these barriers or walls within ourselves that keep us from reaching those who are not believers?

THE WALL OF GUILT

Unfortunately, many believers are afraid of the subject of evangelism and may even plan to miss a church service when the announced sermon topic is outreach. Why is this? The sad truth is that frequently preaching and teaching on evangelism operate by trying to produce guilt.

Pastors can easily and with the best of intentions fall into the trap of berating their congregations with commands to evangelize or illustrations about evangelism that seek to motivate by creating the maximum amount of guilt in those who hear. This may appear to be successful in the sense that everyone vows to do better in the future. Yet, after a period of carefully induced misery, everything returns to the state of minimal outreach, except that those with a tender conscience are carrying a bigger burden of guilt than before. There is an obvious problem here. Jesus promised that He came to set us free—free from sin, free from condemnation, free from a guilty conscience. It ought to be evident to anyone who teaches God's Word that laying a burden of guilt on believers can never be the best motivation to help us make known the freedom from guilt that the Gospel of Christ grants us.

LACK OF CONFIDENCE

Another internal wall is our lack of confidence in our ability to present the Gospel clearly or to answer the challenges that people might put forward against the Christian message. Even the apostle Paul felt this way! He wrote:

> *And pray for us, too, that God may open a door for our message, so that we may proclaim the mystery of Christ, for which I am in chains. Pray that I may proclaim it clearly, as I should.*
>
> —COLOSSIANS 4:3-4

> *Pray also for me, that whenever I open my mouth, words may be given me so that I will fearlessly make known the mystery of the gospel, for which I am an ambassador in chains. Pray that I may declare it fearlessly, as I should.*
>
> —EPHESIANS 6:19-20

Paul was perhaps the greatest evangelist apart from the Lord Himself there has ever been. Yet Paul knew that he needed to ask for prayer to be clear, and he knew that he needed God to give him courage. If this was true for the Apostle to the Gentiles, how much more will it be true for us! We should gladly acknowledge our anxiety and nervousness about our abilities, our embarrassment, our fear, even our sense of shame when we try to tell someone what it means to us to be a Christian. Humility about ourselves is the best place to begin as we think about our responsibility to share the Gospel. Jesus opened his Sermon on the Mount with these words: "Blessed are the poor in spirit, for theirs is the kingdom of heaven" (Matthew 5:2).

Knowing our own fears and weakness is the starting place for all growth, because this knowledge drives us to prayer for ourselves and requires us to acknowledge to others that we are not at all adequate for the tasks to which God has called us. We have all heard people who claim to be evangelists telling us how good at evangelism they are, how bold, how they always know the right words to say. The effect of such boasting is to make us feel discouraged and useless. We think to ourselves, "I could never be like that!"

But when we read in the New Testament about Paul's missionary work, it is not discouraging to us, for we see that Paul was just like the rest of us. He sometimes lacked courage, and he knew that only when he recognized his inadequacy could he do the work that God had set before him. His attitude was:

> *I will boast all the more gladly about my weaknesses, so that Christ's power may rest on me. That is why, for Christ's sake, I delight in weaknesses, in insults, in hardships, in persecutions, in difficulties. For when I am weak, then I am strong.*
>
> —2 CORINTHIANS 12:9-10

So we begin our reflections on our own calling to be evangelists with the confession that we have not done well in the past and that we are not self-confident about our abilities or about our commitment to reach out in the future. We need to know our dependence on the Lord's opening doors for us, and we need to tell Him plainly of our lack of courage, wisdom, and even desire to do this work. Humble prayer will be our starting point. Our understanding and gracious Father promises to give us opportunities to reach out; He assures us of His willingness to help us know what to say; He can even take away our fears and grant us boldness of heart and word.

UNCERTAINTY ABOUT EVANGELISTIC METHODS

A third internal wall many of us struggle with is uncertainty, confusion, and perhaps even distaste about some of the evangelistic methods that are urged upon us and are commonly practiced. We are assured that learning the right technique will make us all bold and eager to witness. "Memorize these verses of Scripture; get hold of these questions. This is a surefire method; it has proven itself effective for many churches. We can show you many testimonies of timid and reluctant Christians who are now emboldened to go door to door and give glowing reports of their success."

I know that God has saved many people through the use of such methods of evangelism. I know too that many Christians have been helped to be more courageous in evangelism and have discovered a new freedom to make Christ known. I do not want to cast aspersions on the trustworthiness of those who give such testimonies or who swear by these methods. However, many believers have heard of and perhaps even know personally people who have been turned off by such approaches. Sometimes the following response is given to those who have such objections: "God was not working in the person who is offended by this direct method; they were perhaps the swine before whom Jesus said we are not to cast our pearls." Or "We are simply plucking the ripe fruit that the Holy Spirit has made ready. Don't worry about the fruit that is not yet ripe. God will take care of the unripe fruit in His own time."

Such responses do not take away the feeling of discomfort entirely. We all remember times when we have been subjected to a smooth and clearly learned presentation given by a salesman or saleswoman for some product, whether insurance, lawn care, carpet cleaning, or a religious message we did not want to hear. We felt taken advantage of, treated as an object, our privacy invaded. Sometimes we even agreed to buy things we did not want, simply to get rid of the persistent person keeping a foot in our door!

Even so, when doubt is expressed about particular techniques of evangelism, we need to respond to such hesitations carefully and biblically. It is not appropriate to assume that the person who feels doubts and hesitations or who even dares to express them is simply making excuses for his or her laziness or for a refusal to be obedient to Christ's command. (We will return to this issue in a later chapter.)

Overcommitment

We may also feel walls of inner anxiety about overcommitting ourselves or wanting to avoid having our privacy and personal space invaded by strangers we really don't desire to know. Many of us are already in over our heads with too many church activities. We may feel like saying (though we usually keep such thoughts to ourselves), "What is this book (or sermon) going to ask me to do now? I already have too much on my plate. Don't burden me with another activity that needs regular commitment!"

It is true that many Christians are involved in entirely too many meetings they feel they want to attend or maybe feel compelled to attend. We sometimes believe the illusion that many programs and a full calendar equal spiritual effectiveness and maturity. We become so busy about the work of being a Christian (along with the necessary task of providing for ourselves and our families) that there is no time left to invite friends, neighbors, or workmates for a meal or simply to have some fun together. Perhaps we need to cut out some of the activities, even go to fewer services and Bible studies, so we have time to become good friends with a few people who are not believers.

These barriers within us demand to be taken seriously. The following questions should help our reflection.

1. What are the walls you face within yourself? Have you felt reluctant to think about evangelism? Has this brought with it a sense of guilt? What do you think has caused your sense of guilt—unhelpful teaching, an unwillingness to obey the commands of Scripture, or a mixture of both?

2. What Scriptures do you think address this issue of guilt about our reluctance to engage in personal evangelism?

3. Do you feel confident about your abilities as one called to "always be prepared to give an answer . . . for the hope that you have" in Christ (1 Peter 3:15)? If not (and it should be hard to say you are confident after reading this present chapter!), what do you sense are your own particular weaknesses with regard to evangelism? (It is

important to learn to be comfortable before the Lord in acknowledging our inadequacies.)

4. Do you feel uncomfortable about some of the evangelistic methods you have read about or been taught? Why the discomfort? What do you think is inadequate about them? Do you think biblical criticisms can be made of them?

5. Are you overcommitted? Remember that Jesus has promised us freedom and fullness of life rather than bondage to a whole new set of rules and Christian activities. What could you cut out of your commitments without compromising your desire to be faithful to the Lord in your family life, your work, and your church?

6. Do you think being faithful to the scriptural command to share your faith will mean more activities and meetings in your life? Why or why not?

21

BARRIERS BETWEEN THE CHURCH
AND THE WORLD I

Acknowledging our need is the primary means of dealing with the walls within us. When we look into our own hearts, we see how important it is to cry out to God and say, "Lord, I am weak, but You are strong! Help me to have confidence in You and in Your desire to save. Help me to believe that Your Spirit can open the heart and mind of an unbeliever. Help me to know that You can overrule the circumstances of my life to bring me into contact with those in whose hearts You are working. Help me to have the courage to make the most of the opportunities You place in my path to share Your truth with those who don't know You. Help me to speak clearly when I try to present Your Good News. Help me to be in some small but faithful way an example of the Gospel that I claim to believe and that I say has saved and is transforming me."

As if the walls within us were not enough, we quickly realize that there are other barriers to communication of the Gospel that exist between Christians and unbelievers as well. What are some of these barriers that the church faces today?

THE LOSS OF TRUTH

In addition to the walls within us, we face walls of unbelief created by the prevailing ideas in our culture. There is, for example, the loss of belief that there is one truth that explains the world. We live in a society where everyone has "his or her own truth." There is the loss of the clear conviction that there is an infinite and personal God who is involved in ruling the nations or in caring for us in our daily lives. Many people in our culture have lost the confidence that there is a transcendent moral law that applies to all people of whatever background or culture and no longer recognize that we live with a constant moral obligation to our neighbors and to the society in which we live. Instead there is simply the commitment to enjoy our own individual freedom and to pursue our own personal happiness. Fewer and fewer of our contemporaries have the expectation that we will all have to give an account to the Supreme Judge one day. Along with this goes the loss of a sense of sin and objective guilt. Younger generations have for the most part lost the hope that we will live forever as physical beings in a real world; indeed, many teenagers have no hope for the future at all.

We may summarize this loss of truth by saying that our society has lost the Christian story. This is tragic because Christianity is the only story that makes sense of our world, that acts as our moral guide, that fills us with a confident hope for our individual futures and the future of our race and of this world. People may still encounter the Christian story in a sentimentalized form as they do their Christmas shopping, but the majority of them no longer hear this story as truth. They only hear it as a fable, as a comforting Christmas tale, just like stories about Santa or Rudolph the Red-nosed Reindeer. Many of our generation still listen to the music of the Christian story, whether in Christmas songs and carols, sacred music like Handel's *Messiah* or Bach's *Oratorio*, or church services. Yet, most of our contemporaries do not understand this music to be making truth claims, nor does it act as a control over life. (We will look further at the problems we face in a postmodern society in a later chapter.)

Perhaps even more unsettling to us is the recognition that these walls of unbelief affect those of us who are within the Christian church as well as those outside. Do we believe firmly that the message of the Gospel is Truth, what Francis Schaeffer called "true truth"? Or have we been touched by the skepticism and uncertainty of the age in which we live, just like our unbelieving contemporaries? Do we secretly think that, after all, the biblical message is wishful thinking or just "my truth" and that others have their own "truth," whether they are Hindus, Moslems, Buddhists, or even atheists?

To the extent that we are affected by this loss of truth all around us, we will feel uncertain about making our good news known. We may feel even more insecure when we ask ourselves, "What do non-Christians believe anyway?" How can we ever become confident in communicating the truth in an age that accepts personal religion but rejects passionately the claim of exclusive truth?

We need to be sure for ourselves that our faith is indeed the Truth. This will mean taking our own questions and doubts seriously and being prepared to work them through so that we come to a place of confidence. It will mean a readiness to answer our own children's questions and to help them become committed to the truth. It will require a willingness to answer the questions and objections of unbelievers, and this will demand some hard study for ourselves both of our own beliefs and of theirs. If we are prepared to respond to doubts and questions and seek to work them through, then we will discover that we have a growing excitement about the truthfulness of the biblical message. We will learn about its strength in facing any objection or attack and about the wonder of the answers that the truth gives to the problems and needs of the culture in which we live.

FAITH WITHOUT LIFE

Yet another wall is raised by the lack of reality in the Christian church. People still mention the scandals of certain tele-evangelists as a primary objection to considering the claims of the Gospel. A store clerk told me I was in a good business when he learned that I was a pastor. He meant it as a compliment, assuming that I was into preaching for financial rewards. Most non-Christians have a very different reaction to those who preach for financial gain! Our hearts are made heavy by the all too frequent failures in the areas of finances, sexual chastity, and marital fidelity among priests and pastors. A student who was in the insurance business before coming to seminary repeated the warning his boss had given the agents during an educational session: "Remember that God is our worst customer!" By this he meant that churches, Christian institutions, and religious individuals who were the quickest to push their Christian commitment were often the slowest at paying their premiums and the worst at keeping their word. This kind of comment ought to make us weep as we reflect on the damage done to the cause of the Gospel by failures in the area of financial integrity. In many churches the members dread sermons on giving, expecting a guilt trip rather than a serious and careful exposition of biblical teaching about finances. Even our own church members sometimes are made to feel that all we want is their money! If believers feel that way, what is the world thinking?

We have to recognize that these problems that are raised by nonbelievers are not only coming from their unwillingness to believe but point to a deep-seated failure among professing Christians to teach and to practice obedience to the commandments of God. Despite all our talk about moral values, the abortion rates and divorce rates are similar in the evangelical community to the rates for the culture as a whole. In a widely publicized poll taken by George Gallup, only about 10 percent of those professing to be believers claimed that their Christian faith had any effect on their daily life.

This is a formidable obstacle in our way as we seek to make God's truth known in our world. We have to acknowledge this with grief and repentance, both to the Lord and to unbelievers who raise this kind of problem as an objection. It is of enormous importance that we do not try to pretend there are no problems in the life of the church today or that it is inappropriate for these problems to create obstacles for non-Christians when we ask them to take the Gospel seriously. The Scripture teaches us that "a gentle answer turns away wrath, but a harsh word stirs up anger" (Proverbs 15:1). When there are failures in the lives of Christians, we need to acknowledge them, and our acknowledgment should be made with sorrow.

This is also true if people raise problems about the past. If, for example, an African-American points to white Christians' ancestors' involvement in the practice of slavery, we ought not to ignore this history, nor should we try to explain it away, nor should we say that it has nothing to do with us. Think how readily (and rightly so) Christians want to point to beneficial ways in which the church influenced the culture in the past, or how proud we are personally of the positive exploits of our own forebears (though these too have nothing directly to do with us). If we want to be appropriately glad for the glories of the past, we ought also to be appropriately ashamed of the failures and sins of the past. We are to acknowledge with genuine sorrow any failures of obedience to God's

Word whether they are past or present. Scripture is a great encouragement to us here, for it is strikingly honest about the failures of the people of God. In addition we see believers confessing to the Lord the sins of their contemporaries and of their ancestors (Daniel and Nehemiah are examples of this).

THE LOSS OF A COMMON LANGUAGE

Yet another wall arises from the lack of knowledge of the Scriptures in our society. More and more people are biblically illiterate. Even those teaching at a seminary, as I do, observe that our students have less knowledge of the content of the Bible each year. This being so, we need to recognize that most of those around us no longer have any true grasp of what the Bible teaches; nor do they understand the language Christians are accustomed to using.

The words that we hear every Sunday in most of our churches and that we use in our prayers are no longer part of the everyday language of our society. People simply do not talk about justification or sanctification, nor about redemption, salvation, or sin. Language that is precious to the Christian is an unfamiliar dialect to most people around us. This means that church as usual and sermons that don't acknowledge this problem are difficult for our contemporaries to relate to, just as computer language is incomprehensible to many of us! (We will examine the kind of language to use in communicating the Gospel in a later chapter.)

Again, some questions may help us to think about how we are affected by the barriers we have discussed in this chapter.

1. What do you believe to be the major barriers that you face as you have tried to make God's Word known or as you think about making it known?

2. Where do you encounter the problem of the loss of truth? How do you see the loss of truth manifested in popular culture?

3. Do you struggle with wondering if it is arrogant or intolerant to claim that Jesus is the only way to know God and to be saved?

4. Have you heard unbelievers criticize the loss of credibility of the church or give you examples of their personally having been let down

by Christians? How did you respond? How do you think Scripture calls you to respond to such criticism?

5. Have you talked to people who have written off Christianity because of failures of the church in the past? Were you defensive in your response? Did you attempt to justify such failures or explain them away? How do you think you should have responded?

6. What examples can you find of the Bible being honest about the failures of individual believers or of the people of God?

7. Is there anyone you need to go to and apologize to for the way you have responded in the past when criticisms were raised against Christians or against the history of the church?

8. Have you found it difficult to come up with words that people can truly understand when you try to communicate your faith? Try to write down in a short paragraph what being a Christian means to you without using any Christian words like *sin* or *salvation*. Try to answer the question, "Christian, what do you believe?" Express your faith in terms that any unbeliever, one with no familiarity with the Bible, could understand.

22

BARRIERS BETWEEN THE CHURCH
AND THE WORLD II

The last wall and perhaps the most difficult for us to acknowledge and overcome is the wall created by our sense of alienation from those around us. Many Christians have been taught to avoid business partnerships or even close friendships with non-Christians. We have learned to "come out from them and be separate" in every area of life (2 Corinthians 6:17). We have assumed that this means we are to avoid all close contact with unbelievers, failing to engage in adequate reflection on other passages of Scripture that call us into the world of unbelief. Though we are instructed to "be separate," a misunderstanding or overapplication of this Scripture can be a barrier to any faithful witness for Christ. A sense of antagonism to the culture and alienation from the culture expresses itself in four ways.

INTIMIDATION

Many of us who are Christians are afraid of the culture around us. We see that it is deeply hostile to the Christian faith. Both the intellectual culture in our universities and the popular culture of television and music are post-Christian and even frequently explicitly anti-Christian. Our response to this is fear—fear for ourselves, fear for our church members (particularly our young people), and fear for our children. Yet Jesus tells us not to fear the world, or even the devil, but to fear only God (Luke 12:4-5).

We need to recover trust in the promises of the Lord to us and to our children and to pray to the One who is able to protect us, keep us safe, and deliver us into His kingdom. Which of us, asks Jesus, is able to add an hour to our lives by fear and anxiety (Matthew 6:27)? In telling us not to fear, He reminds us that He cares even for the sparrows, and that we are worth far more to Him than they are (Matthew 10:28-31). We need to recover trust in the Lord and to recover prayer, both for ourselves as individuals and for our churches corporately. God's Word calls us to repentance, fasting, and prayer rather than to fear when we feel overwhelmed by the opposition from our culture. That opposition is overwhelming, but there is One to whom we can turn who is far greater than the society around us.

CONDEMNATION

The second response of many Christians to our society is to condemn the general culture and to condemn unbelievers. Both in private and public worship we find ourselves congratulating ourselves that we are not like the sinners around us. "They may be homosexuals, adulterers, fornicators, pornographers, drunkards, drug addicts, or violent people, but we are not," we remind ourselves. Then we thank God that we are so different from the world. In our teaching and in our writing as Christians we pour scorn and contempt on the decline of moral standards in the world around us.

Scripture, of course, asks us to be discerning about sin, but is this reaction of condemnation and criticism appropriate? This question is important for us to consider, whether our condemnation is directed toward the culture in general or toward particular individuals whom we identify as the leading enemies of the cause of Christ and of the moral commandments of God. Our condemnation may even be focused on people we know personally in our own neighborhoods and communities. However, consider these words of Jesus taken from Luke 18:9-14:

> *To some who were confident of their own righteousness and looked down on everybody else, Jesus told this parable. "Two men went up to the temple to pray, one a Pharisee and the other a tax collector. The Pharisee stood up and prayed about him-*

self: '*God, I thank you that I am not like other men—robbers,*
evildoers, adulterers—or even like this tax collector. I fast twice
a week and give a tenth of all I get.'"

Jesus told this parable of the Pharisee and the tax collector to warn
us against the mentality of self-congratulation and comparing ourselves with "sinners." He teaches us that God does not hear such
prayers, for they are not the kind of prayers He is willing to hear. The
only prayer acceptable to God is that which begins with a heartfelt
recognition of our own sin and need before God, like the prayer of the
tax collector who

> . . . *stood at a distance. He would not even look up to heaven,*
> *but beat his breast and said, "God have mercy on me, a sinner."*

Judgment, the Bible instructs us, is to begin with the household of
God, not with the world or with unbelievers (1 Peter 4:17). We are called
to judge ourselves, not those around us (Matthew 7:1-5). Indeed, Jesus
teaches us that He did not come into the world to judge the world but
rather to save it:

> *"For God did not send his Son into the world to condemn the*
> *world, but to save the world through him."*
>
> —JOHN 3:17

What was true for Him is also to be true of us who bear His name
(1 Corinthians 5:12). In the context of this passage in Corinthians Paul
is discussing the need to discipline fellow believers who disobey God's
moral law, and he then challenges Christians not to treat unbelievers the
same way as we treat our disobedient brothers and sisters in the faith:

> *What business is it of mine to judge those outside the church?*
> *Are you not to judge those inside?*

The truth is, instead of judging those outside the church, Jesus calls
us to imitate Him by loving our enemies, blessing those who curse us,
praying for those who mistreat us, doing good to those who hate us

(Luke 6:27-28). Rather than becoming involved in a war of words against the unrighteous and the ungodly, we are to give ourselves for them, just as Jesus did. We are called to bear His grace into the world, not His judgment. The time will indeed come for Him to judge, but that is His task and not ours. Our task is to be the messengers of His mercy and love into the world, even to those who are our enemies or who are the enemies of the Gospel of Christ and hostile to the commandments of God.

This problem of Christians judging those we perceive to be our enemies has been made far worse by the culture war that engulfs our society. An intense conflict is taking place in our communities, in our schools, in the media, even in the courts and the corridors of political power: What way of life will govern our culture? Christians who believe that we live or lived in a "Christian America" have awakened and discovered that they do not like what is happening around them.

Increasingly Christians are running for office as Christians or are trying, for example, to get measures on popular ballots banning homosexuals from public life or from having civil rights. Some politicians in this culture war denounce single-parent families as they fight for family values, forgetting or ignoring the fact that the vast majority of single parents are women who have been deserted by their husbands or companions. The great majority of single mothers are not women who have politically chosen an alternate family model. They are, in effect, the orphans and widows on whom God delights to have mercy and for whom He calls us to care.

We fight school board elections over values, sometimes without earning the right to run by giving years of sacrificial service to the schools; then we complain we are being persecuted or lament the moral state of the electorate when we are defeated. Christians, above all people, should be aware that we need to earn respect from unbelievers by our life of service to the community. Once we have earned that respect, then we can hope to be elected to public office, whether that office is the local school board, city or statewide representation, or political service at the national level. Simply standing on a platform of moral values without deeds of righteousness and mercy to back up our words is offensive to non-Christians and is displeasing to the Lord who always asks us to keep words and actions together.

Our newfound political activism is a positive step, but this activism sometimes expresses itself in hostile and even abusive language. We hear jokes about political adversaries, and we are ready to "demonize" them, as if particular individuals now in office were single-handedly responsible for the lamentable moral decay in our culture. Instead of obeying the apostle's command always to communicate with "gentleness and respect" (1 Peter 3:15), we find ourselves in a war of words.

A more appropriate response to our dilemma than this war of words might be repentance for the failure of Christians to be more involved in the political process at the local and national level over the past few generations. Of course, those who have worked to undermine the hold of God's moral law over the consciences and lives of Americans will have to bear their own load before God. But we in the church of Christ bear a far greater responsibility for the present situation and must examine the plank in our own eyes, the plank of our failure to be salt and light in the public square for several generations. We were given so much by the efforts of believers in earlier times, and yet we failed to be faithful in holding fast to that which was good and in serving our communities with the gift of God's moral law.

We ought indeed to be involved in the culture war, but we ought to take our part in humility and repentance and with words of grace, seasoned with salt, not with the crude jokes, the name-calling, the demonizing, the abuse we too often use. Jesus spoke to us very plainly about this:

> *"But I tell you who hear me: Love your enemies, do good to those who hate you, bless those who curse you, pray for those who mistreat you."*
>
> —LUKE 6:27-28

The apostle Paul adds: "Bless those who persecute you; bless and do not curse" (Romans 12:14).

The words of Peter in 1 Peter 3:13-17, when he commands us always to speak with "gentleness and respect," come within the context of discussing appropriate behavior for Christians when others are speaking maliciously against them. Even if we are unjustly attacked by those who are opposed to the Gospel, we are to answer kindly and with our hearts and words filled with the mercy of the Gospel. The Scriptures teach us that we are to *expect* a judgmental attitude from the world. If the world criticized and persecuted Jesus (and it certainly did), then we should not be surprised when it criticizes and persecutes us (John 15:18-20). But this is no excuse for us to retaliate in the same vein. The Christian is called to a higher standard by the Gospel, and if we feel it is an impossible standard, then let us remember that what is impossible for us is possible for God. We are, as Francis Schaeffer used to say, to do the Lord's work in the Lord's way, not in the way the world does its work.

RETREAT

The third response of many of us as believers to the surrounding culture is to retreat from it. Distressed by the world because it is so "worldly," we try to create our own distinct culture so we can avoid sinful society as much as possible. We have our own separate Christian or even Reformed institutions so we will be able to avoid the pollution of the world. We retreat into our churches and all the relationships and institutions associated with them, so that the world will influence us in a minimal way. Then, we think, we will be secure and safe from contamination. I heard an elder in my own denomination begging his congregation to turn their church into a "haven" from the world, so they would be able to have as little as possible to do with "the people out there."

I am not suggesting that all Christian institutions are wrong—for example, schools and colleges or mission agencies and organizations devoted to social action. Clearly such institutions are necessary and good. However, we need to ask ourselves what our motivation is for starting a particular Christian institution. Is our purpose to retreat from the world, or is our purpose to prepare believers to serve in the world?

Jesus prayed that we might be in the world as He was in the world, not that we might retreat from it (John 17:15-18). He described us as salt in the world (Matthew 5:13-14). He said that if we fail to influence our society because we have kept ourselves within the saltshaker of the church, on the shelf of our retreating institutions, then we will be worth nothing at all except to be thrown out and trampled underfoot by men.

If we sometimes wonder why we Christians do so little evangelism, and why the little we do is often ineffective, we need to recognize that this mentality of retreat is one of the reasons.

SEPARATION

On a more personal level, the fourth response of many Christians to our ungodly society is personal separation. We insist that we must keep ourselves and our children set apart from personal relationships with unbelievers. We want to be pure, holy, separate from sinners, and we think the only way to do this is to keep ourselves away from them. But if we want to keep ourselves separate, then, says Paul, we would have to leave the world altogether (1 Corinthians 5:9-13). In the context Paul is discussing church discipline:

> *I have written to you in my letter not to associate with sexually immoral people—not at all meaning the people of this world who are immoral, or the greedy and swindlers, or idolaters. In that case you would have to leave this world. . . . "Expel the wicked man from among you."*

What do we find to help us in our understanding of this subject when we turn to the Gospels? We do not have to look far before we discover that Jesus frequently received criticism from His "righteous" contemporaries. They judged Him because He made Himself a friend of sinners. They reasoned that He could not be a prophet or a holy person or a man sent by God because of the company He kept (Luke 7:39; 15:1-2; 19:7). Jesus answered these accusations by arguing that this was the very reason He was sent into the world—that is, to be a friend of sinners (Matthew 9:10-13; 11:19; Luke 15:1-32). The commandments of God are not about personal separation from sinners; they are about being merciful and loving to sinners and at the same time living in personal holiness and purity.

Consider the parable of the good Samaritan, a parable that teaches us that we are called to a life of serving our enemies and anyone in need of our love. Or consider the parable of the two lost sons, which challenges us to imitate our heavenly Father and to be merciful to the prodigal younger son and to the proud and ungrateful older brother. Or at an even deeper level consider the Gospel itself. Jesus came into the world "to seek and to save what was lost"—that is, you and me (Luke 19:10). He calls us to do the same. We all need to ask ourselves some challenging questions: "Who are our unbelieving friends? Who are the 'sinners' whom we give ourselves to love? Who are the ungodly who welcome us gladly and enjoy being with us?" There is no other way to be like Jesus and to be obedient to His command.

Yet, the reality all too often is that along with fear and condemnation, separation and retreat characterize too many of us as believers. We retire into the haven of the church for our own protection and for the protection of our children. This makes genuine outreach almost impossible. How can we have true communication with people about a gospel of love, self-giving, and the Word made flesh if we distance ourselves from those who need to hear the message? A friend who is not yet a believer put it this way: "The trouble with you Christians is that you wrap yourselves in a cocoon. All your close friends are other Christians. What about pagans like me? Who is going to reach me?"

23

BARRIERS BETWEEN THE WORLD
AND THE CHURCH

Our present chapter turns to consider the barriers that exist between unbelievers and believers. In this chapter we reflect not so much on the barriers we raise to keep the world at bay, but rather the barriers raised by non-Christians. To aid this reflection we need to summarize briefly some of the characteristics of our postmodern generation.

THE FAILURE OF REASON

In an earlier chapter we looked briefly at the loss of truth in our culture. Here we need to think more about this issue. For the past several centuries western nations have celebrated the power of reason. Reason was thought to have brought enlightenment to our societies, and along with this confidence in human reason came optimism about human life and the future. In sharp contrast we live now in a time when human reason is considered to be inadequate to lead us to the truth. Objective truth about the ultimate nature of reality and about the human condition is thought to be beyond human reach. Instead of objective truth it is claimed there is only personal truth: "You have your truth; I have mine."

The pluralistic nature of our society reinforces this. All around us are people with differing religious convictions or with no religious convictions at all. People come to the United States and to other so-called Christian nations from many parts of the world, bringing their religious convictions and practices with them. Major cities like New York,

Chicago, Los Angeles, or Houston have perhaps fifty Islamic mosques in each of them and twenty or more Hindu and Buddhist temples, as well as meeting places for many other religious groups. Our society is increasingly a melting pot of beliefs, ideas, and cultures. The United States today is considered to be the most religiously diverse nation the world has ever seen.

Christians should not be afraid of this diversity; rather, it brings within reach of the churches vast numbers of people who are displaced from their own cultures and their roots, many of whom are open to considering the claims of Jesus Christ. We should see this diversity as an opportunity for evangelism and not something to lament. We pray for such pluralism and the allowance of diversity in a Moslem nation such as Saudi Arabia and in a Hindu kingdom like Nepal. We pray for the legal recognition of pluralism in such nations, for we long for Christian missionaries (especially those sent and supported by our own churches) to have the freedom to proclaim the Gospel. We also pray earnestly that the peoples of such nations will be free to become Christians and practice their faith without fear of persecution.

If we pray for pluralism elsewhere, why should pluralism of belief at home make our lives difficult? Postmodernism, however, teaches that pluralism is the way it ought to be, not just for the sake of tolerance and mutual respect, but because Postmodernism insists that there is no one truth that describes reality. It asserts that our finite grasp on reality is so tenuous that there can be nothing but the belief systems of individuals or cultural groups, and that none of these can claim either the status of Truth or even superiority over any of the others.

One consequence of this postmodern claim is the belief that every person has the right to his or her own views. The right not simply in the sense that everyone's views ought to be respected, and not only in the sense that people should have the legal right to hold their convictions, but in the sense that all beliefs are equally valid. But if all ideas are valid, then they are all invalid, for once one says all religious beliefs are equally true, one has acknowledged in effect that none of them are true, for they all make differing statements about the world, God, humanity, salvation, and the future.

A second consequence of this loss of confidence in reason and a loss of confidence in truth even existing is that western societies have raised a generation of skeptics. If you doubt this claim, then listen to the music of young people. It is deeply uncertain and pessimistic. We live in a generation that has no hope; and the younger people are, the more hopeless they feel.

THE LOSS OF AUTHORITY

A second major characteristic of Postmodernism is the rejection of authority. If there is no truth, then there is no book (the Bible), no body of beliefs (Christian creeds or confessions), no person (the pastor), no social institution (government, church, or family) that can command respect or submission. Readers can supply here their own examples of loss of respect for the authority of persons and institutions. Even as one teaching mature Christians in a theological seminary, I notice an increasing questioning of a professor's right to determine grades or to expect respect in the classroom or to require submission to institutional rules and standards. This is in a context where our students pride themselves on not being postmodern.

This loss of respect for authority leads to the irreverence of Generation X and almost all teen subgroups. Everything that anyone or any group has held to be sacred or precious can be scorned and held up for ridicule. There is a delight in shocking the viewer or listener (just watch music videos or listen to the words of many songs or turn on your TV and watch talk shows or even soap operas). Another element of this is the deconstruction or tearing apart of what has been considered to be authoritative or sacred.

This questioning of all authority means that no style can be judged better than any other style. There is no canon of great literature or art or architecture or music. No culture and no cultural artifacts can be considered higher or more advanced than any other. To claim, for example, that Shakespeare is the greatest dramatist to have written in English is considered by a radical postmodern to be an imperialistic claim, a thinly disguised attempt to impose "Dead White European Male" culture on other cultural and social groups, writings, and artifacts. This same criticism is leveled at any claim to truthfulness for the Bible or for Christianity or for the preaching of the Gospel.

Sometimes this disrespect for authority has a playful element to it, a humorous mixing of styles—past and present, the serious and the comedic. Consider the commercials selling everything from food to deodorants by using a painting like the *Mona Lisa*. "Great" objects can be taken from their context and used in any way at all, especially to add a touch of spice and fun. However, despite the humor and creativity in some of the best of this, there is a serious statement underneath the fun, a questioning of significant cultural icons, an ignoring of the meaning of such icons to those who honor them, a relativism about standards. An example of this is the hotel and casino in Las Vegas, built in imitation of the Great Pyramid, with a full-size model of the Sphinx and Cleopatra's Needles before it. The construction material is not hewn stone but appears to be black glass. One may admire or be amused by the startling creativity of this casino, but the setting and use of these icons is so radically different from their historical setting and significance in Egypt that the transformation trivializes both the copies and the originals.

MORAL UNCERTAINTY

Postmodernism is characterized by moral relativism. There is no "you shall" or "you shall not." There are no transcendent commandments for this generation. No one individual, no group, no authority, no religion, no sacred book, no god has the right to tell anyone else how he or she ought to live. In our society what are the consequences of this loss of moral authority?

The Individual

The individual becomes the moral authority for himself or herself. In place of morality there is left only "my values" or even "my lifestyle." Adults and children are encouraged, on this view, to find their own way, to make their own choices about how they should live. No one else can decide for them, for the individual is considered autonomous—a law to oneself. Quite apart from the reality of our finiteness, which makes it impossible for us to legislate for ourselves (we need our Creator for that), there is the difficulty of our sinful passions that distort our reflection on what is right and good for ourselves. The apostle Paul wrote about this problem in Galatians 5:13: "Do not use your freedom to indulge the sinful nature." The reality of people using their freedom to feed their sinful nature is all around us in contemporary society.

Morality by Consensus

Along with pushing for greater individual moral "freedom," our societies bring moral issues before the public for their input, either in referendums or in opinion polls. What do people think about sex before marriage, or homosexual practice, or abortion, or euthanasia? Such an approach, consulting the opinions of the people about moral matters, would have been unthinkable a generation ago. The novelist William Golding summed it up this way: "When God is dead, when man is the highest, good and evil are decided by majority vote."

It ought to be apparent to anyone who reflects on this notion that majorities often do things to minorities of which it ought to be declared, "This is wicked." Consider the slave trade, or the setting aside of almost every treaty ever made by our national and state governments with Native Americans, or ethnic cleansing in Bosnia or Kosovo, or the treatment of the East Timorese by Indonesia. No majority decision can make brutality and wickedness into ethical behavior. Such a stance is a consequence of our postmodern rejection of moral authority.

Loss of Public Accountability

There is in addition a loss of moral discussion, persuasion, and accountability in the public square. Television and other media companies constantly push the moral envelope to see what people will endure or enjoy, for there is a perverse pleasure in viewing sin. After a few presentations, something we once thought too shocking to watch becomes acceptable. Our consciences become hardened. Those responsible for making media choices feel no need to consult any moral authority or even the people. Attracting audiences becomes the only authority.

Similarly, those in law or medicine or scientific research feel the freedom to do whatever they want within their disciplines. "Should Grandfather die, regardless of what the family wants, regardless of what Grandfather may desire? Then let's sedate him to death." This is not a make-believe situation. This precisely happened to the grandfather of one of our students. When family members visited him in the hospital (he had been admitted for tests), they noticed that he was drowsy and somewhat incoherent, and he also seemed to be thirsty and a little dehydrated. One went to fetch him a glass of water (there was none beside his bed), but a nurse, finding them trying to help him drink, said, "You can't do that! He is on a no food or drink regimen." On inquiry the family discovered that the doctor, without consulting anyone, had decided the old man should die. It was too late by the time the family realized what was happening to prevent his death, and a day or two later their grandpa died.

We should not be surprised by such happenings, even if we are appalled. A nation without moral direction can quickly find that its decisions are being made by "experts" who have little regard for the views of ordinary people. Even moral discussion becomes difficult in such a context, for everything becomes reduced to "my point of view." Once a society moves beyond a shared understanding of moral boundaries, it is very difficult either to talk rationally and courteously to each other or to feel the need to respect or to be bound by others' moral convictions.

PRACTICAL IDOLATRY

Our culture once held precious the Christian story as the account of human life that gives us sense and meaning. By *story* I do not mean that Christianity is a fairy tale, for it is, of course, God's true account of our human origin, reality, and predicament and its resolution in Jesus Christ. I use *story* in the sense of a narrative about the human condition that explains and gives direction to people's lives. Every human society has a story in this sense. Christians are blessed in that we have been given the real story from the perspective of the Creator Himself.

But postmodern society is a society in which there is no longer a shared story to give people ultimate meaning to their lives or hope for their future. The true story has been lost for most people, and there is no other story to bind our society or people's individual lives together. Consequently our contemporaries become idolaters, given up to anything that will achieve the two goals of personal success and vivid personal feelings (Robert Bellah's analysis of American culture at the end of the twentieth century).

Idols of the Mind

People need to believe something about their lives to give them a sense of meaning, purpose, and direction. They may opt for a political ideology, and despite their years of education they will believe anything, no matter how irrational it is. Consider the growth of far-right conspiracy theory groups or white supremacists, even existing within the fringes of the church, who teach that other races are not fully human. Or think of those who still cling to Marxist ideology despite its being so thoroughly discredited with the collapse of the Iron Curtain. Such extreme political theories are not harmless; rather, they can bring enormous destruction into a society. Consider, for example, Nazism and Aryan supremacy in Germany and elsewhere during the thirties or Marxism for more than a generation in the Soviet Union and much of Central and Eastern Europe.

Alternate intellectual idols may be theories about the structure and beginnings of the universe or the origin of life or the nature of human existence. Again such idols may have terrible consequences for individuals and societies—for example, the practice of abortion, infanticide, and euthanasia in so many western countries today, or the widespread use of sterilization in the USA in the twenties and thirties to improve the gene pool.

Idols of the Will

With no transcendent commandments from God to direct their lives, people search for idols for their wills. They will live for anything that provides goals and a sense of direction and purpose for their lives, such as work, ambition, success, money, or even a cult.

Idols of the Heart

With no passion in one's innermost being to love God and to enjoy Him forever, people look for idols for their hearts. They search for anything that will give them pleasure and vivid feelings—sex; relationships; possessions; one's own body; sports; the arts, especially music; drugs; even a religious experience.

Ultimately all idolatry, whether it is of the mind, will, or heart, is destructive to individuals and to societies. The psalmist describes for us the consequences of worshiping idols (Psalm 115:1-8; 135:15-18; the latter is quoted below):

> *The idols of the nations are silver and gold,*
> *made by the hands of men.*
> *They have mouths, but cannot speak,*
> *eyes, but they cannot see;*
> *they have ears, but cannot hear,*
> *nor is there breath in their mouths.*
> *Those who make them will be like them,*
> *and so will all who trust in them.*

Idols may seem powerless, for they are not true gods. But idols do have power, the power to remake their worshipers into their own image. To the extent that we worship any idol, to that extent we will diminish our humanity. Reflect on the example of Scrooge in Charles Dickens's *A Christmas Carol*. Scrooge's worship of money eats away at the fabric of his life and even of his character. All idols are like this. If we live for our job, it will consume us. As it captures more and more of our devotion, it will begin damaging our marriage, family, friendships, health, and ethical standards. If we live for sexual enjoyment and ignore God's directions about chastity, fidelity, and sexual fulfillment, we will hurt others, we will limit our own ability to make deep relationships, and in the end we will even find sexual pleasure harder and harder to achieve and enjoy.

Whatever we worship will make us like itself. This is true for idols, and it is also true for the Lord. If we bow to the one true God, He promises us that He will transform us so that we reflect His image. Unbelievers think that an idol, because it has been chosen and made by them, will be under their control and bring them freedom. The opposite is the reality. Idols always enslave. God, on the other hand, asks us to be prepared to lose ourselves but delights in helping us find ourselves and in giving us perfect freedom. People fear knowing God, for His true character is hidden from them behind a veil of ignorance, superstition, and above all, pride. They are afraid that if they bow before Him, they will be humiliated and ashamed. They want to always be able to say, "I am the master of my fate: I am the captain of my soul" (from the poem *Invictus* by Wallace Ernest Henley). They fear that by yielding to God they will lose the essence of who they are. But the actual fruit of knowing God is very different than what they fearfully envision.

> *Whenever anyone turns to the Lord, the veil is taken away. Now the Lord is the Spirit, and where the Spirit of the Lord is, there is freedom. And we, who with unveiled faces all reflect the Lord's glory, are being transformed into his likeness with ever increasing glory.*
>
> —2 CORINTHIANS 3:16-18

Sadly, most people around us do not know this. They either deny God or turn from Him to idols. When they think there is no one in heaven for them to worship, they will worship something, anything, here on this earth. What we observe in our society is exactly what Paul teaches us in Romans 1:21, 23, 25, 28.

> *They exchanged the truth of God for a lie, and worshiped and served created things rather than the Creator—who is forever praised. Amen.*
>
> —v. 25

PAGANISM

A fifth characteristic of our postmodern society is a return to paganism. Giving up the hope that there are religious answers that can make sense of the world or of human life, people remain religious, for God has placed eternity in their hearts (see Ecclesiastes 3:11). It should be no surprise to us when we see the flourishing of every kind of neo-paganism and of various New Age religions. Many people do not ask, "Is this religion true?" or even "Is it sensible or moral?" They are more likely to ask, "Does this make me feel spiritual?" or "Does this fill for a moment the vacuum in my heart and soul?" Think of the Heaven's Gate cult or of the Branch Davidians as extreme examples of this.

Christians need to respond to this spiritual search with understanding and sympathy. If people recognize that material prosperity is insufficient to satisfy the soul, this recognition should be seen as a good beginning. Such searchers know they are in need, even if they are looking in the wrong place. God does not call us to be afraid of those who become involved in new (or old) religious movements; rather He calls us to honor their desire for spiritual fulfillment and to reach out to them in love.

24

WHAT IS MY NEIGHBOR THINKING
ABOUT ME?

The last chapter gave a brief outline of the characteristics of our post-modern culture. This description of the directions in which so many people around us are moving may seem overwhelming to us, but it leads us to a further question: If many of our contemporaries are embracing such ideas and such ways of life, what do they make of Christians and of what we believe? We perhaps all wonder at times, *What is my neighbor thinking about me? What does my neighbor think of Christianity?*

It was said of the Greeks and Romans of the first century A.D.: "It was not that men became so depraved that they abandoned the gods; but that the gods became so depraved that they were abandoned by men" (quoted in Michael Green's *Evangelism in the Early Church*). This is the reality that we as Christians face in our moment of history. God forbid that anyone would think that I am suggesting that our heavenly Father might be depraved or evil in any way. However, many around us think that our religion is immoral and that the God we proclaim is not worthy of worship, that He is to be judged and rejected as not meeting contemporary standards of goodness and justice. What is it that people find so unworthy about the Christian faith?

THE PROBLEM OF TRUTH

Truth claims are offensive to our contemporaries. As long as we say, "This is *my* truth," no one minds or pays us any attention; but we are considered arrogant when we claim that what we believe is *"the* truth." As I write this I have before me an article from a current newspaper about the Southern Baptist Convention's new guidelines on communicating the Gospel to Jews. That document has drawn a firestorm of criticism because it is evident that the Southern Baptists are claiming that Christianity is true and that therefore they consider other religions to be false. The newspaper reporter and the Jewish community alike find such a claim to be proud beyond measure, intolerant, and therefore intolerable.

THE PROBLEM OF CHRIST

Exclusive claims are offensive. The exclusiveness of Christianity follows necessarily from our truth claim. Once we say that Jesus is the Son of God, the true God Himself, then we submit to His insistence that He is *the* way, *the* truth, and *the* life. When it becomes clear to our contemporaries that we believe Christ is the only way to God, that His name is the only name given under heaven by which people can be saved, then we are regarded as intolerant and unloving. Tolerance is understood to mean not simply respect for a person and for his or her views, but not saying openly or even hinting by implication that his or her views might be wrong and might need to be changed.

THE PROBLEM OF MORAL LAW

Absolute moral commandments are offensive. As long as we say only, "This is *my* chosen way of life; these are *my* values," we are accepted. But as soon as we say, "You shall not!" or "This is God's commandment for all men and women," we are considered to be disrespectful, intolerant, judgmental, and self-righteous. The statement that there is one set of moral commandments for all people is regarded as an immoral statement. If we say that we know for certain what is moral for others as well as for ourselves, we are judged to be immoral.

THE PROBLEM OF JUDGMENT

The judgment of God is an offense to our contemporaries. Personal freedom to do as one wishes is the greatest idol of those around us. The notion that God will hold us accountable at the end of our lives for our lifestyle is considered outrageous. God is declared to be immoral because He sets Himself up as the judge and measure of human behavior.

THE PROBLEM OF AUTHORITY

The claim of authority for our churches, for their teaching ministry, for our pastors is unacceptable and offensive today. For our contemporaries our religion is just one among many; it has no greater claim to respect than that of any other religious group around us, even the most extreme, such as Heaven's Gate. People go shopping for a religion or church just like they try out different restaurants and cuisines.

I use this image of trying out restaurants and sampling different kinds of foods because this was the way a television interviewer described her own approach to religious worship. After she had interviewed me on a Sunday morning show, we were having a conversation about the issue of truth, a result of her being surprised by my statement on the show that I believed Christianity to be *the* truth. "That is a completely new idea to me," she said. "I visit different religious services just as I try out various ethnic restaurants." One week she tried Baptist, another Episcopalian, another Catholic, another Jewish, another Presbyterian, another the Ethical Humanist Society. When I spoke to her about truth and the need to find a church that proclaims truth with authority, she was amazed; she had never heard anyone speak in this way before. Our claim to be the one true religion, to belong to the true church, is simply unbelievable and unacceptable.

All this presents us with a tremendous challenge. How will we respond? We have already learned that fear, judgment, retreat, and separation (withdrawal) are not biblical options. Jesus calls us into the world, and He calls us into the world as gracious ambassadors of His message of grace. What will this mean for us?

He calls us, first, to pray about His Spirit's convicting people of sin and righteousness and judgment (John 16:8-11). He calls us to pray that He will send laborers out into the harvest field, a field that sometimes seems impossible for us to labor in, but where all things are possible to Him. He calls us to pray that He will give us an open door to those around us. He calls us to pray that we might speak the truth with courage and with clarity.

Second, He calls us to love our neighbors as we love ourselves, and many of our neighbors are postmoderns. He calls us not to be offended by their offense at what we believe but rather to turn the other cheek and to be prepared to be hated by the world without cause. He calls us even to consider it a blessing to be persecuted for what we believe and for living righteously. He calls us to take up the cross and follow Him. To take up the cross means to love, to serve, to befriend, to give ourselves for those around us, even when they are shocked by what we believe. Are we willing to live the kind of life of self-sacrifice that Jesus lived for us?

Third, He calls us to be prepared to speak his word with "grace," "respect," and "gentleness" (Colossians 4:5-6; 1 Peter 3:15-16). The message we believe, the message that has saved us, is a word of grace. It is that grace that is to be carried into the world in our hearts, in our lives, in our attitudes, and in our words. There is no other way to be a faithful disciple of Jesus Christ.

Jesus' teaching and example get under our skin! He challenges us to set aside the barriers that are so much a part of our lives. He even commands us to imitate our heavenly Father by loving our enemies and doing good to them. He asks us to make ourselves vulnerable by showing mercy to "sinners" and becoming friends with them. For most of us this would mean some radical changes in our lives. We would have to set some different priorities in regard to how we spend our time and where we use our energies.

25

THE PHARISEE WITHIN

Jesus calls us to befriend sinners, enemies, and our postmodern neighbors. We may (and we need to) wrestle with the question, "Why do we find this so difficult?" Or "Why can't outreach be just to 'nice' people who think like us and who share our values, whose ideas are not strange and different, who have the 'right' political and social views, whose lives are 'together' already?"

Just verbalizing these questions exposes their folly, even though this is probably how most of us feel! Clearly it is the way many of Jesus' contemporaries felt, for they constantly criticized Him for the company He kept, for the people He ate with, for those He allowed to come close to His life. What are the underlying problems here? Those most vehement in their criticism of Jesus were the most zealous for God's name and God's Law in that society; they were the "church" group of the time that we know as the Pharisees. There is more than a little of the Pharisee within us all; so we will consider a few of the criticisms that Jesus, in turn, leveled at those who criticized Him. What are the basic characteristics of a Pharisee as Jesus saw them?

PRIDE

The most fundamental of all human sins is pride. It was at the root of the sin of Adam and Eve and was the reason for the ruin of Lucifer. Pride is at the heart of all unbelief. Pride stands in the way of any person acknowledging his or her need of Christ. Pride prevents us from being reconciled to one another when our relationships are disrupted by sin.

This self-serving aspect of our fallen nature does not just disappear when we are converted, though it does receive a mortal blow when we are humbled before Jesus. Pride takes our whole lifetime to die.

In an earlier chapter we looked briefly at Jesus' parable of the Pharisee and the tax collector (Luke 18:9-14). In this parable Jesus addressed the problem of pride. The Pharisee stood in the temple praying about the difference between himself and other people, who were "evildoers" and enemies of God's laws. Jesus admonished the Pharisee for not offering acceptable prayers to God. He was simply congratulating himself, making himself feel good before God and in his own eyes by comparing himself with others. The "sinner," in this case a collector of taxes, did not look at other people, nor did he presume even to lift his eyes to heaven. Instead he cried out to God for mercy. God justified that man rather than the Pharisee.

How often is our internal dialogue about ourselves and others filled with pride like that of the Pharisee? How many of our private and public prayers would seem like the Pharisee's to an objective ear? How much of our public worship or our preaching and teaching sound to Jesus like the Pharisee's words as He, Jesus, listens in on our church services?

Scripture teaches us that God resists the proud but gladly receives the humble. Humility is to be a lifelong attribute, not simply the attitude of our hearts when we first come to Christ. Every day we are to remember our own need of God's mercy, the problems and failures in our own lives, rather than making ourselves blind to our own sins by concentrating on those of others. So deep is the problem of pride that even God's good gifts to us can readily be turned by us into means of self-congratulation. This is true with spiritual gifts; it is true with any special blessing that we receive from God. Even biblical knowledge can make us proud, not because sound biblical knowledge is a problem, but because of the pride in our hearts that clasps on to anything that will help us to feel a little better about ourselves than about our fellow believers. Consider Jesus' words, "If you were blind, you would not be guilty of sin; but now that you claim you can see, your guilt remains" (John 9:41), or those of Paul: "We know that we all possess knowledge. Knowledge puffs up, but love builds up. The man who thinks he knows something does not yet know as he ought to know" (1 Corinthians 8:1-2).

Whatever our strength as individuals, whatever blessings and gifts

God gives us, these are the places in our lives where we have to be most on guard against pride. For example, if the strength and glory of our church or denomination is teaching and sound doctrine, then that is where pride will most likely enter in. That will be the area where we will indulge in self-congratulation before God; that will be where we turn our spiritual strengths into a weapon against others. More than anything else in our prayers for ourselves, we need to pray for a humble and grateful heart and clarity about the ease with which we become self-serving and full of pride.

A CRITICAL SPIRIT

Closely related to the problem of pride is our tendency to be more critical of others than we are of ourselves. Jesus addressed this issue in the Sermon on the Mount:

> *"Do not judge, or you too will be judged. . . . Why do you look at the speck of sawdust in your brother's eye and pay no attention to the plank in your own eye? How can you say to your brother, 'Let me take the speck out of your eye,' when all the time there is a plank in your own eye?"*
> —MATTHEW 7:1-4

Whether the person in our mind's eye is a fellow believer or an unbeliever, we all tend to spend more time thinking about the faults of others and to use higher standards when we criticize others than when we turn our attention to our own failings. Why is this? It is easier to criticize others than to criticize ourselves, and it is more comfortable to pick at someone else's weaknesses and shortcomings than it is our own. We would have to change if we looked at ourselves as critically as we look at others, and that would be costly and painful!

We can indulge in gossip within our own hearts or carry on an internal running commentary about someone else's failings with pleasant complacency. Occasionally we all gossip, sometimes even under the guise of spirituality, as, for example, when a prayer meeting or a Bible study becomes an excuse for talking about the weaknesses and failings of others. Even our sermons can turn into sessions for criticizing who-

ever, in our or some other church or in the society around us, is our particular source of self-righteous scorn at the present time. How virtuous
we can feel as we expose the enemies of God and of Christian values!
Jesus' words from the Sermon on the Mount confront us in our
hypocrisy:

> *"In the same way you judge others, you will be judged, and with
> the measure you use, it will be measured to you. . . . . You hyp-
> ocrite, first take the plank out of your own eye."*
> —MATTHEW 7:2, 5

Jesus challenges us to look to our own sins. *I* am the one I have to
concentrate on changing, not my wife or husband, not my relatives, not
my friends or neighbors, not my work colleagues, not politicians I dis-
like, not my enemies. Go to work on Number One! Judgment is to begin
with my own temple of the living God, my own heart, not my fellow
believers, and not the world.

EXTERNAL SPIRITUALITY

Another related failing of our internal Pharisee is placing our emphasis
on outward acts of religious practice and on the public appearance of
spirituality. We pride ourselves on our church attendance. We pray more
fervently in the hearing of others than in the privacy of our rooms. We
make sure others know when we give. We parade our devotion to God
by talking about our daily Bible reading, our fasting, or our commitment
to involvement in church activities. We let everyone be aware that we
hold some church office. Jesus repeatedly addressed this issue. See, for
example, Matthew 6:1-18, 15:1-20, and 23:1-28. Why are we so easily
tempted to fall into this trap of showing off our spirituality? There are
several reasons.

First, we like to be thought well of by others. We want to make a
good impression on our fellow Christians and to represent our
Christianity well to non-Christians. Partly this is good. We desire to
follow the biblical injunction to avoid every appearance of evil
(1 Thessalonians 5:22 and elsewhere). But the focus of our devotion may
easily become skewed. For whose attention am I praying? Why am I giv-

ing? Why fasting? The Lord calls us to have true devotion in our hearts to Him and not to be concerned about whether others think I have a good prayer life or if I give enough or if I appear sufficiently religious.

> *"When you pray [give, fast], do not be like the hypocrites, for they love to pray . . . to be seen by men. . . . When you pray, go into your room, close the door and pray to your Father, who is unseen. Then your Father, who sees what is done in secret, will reward you."*
>
> —MATTHEW 6:2-3, 5-6, 16-18

Second, we easily begin to congratulate ourselves on our spirituality if others are commending us. Pride creeps in again, and we readily forget our spiritual poverty. In reality how cool is our devotion, how lukewarm our love, how weak and inconstant our zeal!

Third, these outward evidences of religious life are so much easier to accomplish than is true obedience to God's commandments about justice, mercy, and faithfulness. We all hanker after an easier path to spiritual maturity than the one God has laid down for us. To all of our excuses Jesus' response is the same: "What does it truly mean to love God with all your heart and soul and mind and strength, and what does it mean to love your neighbor as yourself?"

A COMFORTABLE LIFE

A fourth characteristic of a Pharisee's heart is a desire for comfort. Opening our lives up to "sinners," "enemies," and people who are "different" will make us vulnerable. It may not be entirely safe. It may be messy. It will certainly be costly in terms of time and energy. It is much easier to criticize unbelievers and sinners or simply to keep them at a secure distance than to do something for them. We become frightened. "What will be the effect on our families? Will I be able to cope myself? Will I be any good at this?"

We all desire to grow a hedge of comfort, privilege, and security around our lives; within this private space we feel that we can be in control and nothing too demanding will come our way. So we take refuge in making speeches about problems in our culture, or in listening to sermons denouncing those who cause the problems, or we may even give to a ministry that does something about them. This helps us feel better.

But instead of making us feel better, Jesus discomforts our hearts and our lives:

> *"Go and learn what this means: 'I desire mercy and not sacrifice.' . . . You have neglected the more important matters of the law—justice, mercy and faithfulness. . . . If anyone would come after me, he must deny himself and take up his cross and follow me. For whoever wants to save his life will lose it, but whoever loses his life for me will find it."*
> —MATTHEW 9:13; 23:23; 16:24-25

26

MEMORIZED SUMMARIES OF
THE GOSPEL

In our last chapter we saw that a key to outreach is learning to recognize the Pharisee within each of us. Daily we are to humble ourselves gladly before the holiness and mercy of Christ. As those who slowly and painfully are coming to know our own hearts, we ought to be more ready to give ourselves in the service of reaching out to our neighbors, whoever they may be. At this point in our study we need to turn to another very basic question. What is it that we should communicate to people? You may feel as you read this, "That is an unnecessary question! Every Christian knows that the Gospel is as simple as ABC." What is this ABC?

> A—You are a sinner.
> B—Christ died for you.
> C—Repent and believe in Him.

Much training for evangelism specializes in teaching some readily remembered form of this ABC or something similar. The trainee learns a simple outline of the Good News that needs to be imparted to a non-Christian or is taught a set of questions to ask and answers to give to the unbeliever. Is this approach right or wrong? Is it helpful? To answer these questions we need to turn to Scripture itself.

There is indeed a basic content to the Gospel, a content that can be summarized simply. It is also clear that this basic content needs to be communicated to the non-Christian. Think, for example, of Paul's words in the first five verses of 1 Corinthians 15:

> *Now, brothers, I want to remind you of the gospel I preached to you, which you received and on which you have taken your stand. By this gospel you are saved, if you hold firmly to the word I preached to you. Otherwise, you have believed in vain. For what I received I passed on to you as of first importance: that Christ died for our sins according to the Scriptures, that he was buried, that he was raised on the third day according to the Scriptures, and that he appeared to Peter, and then to the Twelve.*

In this passage Paul teaches us that there are indeed gospel truths that are of first importance:

1. Christ's death for our sins in fulfillment of Old Testament promises.
2. Christ's burial in a grave.
3. Christ's resurrection in agreement with the prophecies of Scripture.
4. Christ's appearances to the apostles and others, proving that He was alive.

Another example of such a presentation of the basics of the Gospel comes in Peter's challenge at the conclusion of his sermon on the Day of Pentecost, recorded in Acts 2:22-40:

> *"Jesus of Nazareth was a man accredited by God to you by miracles, wonders and signs. . . . You . . . put him to death by nailing him to the cross. . . . God has raised this Jesus to life, and we are all witnesses of the fact. Exalted to the right hand of God, he has received . . . the promised Holy Spirit. . . . God has made this Jesus, whom you crucified, both Lord and Christ. . . . Repent and be baptized, every one of you, in the name of Jesus Christ so that your sins may be forgiven. And you will receive the gift of the Holy Spirit. The promise is for you and your children and for all who are far off."*

On this occasion our summary of Peter's words has additional elements along with those we find in 1 Corinthians 15:

1. Jesus' miracles attest to His favor in God's sight.
2. He was put to death in fulfillment of God's purposes.
3. Jesus was raised from the dead, and there were witnesses. (The context makes clear that His resurrection was in fulfillment of the promises of Scripture.)
4. Exalted as God's equal and heir, He received from the Father the Holy Spirit whom the prophets had said would come.
5. Jesus was put to death at the hands of sinful men, but by His resurrection God has declared Him to be the divine Lord and also the promised Messiah.
6. You must repent of your sins and believe in Jesus so you can be forgiven.
7. When you believe, you will receive the Holy Spirit.
8. This promise of salvation is not only for you and your children but for the whole world.

A third example of a condensed presentation of the Gospel comes from the words of Jesus Himself to the disciples in the upper room when He appeared to them after His resurrection:

> *"This is what I told you while I was still with you: Everything must be fulfilled that is written about me in the Law of Moses, the Prophets and the Psalms. . . . This is what is written: The Christ will suffer and rise from the dead on the third day, and repentance and forgiveness of sins will be preached in his name to all nations, beginning at Jerusalem. You are witnesses of these things."*
>
> —LUKE 24:44-47

Once again we can set out Jesus' words as a set of points to be readily remembered:

1. The prophecies of Scripture were fulfilled in Jesus Christ.
2. Jesus suffered and died.
3. He rose from the dead.

4. People must repent and have their sins forgiven through Jesus.

5. This message is to be made known not only among the Jews, but also to all nations.

6. The apostles were to be witnesses of these facts of Jesus' death and resurrection, of their meaning, and of God's purposes for the whole world.

As we consider these three examples of summaries of the Gospel, there are several matters of importance to note. First, these summaries can only be made if we extract the words of Jesus, Peter, or Paul from their wider context. Jesus' words are taken from a lengthy session of teaching about the fulfillment of Old Testament prophecies in His life, death, and resurrection. Peter's words are his challenge at the end of a long sermon that itself is set in the context of the pouring out of the Spirit on the Day of Pentecost. Paul's words come from the introduction to his discussion of the importance of the historical nature of the resurrection.

Second, we have only been able to make these summaries by leaving out parts of what was originally written in their immediate context. This is noted by the use of ellipses. Peter's words, for example, come from a sermon that appears in the Acts text as Luke's extracts (a sermon that in its original form would have been much longer than the twenty-five or so verses found in Acts 2. Luke adds in 2:40, "with many other words he warned them").

Third, each of these summaries of the essential truths of the Gospel is slightly different from the others, though there are clearly some common features:

1. Old Testament witness to the coming events and the import of Jesus' ministry.

2. The reality of Jesus' death for our sins.

3. The historical fact of the resurrection of Christ.

4. The necessity of repentance and faith.

5. Apostolic testimony to these truths.

Even the diversity we have noted in these three simple examples does not begin to cover the range of presentation of the Gospel that we find within the New Testament. In fact, the three examples we have examined are fairly similar to each other, and if we look at the settings from which they are taken, it should be apparent why this is so. Two of them come from a context where believers are being addressed, while one, Peter's sermon on the Day of Pentecost, is an address to unbelievers who are primarily Jewish (along with some Gentiles familiar with Judaism and the Old Testament—see Acts 2:11).

However, when we turn to a very different situation—for example, Paul's talk on Mars Hill in Athens—we cannot make a summary that is anything like those above. If we study Acts 17:22-31 carefully, we might extract the following statements that express the Gospel as Paul communicated it to the Athenians:

> "... *The God who made the world and everything in it is the Lord of heaven and earth ... in him we live and move and have our being ... we should not think that the divine being is like gold or silver or stone—an image made by man's design or skill. ... God ... commands all people everywhere to repent ... he has set a day when he will judge the world with justice by a man he has appointed. He has given proof of this to all men by raising him from the dead.*"

The people to whom Paul was speaking were Gentiles who had no knowledge of the Bible. Paul's central emphasis was not the death and resurrection of Jesus, nor the fact that Christ is the Messiah, the Son of God promised in the Old Testament. Rather, he stressed the existence and nature of God. We might summarize this message as follows:

1. God is the Creator of all things.
2. We are dependent on God for our life and for everything.
3. Our human nature is derived from His nature.
4. Idolatry is folly, for an idol is less than the man who makes it.
5. God commands us to repent of our idolatry and worship only Him.
6. Judgment Day will come, and God's representative will bring true justice to this world.

7. The resurrection of Jesus Christ from the dead proves that
He will be that great Judge.

This summary is remarkably different from the three we examined
earlier. If we ask why, the obvious answer is that these pagan unbelievers did not have the same knowledge of the Scriptures possessed by
the hearers in the other three examples we considered. We will return
to this issue in later chapters, but for now we need to ask the question,
"Does this mean that it is without value to learn a summary of the
Gospel?" Or we might ask in perplexity, "Are you saying that the
Gospel cannot be simply summarized?" Of course neither of these is
the point being made!

There are, of course, truths that people need to know to become
Christians. Simply because Christianity is true, because it is the truth
about the world in which we live and about human life, what we believe
can be expressed in a set of statements. The New Testament's baptismal
formula is one simple expression of this: "I baptize you in the name of
the Father and of the Son and of the Holy Spirit" (Matthew 28:19). A
new Christian can state his or her faith in this way:

I believe in God the Father, the Creator of all.
I believe in God the Son, my redeemer.
I believe in God the Holy Spirit, who has given me new life.

Having confessed this faith, the new convert is baptized into the
name of the triune God. It seems probable that the early creeds were simply an expansion of this baptismal formula, having three paragraphs,
one for each member of the Trinity, setting out what a convert was
expected to profess when he or she came to be baptized. Today whenever someone is baptized as a believer, he or she is asked questions
expressing the fundamental beliefs and commitments that are at the
heart of being a Christian. Those I have used for many years are set out
later in this chapter.

Clearly it is helpful to have, both for oneself and for one's church,
a summary of Christian beliefs. Public confession of our faith, reciting
a biblical passage or one of the early creeds, unites us with Christians
throughout the world and all through the history of the church. We

know that we do not stand alone with our own private beliefs; rather we are part of the people of God who come to Him through our Lord Jesus Christ, a people from every stage of history and from every nation on the face of the earth.

Such a summary of our faith is also useful for teaching our children. The statement of belief and commitment, the *Shema* (found in Deuteronomy 6:4-6), was given by God to His people for this very purpose:

> *Hear, O Israel: The* LORD *our God, The* LORD *is one. Love the* LORD *your God with all your heart and with all your soul and with all your strength. These commandments that I give you today are to be upon your hearts. Impress them on your children.*

In evangelism also, a clear statement of what we believe as Christians will be helpful in communicating the Gospel. There have been times when people have approached me, as the Philippian jailer approached Paul (Acts 16:29-34), asking, "What must I do to be saved?" One can reply as simply as Paul did on that occasion: "Believe in the Lord Jesus, and you will be saved."

Of course, the text then adds: "Then they spoke the word of the Lord to him." Paul had many other things to say to this man and to his household in addition to that simple summary of what it means to be a Christian. But that one sentence—"Believe in the Lord Jesus and you will be saved"—was indeed a good starting place for Paul's presentation of the truth to the jailer and his household.

It is valuable for all believers to have a clear outline of the basic truths of the Gospel in mind. On occasion I have gone through the five questions below, one by one, when someone has said to me, "What must I believe to become a Christian?"

FIVE QUESTIONS EXPRESSING BASIC CHRISTIAN CONTENT

1. Do you believe that God exists, that He is not just an idea or a projection of the human mind, but that He exists as the infinite, personal God, the God who is the Creator of the universe, the God who is one and yet three—the Father, the Son, and the Holy Spirit?

2. Do you acknowledge that you have many times done, said, and thought things that you know to be wrong, and that if God, the righteous Judge of all people, were to judge you as you deserve, He would have no alternative but to condemn you?

3. Do you believe that Jesus Christ is the Son of God, the eternal Second Person of the Trinity, and that He was born into this world as a human baby? And do you believe that in His perfect life, His sacrificial death on the cross, and His historical resurrection from death He did everything that was necessary to restore you to fellowship with God, our heavenly Father?

4. Have you personally accepted this work of Christ on your behalf, and have you believed the promises of God, promises such as "Whoever believes in the Son has eternal life" (John 3:36), so that you are able to say without any pride or presumption, "I know that I am a child of God, born into His family through the love and atoning death of Jesus Christ"?

5. Do you now commit yourself to seek to serve God in all your life, knowing that you are weak and prone to fall into wrongdoing, and that therefore you will need to depend on the help of the Holy Spirit, and knowing also that at times this obedience will be difficult and costly, but that ultimately it will bring the complete fulfillment of yourself as a person made in the image of God and restored to that image through Jesus Christ?

Even when I have used these questions or other summaries of the Gospel, I have not insisted on "getting through my presentation" without discussion or questions. Always, even when using such a summary, I am committed to listening to unbelievers, to encouraging unbelievers to ask their questions. Always I am ready to change, shorten, or expand the summary. In other words, I must be ready to have a genuine conversation with the individual before me rather than giving him or her "the pitch" as if I am a salesman who is eager to get through my presentation as quickly as possible and make my sale.

What is essential to understand is that while a summary of our faith can be made, and a summary is frequently very useful in making the Gospel known, we must not assume that evangelism will mean simply learning and saying any particular set of words. To think that it does mean learning and saying a particular set of words ignores the particular personality and circumstances of the one to whom we are speaking. To ignore someone in this way is dishonoring to the person and dishonoring to God who made him or her a special individual.

Read the Gospels to see how Jesus made the truth known. Every conversation Jesus had was different, for Jesus treated the people He met as individuals. To Jesus each person is unique. Each is made in God's image and therefore is of infinite value to Him. Each is loved so much that Jesus was prepared to die for him or her. Each is worth the Savior's being patient and generous in the expending of His time. Each longs to be listened to and to receive the full attention that Jesus gives him or her. Each needs the same ultimate truths expressed in the particular way that he or she can hear them. Jesus is to be our teacher and our model in these matters.

MAKING THE GOSPEL KNOWN

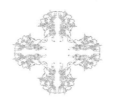

27

ALL THINGS TO ALL PEOPLE

As we grow in our faith, we learn to treasure more and more those truths that are at the heart of the Gospel, those truths that have set us free. We may have a favorite hymn or spiritual song that sets these precious truths out for us; or we may recite the Apostles' Creed or a series of catechism questions; or we might memorize several passages of Scripture that express for us what is central in our understanding.

It is right and good to desire to be able to summarize and record clearly and simply what we believe, for Christianity is the truth and has a particular message that is to be believed. Christian faith is not a matter of private opinion and conviction, though the truth that is for all must be personally believed and appropriated by each individual. Christian faith is not only a deep personal and emotional response to Christ, though our sorrow over our sin ought to be deep, our love for Christ ought to be joyful, and our delight in the truth should fill our hearts with gladness. But our Christian faith is the truth, and without that truth our personal belief and our emotional response would be empty and in vain. As truth, what we profess can be and must be set down in propositions, propositions that can be easily stated and readily understood.

Yet as we saw at the end of the last chapter, each biblical summary of our faith is different from every other one, but not because the truth changes, and not because the truth ought not to be simply stated. Rather, each biblical summary of our faith is different because each time that truth is made known, the situation is different. When we are communicating the Gospel to someone we know and love, or even to someone we meet for the first time, our communication is not merely to be a matter of stating the central truths of the Gospel in some form that we can readily memorize, whether that form be a creed, a set of catechism questions, a hymn, a song, or even some Scripture verses. The focus in evangelism is not to be whatever is easy for us, but the particular person to whom we are speaking. Communicating the Gospel is a personal endeavor, one person to another, and therefore we must be prepared to be flexible. (Of course, at some point in a relationship or in a conversation a summary may be appropriate, and then what we have memorized will become useful.)

There are three basic reasons why we need to be flexible in what we say to people, and we learn of these reasons from the example of Jesus and the apostles and from the clear teaching of Scripture.

First, we are to treat people with respect and dignity, for every person we meet is a unique individual, made in the likeness of his or her Creator. People are not robots who can be programmed like a computer with a prepackaged deal; to treat them as if they were is to deny their dignity, despise their individuality, and dishonor the God who made them. We all know this instinctively, which is why people rarely will use prepackaged programs with people they know and love. Such programs are designed for strangers, not for people I share a home with or work alongside day by day. (Though even in those latter situations there will be times when a learned summary may be helpful, just as it may be helpful for our own hearts when we need to remind ourselves of the truths that have set us free.)

Second, because of this uniqueness and because of the differing circumstances of each person's life and history, every individual we meet is at a different stage in his or her spiritual journey from every other person. This demands that we discern where they are on that journey, rather than taking the lazy route of ignoring where they are and simply fulfilling our obligation by insisting that they hear what we wish them to hear.

Third, we know that our heavenly Father loves people far more than we do and that it is the Father who will draw them to Christ. God does what we can never do when He softens the rebellious heart, convicts someone of his or her sin, and grants him or her faith in Jesus Christ. The field of salvation is God's, and we are laborers in His field, called to be faithful in living and making known the truth that He has entrusted to us. Paul expresses how we are to view our part in evangelism in 2 Corinthians 4:5-7:

> *We do not preach ourselves, but Jesus Christ as Lord, and ourselves as your servants for Jesus sake . . . we have this treasure in jars of clay to show that this all-surpassing power is from God and not from us.*

The Bible, then, does not give us a simple method or a technique that we can learn that will turn us into good communicators. However, God's Word does teach us some basic principles of communication. It is these principles that need to govern us as we seek to reach out with the Gospel. Where do we find them? We will turn to two primary sources. One is the account of the apostle Paul as he went about proclaiming Christ, recorded for us by Luke in the book of Acts. The other is the record, set down by the four Gospel writers, of the way Jesus Himself made the truth known. As we examine these examples of the evangelism of Paul and Jesus we will use additional passages of Scripture to support and supplement our study.

PAUL AMONG HIS CONTEMPORARIES

As we read the Acts of the Apostles we find in the middle section of the book that Luke records for us three missionary or evangelistic messages delivered by Paul in three very different contexts.

The Synagogue

The first is a sermon given to Jews and to God-fearing Gentiles in a synagogue, found in Acts 13. Luke tells us (14:1) that Paul's custom, when he arrived in any city, was to go to the synagogue on the Sabbath day and begin his evangelistic ministry there. Paul must have followed this pattern on many occasions during his missionary journeys, but Luke has written down one example for us in detail. Acts 13:14-52 describes Paul's visit to the synagogue in Pisidian Antioch, a city in the center of modern-day Turkey. In Paul's day this particular city of Antioch was in Pisidia, the southern part of the Roman province of Galatia.

Pagan Polytheists

The second message is found in Acts 14:8-18, where Luke describes for us the visit of Paul and Barnabas to the city of Lystra in Lycaonia, again in the province of Galatia. This time the audience was completely different. The people Paul addressed were uncultured pagans who were polytheists; that is, they believed in the many traditional gods of the ancient Greek and Roman worlds. Many of the Gentiles Paul met on his journeys would have had similar ideas to these pagans in Lystra.

Cultured Pagans

The third is different again and is set down in Acts 17:16-31. This time Paul is in Athens, both then and now one of the most prominent cities in Greece, at that time part of the Roman province of Achaia. Paul on this occasion was speaking to more thoughtful pagans who were educated in the philosophy of their time.

Clearly we are to understand that it is not accidental that Luke gives us these three messages rather than, for example, three synagogue sermons or three talks to cultured pagans. Luke intends for us to learn from Paul's example. All Scripture is set down for our instruction, not only those parts of Scripture that contain direct commands to us (though Paul does, in fact, command us—1 Corinthians 4:16: "I urge you to imitate me"). But in the same letter he also writes (1 Corinthians 11:1), "Follow my example, as I follow the example of Christ."

We should therefore seek to discover how Paul communicated the Good News to his contemporaries, so that we can better make known that same Good News in our own day.

We find Paul, then, in three varied settings; yet we will discover that in these very diverse contexts the same basic principles governed Paul's presentations. To summarize Paul's practice we may say that he developed principles of communication from his desire to be all things to all people for the sake of Christ, for the sake of the Gospel, and for the sake of those to whom he went with the Good News. Paul expressed this commitment with great power in 1 Corinthians 9:19-23:

Though I am free and belong to no man, I make myself a slave to everyone, to win as many as possible. To the Jews I became

*like a Jew, to win the Jews. To those under the law I became
like one under the law (though I myself am not under the law),
so as to win those under the law. To those not having the law I
became like one not having the law (though I myself am not free
from God's law but am under Christ's law), so as to win those
not having the law. To the weak I became weak, to win the
weak. I have become all things to all men so that by all possible means I might save some. I do all this for the sake of the
gospel, that I may share in its blessings.*

Among people of whatever race, culture, or religious background,
Paul's desire was to be a servant to them. He would shape his presentation of the message to fit the understanding of his hearers, and his own
pattern of living to their patterns of life. Of course, the message itself
stayed the same, and Paul never compromised his own obedience to
Christ in adapting his lifestyle to that of those he served; yet he presented
himself and the Gospel in very different ways to reach very different people. We, too, are to regard ourselves as servants of everyone we meet, so
that we also might find opportunities to "save some."

JESUS, PAUL'S MODEL

In this diversity of presentation of the truth Paul modeled himself on
Christ. When we read the Gospels we find Jesus talking to a great variety of people—Jews, Samaritans, and Gentiles; rich and poor; healthy
and sick; male and female; Pharisee and Sadducee; tax collector, lawyer,
fisherman, soldier, prostitute, farmer, teacher . . . Jesus addressed each
person as an individual, for He regarded Himself as one who had come
to serve those who are lost in order that they might be found. Jesus was
and is all things to all people. Among the Pharisees and teachers of the
Law Jesus showed Himself to be a master of theological discussion (even
at the age of twelve!). Among the farmers, fishermen, and homemakers
of rural Palestine and Galilee Jesus used stories from everyday life to
communicate His message.

Jesus came to seek and save those who are lost, whoever they are,
and so He committed (and commits) Himself to love and serve each
individual and to shape His words so that they spoke to the mind and

innermost being of each person standing before Him. This is the heart of the Good News: Christ has loved each one of us and has died for each one of us.

We saw in an earlier chapter that each one of us has a different story to tell as we reflect on how God's Spirit brought us to our knees to acknowledge our need of Christ. No two stories of conversion are ever exactly alike, for we are all unique individuals. This very nature of the Gospel, which has itself been all things to each one of us, is found in all of Jesus' conversations with people and in all of Paul's presentations of the Gospel. This nature of the Gospel must govern our lives as we serve unbelievers and must govern our words to them, just as it governs our hearts if we have indeed come to know Jesus Christ as Savior and Lord.

28

Showing Respect—Principle I

Jesus and His disciple Paul regarded themselves as slaves of those to whom they spoke. Their fundamental motivation was love for their hearers, a selfless love, a love that led them to regard other people more highly than themselves. This self-sacrificing love moved the Son of God to leave His heavenly glory and in deep humility come and share our life. This same love led Him to the cross to give Himself up to death for us. It was this love of Christ that constrained Paul to follow in his Savior's steps.

Such love is also to constrain us in every relationship we have and in all our attempts to communicate the Gospel. But what will this mean in practice? As we study the example of Jesus and Paul, we find a series of principles that expressed their love for their hearers and that governed their commitment to make the Gospel known. These same principles are to govern our practice of evangelism.

We begin with *respect* as the first principle that is to rule the attitude of our hearts toward unbelievers and to be expressed in all our conversations with them. As we study the practice of Paul we find him showing respect for his three very different groups of hearers in the cities of Antioch, Lystra, and Athens.

Paul in Pisidian Antioch (Acts 13:13-43)

As he traveled, Paul would go first to the synagogue in each new city to which he came. In the early years of his missionary work he knew that he could expect a warm welcome in the synagogues and an invitation to teach God's Word. The Jewish custom at that time was to invite a visitor to share with those gathered if he so desired, and Paul happily took advantage of such invitations. In addition, of course, Paul went to the synagogue first because the Jews were his own people whom he loved, and he longed for them to come to know their Messiah.

When Paul stood up to speak, he addressed those assembled as "men of Israel and you Gentiles who worship God" (v. 16), as "brothers, children of Abraham, and you God-fearing Gentiles" (v. 26), and as "my brothers" (v. 38). Notice how Paul carefully included in his words those Gentiles present at the synagogue service. They, too, were his brothers. Not many Jewish teachers of Paul's day would have spoken in this respectful way to Gentiles. The gracious words to his fellow Jews might seem readily understandable to us because these were Paul's own compatriots who shared his cultural heritage, traditions, and moral convictions. And yet, remember that it is these same "brothers," fellow citizens of Israel, who persecuted Paul again and again. In fact, there in Antioch Paul was driven from the town at the instigation of his fellow Jews (v. 50).

PAUL IN LYSTRA (ACTS 14:8-20)

Luke presents Paul in Lystra in a setting that could not be more different from the city's synagogue. This time we find Paul among pagans so trapped in religious superstition that when Paul and Barnabas healed a lame man, the people's reaction was to assume that Paul and Barnabas were gods. A local legend recounted how Zeus and Hermes had once appeared in human form in that region. So when the crowd saw the miracle of healing, they wanted to sacrifice bulls to Paul and Barnabas, concluding that the gods Zeus and Hermes had appeared in human form once more. Because Paul was the main speaker, they decided that he must be Hermes (a god known for his wise speech) and that Barnabas was Zeus.

Paul and Barnabas responded by trying to prevent the sacrifice from taking place. However, even as Paul sought to stop the crowd, he appealed to their common humanity: "Men, why are you doing this? We too are only men, human like you" (v. 15).

Paul's attitude was not, "How can you be so stupid? I would never, thank God, stoop as low as you!" Rather, even when faced with such rampant paganism, he never lost sight of the true humanity of these people, nor of his own shared identity with them.

PAUL IN ATHENS (ACTS 17:16-34)

When Paul arrived in Athens, the situation was similar to that in Lystra in that the city was full of idols and pagan temples. There was, indeed, sophisticated philosophy in Athens; in fact, the city had schools of philosophy that had already for many centuries been widely respected and influential, not only in Greece but across the ancient world. Yet the majority of Athenians were just as pagan and superstitious as those in Lystra. Paul clearly found their idolatry deeply distressing (v. 16), and some of the Athenians were not exactly respectful to Paul, declaring him to be a "babbler" (v. 18).

Despite this sarcasm there was so much interest in Paul's message that he was invited to speak to a gathering of the Areopagus, for, as Luke records (v. 21), "All the Athenians and the foreigners who lived there spent their time doing nothing but talking about and listening to the latest ideas."

The Areopagus was the highest court of Athens to which difficult legal cases were appealed, and also the meeting place for the discussion of religious and philosophical ideas. If we want to try to picture a similar setting today, we should imagine Paul being invited to speak to the Arts and Humanities faculties of all the universities in a city like Los Angeles or New York in the USA or Oxford or Cambridge in England.

Paul showed honor for them when he addressed these pagan thinkers: "Men of Athens! I see that in every way you are very religious" (v. 22).

These words should be read as respectful rather than as sarcasm or flattery. Flattery was forbidden at the meetings of the Areopagus, and Paul, in principle, rejected sarcasm. Besides, sarcasm would have angered his hearers rather than winning a hearing for his words. Reading through Paul's speech, we see that he treated them with dignity and engaged them with respect.

PAUL IN EPHESUS (ACTS 19:23-41)

We find Paul in another pagan setting in the city of Ephesus. Paul's preaching caused a riot in Ephesus, not because of his attacks on the local religion, but because so many people were being converted to Christianity or were becoming interested in the Christian faith that the tourist trade (silver images of Diana's temple) was falling off. (People came from all over the Roman Empire, and even from beyond its borders, to visit the magnificent temple of Diana there, for it was one of the seven wonders of the ancient world.) Yet when quelling the riot, Alexander, the city clerk, was able to quiet the crowd by reminding them that Paul and his companions had not robbed their temples, nor had they blasphemed their goddess (v. 37). Despite the awful practices (sometimes including human sacrifice) that accompanied the worship at these temples, Paul could not justly be accused of speaking blasphemously or disrespectfully about the gods those people worshiped.

This is much more challenging to us than may be immediately apparent. We may feel that, yes, we ought to respect people, but, no, it is not possible for us to respect their ideas and their false religious thinking. Is it not the Christian's calling to ridicule false beliefs and to dishonor false gods? An illustration may help our reflection on this.

An Example of Disrespect

As a teacher of evangelism and apologetics I receive (often unsolicited) newsletters from many Christians involved in outreach ministries. One letter that comes sporadically is from a self-titled "evangelist to Moslems." This particular evangelist travels to a university campus and gives talks advertised specifically so Muslims will attend. But his intention is apparently to attack Islam as blasphemous and utterly false. He is so aggressive in his approach that frequently he has to be escorted from the university by the campus police to prevent a riot and for his own safety. He seems to regard this as a triumph for the Gospel and as proof that he is honoring Christ and being persecuted for his faithfulness. I have no desire to impugn his motives, his love for the Lord, or his zeal for evangelism. Yet when Paul's preaching resulted in a riot, even an unbeliever could acknowledge that he had not uttered blasphemy against Diana or dishonored her or her worshipers. His words to them about their religion were respectful and gracious. This same pattern of behavior is apparent throughout the book of Acts.

PAUL IN THE COURTROOM (ACTS 24, 25, 26)

In these three chapters Luke gives us accounts of some of the events that followed Paul's arrest. The apostle appeared first before Felix, the Roman governor, then before Felix's replacement, Festus, and then before Agrippa the king. In each case we see Paul speaking respectfully, giving honor to whom honor is due (Romans 13:7; 1 Peter 2:17). To Felix he said:

> *"I know that for a number of years you have been a judge over this nation; so I gladly make my defense."*
>
> —ACTS 24:10

Later, having been held for two years, Paul appealed to Caesar and was brought before King Agrippa. It is evident that his respectful words were not mere form; rather Paul clearly considered the monarch to be knowledgeable and thoughtful.

> *"King Agrippa, I consider myself fortunate to stand before you today as I make my defense against all the accusations of the Jews, and especially so because you are well acquainted with all the Jewish customs and controversies."*
>
> —ACTS 26:2-3

Reading through Acts chapter by chapter, we could multiply these examples of respect shown toward unbelievers. We find this pattern of behavior uniformly among the apostles whose practice is recorded for us in the book of Acts. We can be assured that this respect is self-conscious on their part, for in their letters they command us to live the same way. Peter writes:

> *Always be prepared to give an answer to everyone who asks you to give the reason for the hope that you have. But do this with gentleness and respect.*
>
> —1 PETER 3:15-16

Paul's words are similar:

Let your conversation be always full of grace, seasoned with salt, so that you may know how to answer everyone.

—COLOSSIANS 4:6

Both of these apostles are explicit. Non-Christians are to be treated with "grace" and "respect." Our words to them must be honoring, no matter what they believe, no matter how they live, no matter how they speak to us or how they speak about us and about our faith.

A question arises for us at this point. If the New Testament is so clear, why do so many of us have such a problem with this? Our attitude quite commonly is, "How can we respect people who are sinful and who believe in such foolish things?" Or "Surely you don't expect me to show honor to people who not only disobey God's commandments themselves, but teach publicly that others should disobey them?"

An Offense to Heaven

On one occasion I was addressing the faculty of another seminary about biblical principles for communicating the Gospel. I could see that one listener was becoming increasingly angry, and he finally burst out, "How can you ask me to respect unbelievers and sinners? They reek to heaven." This was a good question, for of course it is true that sin is an offense to the nostrils of God. Because sin is so offensive to God, it ought to be distressing to us, just as it was to Lot (2 Peter 2:7-8) and to Paul (Acts 17:16)! What answers can be given to such questions and charges? How is respect toward the ungodly possible?

THE IMAGE OF GOD

Scripture teaches us that all people bear the image of God. This is the foundational statement of the first chapter of Genesis about what it means to be human (v. 27):

So God created man in his own image, in the image of God he created him; male and female he created them.

God is infinite, but we are finite. However, He is personal, and so are we. We are made for relationships, for love, for being like God in righteousness, to be history makers, to create, to have dominion. In Psalm 8 David asks a very similar question to that asked by the professor mentioned above:

> *When I consider your heavens,*
> *the work of your fingers,*
> *the moon and the stars,*
> *which you have set in place,*
> *what is man that you are mindful of him?*

David, inspired by the Spirit, answers his own question:

> *You made him a little lower than the heavenly beings*
> *and crowned him with glory and honor.*
> *You made him ruler over the works of your hands;*
> *you put everything under his feet.*
>
> *—vv. 3-6*

God has given us such great dignity as those who are made in His image that, as the psalmist says, even God Himself is "mindful" of us. If God is respectful of the glory of our humanity, how much more should we honor the divine image in all those we meet? The apostle James reminds us of this very fact when he rebukes his readers for failing to show respect for their fellow human beings:

> *With the tongue we praise our Lord and Father, and with it we curse men, who have been made in God's likeness. Out of the same mouth come praise and cursing. My brothers, this should not be.*
>
> *—JAMES 3:9-10*

THE REALITY OF SIN

Yet the fact remains that people are sinners. Does this mean that despite acknowledging that people bear God's image we are to despise them for their sin? Precisely because they are sinners we are to look at them with mercy and gentleness, for they are in need of Christ's forgiveness. When we see sin in others, we are not to dishonor them, nor are we to thank God (as did the Pharisee described by Jesus in Luke 18:11-12) that we are not like them. Rather, we must remember that we, too, are sinners. When it comes to failure to obey God's commandments, we all stand on a level playing field before God. The only way we can approach God is to acknowledge our unworthiness before Him. We can never look down on anyone as unworthy of our love, honor, and respect or we would be disqualifying ourselves. Whoever they are, whatever they have done, we are one with them in human dignity, and we are one with them in human shame. God's response to our sin is grace, the grace of Jesus Christ. Our response to the sin of others is to be the grace that has been extended to us.

29

JESUS SHOWS THE WAY

I imagine that one response to the previous chapter might be to say that I am replacing one technique of evangelism with another—respect! But being gracious and being respectful can never be thought of as mere techniques to make me a better evangelist. If I were to treat these as techniques and attempt to put on a respectful demeanor and adopt gracious words whenever I encounter an unbeliever, my life would become a hypocritical show, a pretense. God hates such dissimulation, and so must I. Respect and graciousness are to flow from a heart that is being changed by the way God has come to meet me in Christ; they must arise from genuine love and a proper regard for my neighbor's true dignity.

As in everything else in our Christian life, Jesus shows us the way. We turn now to His encounter with the woman at the well, recorded in John 4:1-42, a perfect illustration of the manner in which we are called to relate to unbelievers. Jesus had a brief meeting with this Samaritan woman, but His conversation with her led to a two-day stay in the village of Sychar. As a result of this, many more of the villagers came to believe in Him. What can we learn from Jesus as He met and talked with this woman?

In our reflection on this passage we should note that Jesus was giving His disciples an example of fulfilling the Great Commission. On this occasion Jesus was traveling northward from Judea to Galilee. To make this journey Jesus did not need to go through Samaria, and in fact most Jews would not take the shortcut through Samaria without compelling reasons. They would travel by the longer road around Samaria to avoid contact with its people. They had a saying that if one met a Samaritan walking along the road, one should walk into the ditch to avoid contact even between the two shadows!

Jesus was not in a hurry (he stayed two extra days!), but He had compelling reasons to go through Samaria. (In the Gospels we read of Jesus making the truth known in Jerusalem, in Judea, in Samaria, and beyond to the Gentiles in Syria as well as to those Gentiles who lived in Judea or had occasion to visit.) On this particular occasion John draws attention to the divine constraint that burned in Jesus' heart to be the Savior not only of the Jews but of the whole world: "Now he had to go through Samaria" (v. 4).

Who was this person that Jesus felt constrained to meet? We might say that the woman at the well had four problems or barriers that stood between her and Jesus and made it very unlikely that the two of them would ever have any social contact, much less a serious and lengthy discussion about the truth of God's kingdom.

THE PROBLEM OF RACE

Her first problem was her race. As a Samaritan she was the wrong race, at least from the perspective of the Jews. The Samaritans were a mixed race. They were partially descended from the remnants of the ten northern tribes of Israel who had originally inhabited the land, but they were no longer purely Israeli, for their ancestors had intermarried with the other peoples who had been moved to Samaria by the Assyrians in their policy of conquer and resettle (2 Kings 17:21-24). The Jews avoided and despised people of mixed race even more than "pure" Gentiles.

THE PROBLEM OF FALSE RELIGION

Her second problem was that as a Samaritan she had the wrong religion. The Samaritans' religion blended the worship of the true God with the pagan idolatry of the peoples from around Assyria who had been settled there in the northern part of Israel (2 Kings 17:21-41). They accepted only the books of Moses as Scripture and had built their own temple on Mount Gerizim, a temple that had been burned down by the Jews in 128 B.C., so fierce was the religious hostility between these two peoples. The Jews despised the Samaritans as heretics, and again this contempt was even more severe than their contempt for outright pagans.

THE PROBLEM OF GENDER

The Samaritan woman's third problem was her gender. She was, obviously, a woman. Jewish rabbis or teachers did not at that time have women as disciples, for it was thought that women were incapable of serious reflection on God's Word. Women were also not allowed to be witnesses in court, for they were considered by the rabbis to be irrational and untrustworthy. There was even a prayer of the Pharisees in which they apparently prayed, "Thank You, God, that I am not a Gentile, but a Jew; that I am not a slave, but am free; not a woman, but a man."

The practice of Jesus was very different. He taught women as His disciples; He appointed women to be the first witnesses of His resurrection and to make their witness known to the apostles.

THE PROBLEM OF SIN

The woman's fourth problem was sin. Her sin was not a secret but was in full public view; nor was it a "respectable" sin. This woman was considered by all to be a sinner; she had been married five times and was now living with a man outside of any marriage contract. Such a woman in that culture would have been regarded as little better than a prostitute, and prostitutes were despised as "gross sinners" by teachers of the Law. Divorce was fairly easy for men at that time. If they found another woman more to their liking or if they found fault with a wife for any reason (Matthew 19:3), they could divorce her (that was the understanding of the more liberal wing of the Pharisees, and apparently there was a similar approach among the Samaritans). The woman in such a situation was always viewed as the one at fault; so a woman divorced five times was a woman despised by everyone, having been passed from man to man, having a very low social status, a "true sinner"!

Consequently this Samaritan woman was unacceptable not only to Jews but even to her own people. That is probably why she was at this well some distance from town, alone, at an unusual time of day.

These four problems created insurmountable barriers for Jews of Jesus' day, keeping them from reaching out to her. In earlier chapters we identified some of the barriers that stand between believers and unbelievers today. Could anyone reading this book possibly assert that the barriers they face are higher or more problematic than those Jesus encountered on this occasion? Reflecting on the way Jesus spoke to the Samaritan woman should help us see that it should be readily possible for us to set aside any of the barriers that confront us.

Who is it who meets this mixed-race, heretical, wrong-gender sinner? It is, of course, Jesus, who is described in this passage as:

> *The One who gives living water.*
> *A prophet.*
> *One greater than the patriarch Jacob.*
> *The Messiah.*
> *The "I Am."*
> *The One who can tell us everything we ever did.*
> *The Savior of the world.*

How does the Son of God meet the woman at the well? How does the One who is both God and man, who in His Godhead and His manhood is holy and separated from sinners, relate to this person who has so many barriers existing between Himself and her?

SETTING ASIDE CUSTOM

Jesus broke His culture's customs and laws by asking her for a drink of water (v. 7). In reflecting on this seemingly very ordinary request we should note that Jews did not drink or eat from containers used by Samaritans. Rabbi Eliezer taught: "He that eats the bread of the Samaritans is like one that eats the flesh of swine." Yet Jesus broke His people's social customs, in fact the Jewish law of the time, to ask her to use her container to draw water from the well for Him and then give Him a drink from this vessel that she had handled. She was amazed because she was aware of the extraordinary nature of His request:

The Samaritan woman said to him, "You are a Jew and I am a
Samaritan woman. How can you ask me for a drink?"

—v. 9

Notice how John draws attention to her amazement that Jesus was
talking to a woman as well as to a Samaritan. His disciples, too, were
surprised to find Him talking with a woman when they returned (v. 27).
This surprise shows how little they yet knew Him! Jesus set aside the
usual barriers; He ignored social custom, even Jewish law, in order to
reach out to her. He acted as if the problem of race did not exist at all.
For Him the fact that she was a woman was not an issue to consider. He
treated her respectfully as a social equal.

Our churches have many social customs and regulations that keep
us apart from people. Jesus calls us to discard them for the sake of the
Gospel and out of respect for the people from whom those customs and
regulations separate us.

REVEALING OUR NEEDS

Jesus showed His vulnerability and need to her. The Creator of the
world, who needs nothing from anyone, asked her for a drink. He dig-
nified her by acknowledging His need of what she could do for Him. He
showed His vulnerability to her. He was thirsty and tired, and she could
help Him. We find Jesus doing this on numerous occasions—for example, with Zacchaeus the tax collector in Luke 19:1-9 when Jesus invited
Himself to Zacchaeus' home for a meal, and with the prostitute who
anointed His feet as recorded in Luke 7:36-50.

So often as Christians we behave as if we have everything to give to
the non-Christian and nothing to receive. We imagine that it would be
demeaning for us to acknowledge any weakness or need. Christians are
supposed to "have it all together," and we fear that letting unbelievers
see that we don't might bring discredit on us and on the Gospel. This is
folly, for the truth is that we are always weak and needy, and the Gospel
is not served by pretending otherwise. To acknowledge, as Jesus does,
our need of the kindness, gifts, wisdom, or advice an unbeliever can give
us is encouraging and ennobling to those who might have been led to
expect only scorn or condescension from us.

RESPECTFUL DISCUSSION

Jesus treated the Samaritan woman as a rational and thoughtful person. No teacher (and no man) had ever spoken to her in this way before! But Jesus entered into a theological discussion with her about the patriarch Jacob, about the proper place of worship—Jerusalem for the Jews or Mount Gerizim where the Samaritans worshiped, and about the coming of the Messiah. The Samaritans expected the Messiah and called him the "Taheb," the "Restorer," on the basis of the promise of a great prophet like Moses who would teach all the truth, a promise made in Deuteronomy 18:17-19. In discussing theology with her, Jesus was again demonstrating respect despite her race, her wrong theology, her gender, or her sin. Are we prepared to take people and their theology seriously and respectfully, even if they are heretics, as, for example, the Jehovah's Witnesses or the Mormons or those who follow a New Age Jesus?

GENTLENESS AND GRACE

Jesus approached the Samaritan woman graciously. He spoke to her with grace and gentleness even about her sin, which clearly weighed heavily upon her ("everything I ever did," v. 29). In her mind it was this aspect of what he said that caused her to draw the conclusion that He was a prophet (vv. 16-19), and this in turn led to Jesus' plain declaration that He is the Messiah and to her response of faith in Him. How do we respond to the sin that is frequently so apparent in people's lives? Do we become guarded, reserved, and withdrawn? Do we communicate disapproval and personal rejection? Is scorn and contempt revealed in our tone of voice and our facial expression?

It is apparent that Jesus did not approach the Samaritan woman this way, nor anyone else He ever met. Yet as we reflect on this encounter or any other recorded in the Gospels, we need to remember that for the Son of God all of us should be outcasts. We should be outcasts socially from His presence as the One who is God. We should be outcasts religiously and theologically, for we are all confused in our thinking (not one of us has all our doctrine correct). Above all we should be outcasts as those who have sinned and who therefore have no right of entrance to meet with Him, the Holy One.

Yet Jesus has come to each of us with the same grace, gentleness, and respect with which He came to the woman at the well. He met each of us where we were, and He led each of us through our confusions to the knowledge of the truth. He has shown us our sin without making us feel rejected and condemned by Him; instead we have known that we are loved, forgiven, welcomed, and accepted by Him. He who needs nothing from us has asked for our friendship and even declared Himself not ashamed to be called our God (Hebrews 11:16). He has entrusted us with responsible tasks in His service, just as He commissioned this Samaritan woman to bear the Good News to her neighbors, which she promptly did. He sent her as a teacher of the truth to her own people, and her words to them were so effective that they in turn pled with Jesus to stay two more days in that village. The result is that many of them met with Him and became believers.

Are we prepared to learn from Jesus' example and "go through Samaria"?

QUESTIONS FOR FURTHER REFLECTION

1. What would it mean for you to "go through Samaria"? What groups of people are equivalent to "Samaritans," "heretics," or "sinners" for you? Can you think of people you know for whom a commitment to follow Jesus' example will require you to begin treating them differently?

2. Are there people you have had trouble respecting in your family, in your neighborhood, or in your workplace? What practical steps could you take to build a new relationship with people whom you might have treated without due respect in the past?

3. What to you are the most striking aspects of Jesus' encounter with the woman at the well?

4. What other examples can you think of from the Gospels that demonstrate Jesus' respect for people, either encounters already noted in the text of this book or perhaps some not yet considered?

5. Are there individuals who are not believers whom it might be wise to ask to do something for you? Are there those for whom it might be important to reveal your vulnerability and need?

6. Who are the "Samaritans" for your church? What might it mean for your church, as a congregation, to be ready to "go through Samaria"? What changes in attitude and practice might have to be made?

30

BUILDING BRIDGES FOR THE
GOSPEL—PRINCIPLE II

God commands us to respect non-Christians as persons made in His likeness. Because people are in the image of God, they have His nature stamped indelibly in their hearts. In addition they live in God's world, for there is no other universe than the one God has made. These two realities constrain the thinking of every man and woman on the face of this earth, so that even when they do not bow before God, truth will make itself known in their ideas.

This brings us to the challenge to take this need for respect a step further. We discover that Paul not only respected his hearers as people made by God but also made the effort to find ideas he could approve. Paul built a bridge to his hearers by searching for aspects of truth in their thinking and of virtue in their lives that could be commended. To support this claim we will look again at two of Paul's messages in Acts, the one that Paul preached to Jews and to God-fearing Gentiles in a synagogue and the one that he gave to educated pagans in Athens.

THE SERMON IN THE SYNAGOGUE IN PISIDIAN ANTIOCH (ACTS 13:16-41)

In this context Paul was able to take much for granted, for the Jews and God-fearing Gentiles listening to his words had the same religious background as he did. What beliefs did they have in common?

1. He and his hearers believed in the one true God who had revealed Himself to Israel.

2. They were familiar with the Old Testament and regarded it as inspired—that is, the inerrant Word of God.

3. They knew the history of Israel.

4. They were committed to obeying the Law of Moses as God's commandments.

5. They expected the Messiah promised by the prophets.

6. They knew they would answer to God one day for the way they had lived.

7. They knew something about the ministry of John the Baptist.

8. They had heard about the teaching and life of Jesus of Nazareth.

You might be thinking as you read this, "All this is obvious! Why are you stressing it?" It is important to draw attention to these eight common convictions, for each of these beliefs that Paul could take for granted were a point of contact with his hearers; and if we read Paul's sermon carefully, we will see that he used all eight of them in his message. Paul's sermon was very carefully constructed to build on what they already knew.

In addition, we can ask the question, How did Paul begin his sermon? Did he commence with an attack on their disbelief, on their failure to obey the Law, on their refusal to worship Jesus? No! Paul began by commending them for their desire to worship God. Their knowledge of the truth and their worship of the one true God were the bridges Paul used to communicate the message of Christ.

THE MESSAGE ON MARS HILL (ACTS 17:22-31)

In Athens Paul had a very different audience. The people listening to him on Mars Hill knew nothing of the God of Israel or of the Old Testament. The idea of a Messiah would be meaningless to them. What could Paul build on when speaking to these pagans?

1. They were religious people.

2. They had a desire to worship and a longing to know God.

3. They believed that God must be greater than human persons.

4. They were aware that God cannot be dependent on gifts from human beings.

5. They realized that God does not dwell in temples as if He needs His own house.

6. They knew something of the dignity of being human, that there is a godlike quality to human existence.

Paul built on these ideas that were widely held among more thoughtful pagans. But the important issue to notice here is that all of these points contain an element of truth about God and about humanity. They certainly are not the whole truth about the one true God, but Paul's hearers in the synagogue didn't have the whole truth about God either.

Once again we can ask the question, Where did Paul begin? Did he begin by attacking their idolatry or their endless speculation that never arrived at the truth or their love of argument for its own sake or their devotion to rhetorical skills regardless of the truth or falsehood of the subject? No! Paul began by commending them for their religious longings, for their desire to worship:

> *"Men of Athens! I see that in every way you are very religious. For as I walked around and observed your objects of worship, I even found an altar with this inscription: TO AN UNKNOWN GOD. Now what you worship as something unknown I am going to proclaim to you."*
>
> —vv. 22-23

Paul was not flattering them or being sarcastic about their religion but was identifying a point of contact he could use for communicating the Gospel. Their religious nature and the altar to the unknown god became bridges for declaring who God truly is. Paul's commitment was to ask: "What is right with their thinking? What can I commend about their way of life?" So often we think of dealing with the ideas of non-Christians as a matter of attack: "What is wrong with their thinking?

Where can I attack their ideas and way of life?" Paul seems to have taken just the opposite approach.

"How is this possible?" some may ask. We are often told there is no common ground between the believer and the unbeliever because of the biblical truth that the unbeliever is in the kingdom of darkness while the believer is in the kingdom of light. We know that in such persons' thinking the unbeliever is an enemy of God and of the truth of the Gospel. We know too that "out of [the heart] are the issues of life" (Proverbs 4:23, KJV), and that the unbeliever's heart is in rebellion against God. But the conclusion is drawn from these facts that it is wrong to search for truth or goodness in unbelieving thinking or life. This is an important issue, and we need to think about it carefully.

It is true that believers and unbelievers are in different kingdoms. Unbelievers are indeed enemies of God in their minds. Their hearts are in rebellion against God and the truth. But they never escape the real world. No man or woman inhabits the world of his or her own belief system. Whether people like it or not, there is only one world, the world that God made, and they have to live in it and function in it as God has made it. In addition, people never escape their own humanity. They are in the image of God because that is the way God made them.

Consequently, there will always be contact points for the believer to find. There will always be elements of the truth in any unbelievers' thinking because they have to live in God's world. There will always be signs that individuals still bear God's image in their deepest being, for God has not abandoned humanity. People have not become demons; so there is always something to commend in their way of life.

BUILDING BRIDGES TODAY

Just as Paul built bridges to Israelites and to pagans, so we are to learn from his example and build bridges to our contemporaries. If we are to apply this principle to our own attempts at outreach, we need to reflect on the state of religious belief and church commitment in our society. Approximately 45-50 percent of the population in the USA is church-going, and the other half is unchurched. (The figures of the churched include those who belong to the Jehovah's Witnesses and to the Mormon church, etc.)

Churchgoers

Our first task will be to discern to whom we are speaking—a churched or an unchurched person. Do people identify themselves as in some sense "Christian"? Are they in a sense equivalent to the Jews or God-fearers Paul addressed in Acts 13? If they do describe themselves as "Christian," what can we take for granted?

> 1. Do they believe in God?
> 2. Do they have some respect for the Bible (and do they read it)?
> 3. Do they have a sense of needing to live in obedience to God's laws?
> 4. Is Christ someone they know about and admire?
> 5. Do they acknowledge an afterlife and the possibility of judgment?

If people hold the above convictions, and almost half the population in the USA does share these views, then these beliefs provide us with a basis for discussion. We can commend them for their admiration for Christ or their respect for the Bible or another of the above or similar points. From this beginning we can build to a clear presentation of the Good News.

It is important to note here that many who would answer the above questions yes might nevertheless be faraway from a biblical understanding of any of them. Most are likely to be much further away from biblical understanding than a first-century Jew or Gentile God-fearer. The great majority is biblically illiterate (this includes many churchgoers); consequently their ideas about God, Christ, Christian doctrine, scriptural stories, and God's commandments are likely to be very vague. However, there is frequently some little piece of ground on which to build a bridge. Where biblical knowledge is so poor, it is important to remember that the Christian's message that God exists and who that God is, the personal and infinite God, the God of love and justice, is the beginning of the Good News.

Spirituality

Where do we begin if the person for whom we are praying and to whom we long to communicate the truth is not a churchgoer? We need to discern whether he or she is a person who is interested in spirituality, including spirituality of the New Age variety. Studies suggest that perhaps as much as a quarter of the population in the United States has at least some acquaintance with "new" forms of spirituality. If this interest is present, what can be taken for granted?

1. Do they sense a need to worship?
2. Is there a belief that spirituality is important?
3. Do they see that materialism is inadequate to satisfy the heart's longings?
4. Are they searching for inner peace?
5. Have they given up on the church for the satisfaction of their spiritual needs?
6. Are they concerned for the protection of the environment?

Here again there are hopes, needs, and insights that can be commended. People are right to recognize that they are spiritual beings. Their understanding of the bankruptcy of a culture that pursues only material goals is to be praised. Their abandoning of whatever church was in their background may well have been an appropriate response to false teaching or spiritual morbidity. God has indeed called us to care for the world in which He set us. Any of these points (and many more) is a starting place to use as a building block to move toward declaring the truth.

Secular People

What if my friend, family member, or workmate is a thoroughly secular person who sees no need for God or spirituality at all? Even if this is the case, this does not mean that an individual is not religious. Every human being is religious in the sense that he or she puts his or her trust in *something*. This is true whether that something is the future of the human race, science and technology, human ability to think rationally, the goodness of fellow men and women, family, money, work, sex, pleasure, self, or some other source of hope. The challenge for us is to find out where the person's trust lies.

The French thinker Blaise Pascal expressed it this way: "Every man is already committed." Almost everything in which people put their trust is one or another of God's good gifts to us. People are worshiping and serving some part of the created order rather than the One who made life with all its marvelous variety. Because this is so, even though we will have to challenge this idolatry at some later point in our discussions, these gifts of God are in themselves good and are to be treasured and therefore can be properly used as bridges to share the truth.

Another tack might be to seek to discover where the person is in contact with the universe as God made it. For example, do they see the need for some kind of moral values, or are they concerned about moral breakdown in our culture? This will be a bridging point for a growing number of people across the world today. Many people start attending church or begin to be open when they have to face the challenge of trying to raise children in the contemporary moral climate. They may have been deeply influenced by moral relativism themselves in their own personal life, but they become deeply concerned about how to give their children some kind of moral direction. This concern is right and ought to be commended.

The longing for a moral foundation has been one of the major factors in the open door for the Gospel in the former Soviet Union. After seventy years of the denial of moral absolutes by leaders who were Marxists, Soviet society is now in a state of acute moral degeneration. Consequently many people are searching for some basis on which to rebuild their personal lives and their society.

The Cynic

Some of you reading this may be thinking, "But my friend is a complete cynic. Surely here is someone who has turned their back on God's gifts and is beyond reach!" If a person is deeply cynical, does this mean there is no point of contact? With every person we need to discover what it is that he or she holds dear in his or her heart. Their humanity, from which they cannot escape, will mean there will always be something good and true treasured by them. An illustration may help here.

James knew several Christians, both in the context of his work as a financial analyst and through his involvement in sports. He often met these believers socially, and he liked to boast of his cynicism and at the same time attack their Christian commitment as naive wishful thinking: "You Christians are not man enough to face up to the cold reality of death and ultimate absurdity. You take refuge in pious platitudes. Your faith is just pie in the sky by-and-by." Yet in getting to know James better, it became evident that he was a man with a deep love for his wife, for his children, and for his grandchildren. Tom, one of his business associates, openly rejoiced with James in the deep pleasure he took in family life. This was Tom's bridge. Later he was able to say, "James, your cynicism sounds very realistic and brave, for there truly are many things about life that give us cause for pessimism. However, in my experience it seems that no one is totally cynical. Every cynic has a sacred corner where he does not allow his cynicism to intrude. For you your family is that sacred corner. In the things that are precious to you, James, you are not a cynic at all."

Tom's statement made James think. The time will come in every contact to make such a challenge. That time comes only when we have earned the right, when we have built a sufficient relationship, so that the wounds we give will be experienced, as Proverbs says, as "wounds from a friend" (27:6). But, before the time for challenge comes, we need to find a starting point, a point to commend the person for whatever good quality or insight that he or she has. These elements of truth, these gifts of grace, are God's bridges for the Gospel.

31

UNDERSTANDING WHAT OTHERS
BELIEVE—PRINCIPLE III

It should be evident from the past chapter that if we are going to build bridges for the Gospel, it will be necessary to seek to understand the way non-Christians are thinking, to understand what they believe and why they believe it. This commitment to understand the beliefs of non-Christians is our third basic principle of communication. It should arise from our desire to respect every unbeliever simply because every man, woman, and child on this earth bears the image of God.

Such a commitment will lead the believer to deal with the actual thinking and beliefs of non-Christians rather than conducting evangelism as if it were a war of dirty tricks, in the manner of so much political campaigning. Most people long for candidates to address the issues rather than spending their time attempting to destroy each other's character, credibility, or record. Christians can very easily develop this same mentality, regarding others as "the enemy" or "our opponents" whose way of life and cherished beliefs we feel free to caricature and misrepresent. It should not take too much imagination to reflect on how damaging such a strategy is to effective evangelism. It also, of course, is dishonoring to anyone made in the likeness of God, and most importantly it is disobedient to our heavenly Father.

It is not that the Christian has no enemies! Scripture teaches us that there is indeed an enemy, Satan. He is described as the adversary, the accuser, our foe, the evil one, the ruler of this world's darkness, the god of this age, a liar, a murderer. He is the prince of dirty tricks! He is the enemy of believers. But he is also the enemy of unbelievers, for he desires to keep them in a state of blindness; he works at keeping them captive to do his will in order to prevent them from coming to a knowledge of the truth.

Understanding that Satan is not only the enemy of believers but also the enemy of unbelievers should help us see more clearly why we are called not to abuse, insult, or condemn people around us no matter what they believe or how they live. This is true even if they abuse, insult, misrepresent, or even curse us or curse the Christian message. Rather, we are called to pray for all, including those who may oppose or hate Christianity, to think about them with respect, and to speak of and to them with words that are gracious. The unbeliever is a hostage of the implacable enemy of our souls. In a sense we are on the same side of a war rather than on opposing sides. Our desire should be to help release those who are captives. That was certainly the purpose of Christ in coming into this world.

So if we are to take seriously this task of setting the captives free, it should be obvious that caricaturing or misrepresenting the ideas of unbelievers will be no help to us. It will simply alienate people, for they will rightly be offended by our failure to treat their beliefs seriously. As well as failing to show respect, we will make our work more difficult by unnecessarily wounding their pride. There is, then, an obligation to understand what others believe if we are going to communicate God's truth effectively.

We turn again to the example of the apostle Paul. Throughout the book of Acts we find Paul demonstrating a deep understanding of the ideas, beliefs, and practices of those to whom he communicated the Christian faith.

JEWS AND GOD-FEARERS (ACTS 13:16-41)

When addressing those at the synagogue, Paul was speaking to a mixed gathering of his fellow Jews and God-fearing Gentiles. The God-fearers were Gentiles who attended the synagogue because they had been attracted to the teaching about the one true God and to the high moral code revealed in the Old Testament Law. Paul, a zealous Jew himself, was, very obviously, thoroughly familiar with the beliefs, the Scriptures, and the culture of those meeting in the synagogue. Because of this we tend to ignore the understanding of his hearers' beliefs displayed in this message. But a careful reading of Paul's words in Pisidian Antioch will show them to be a masterful exposition of Old Testament teaching and its fulfillment in Christ.

THE GREEKS IN ATHENS

We will look at Acts 17:22-31 in rather more detail because here we find Paul speaking in a context that is far removed from the synagogue. Thinkers from Greece and from all over the Greco-Roman world and even beyond it were attracted to the schools of philosophy and rhetoric in Athens. For centuries, back to the time of Plato (c. 428-347 B.C.) and even earlier, there had been academies in Athens to study and to discuss the meaning of human existence and every other major philosophical question. As Luke puts it:

> *All the Athenians and the foreigners who lived there spent their time doing nothing but talking about and listening to the latest ideas.*
>
> —v. 21

These Athenians and foreigners had a very different worldview than that of the apostle. Yet Paul showed a deep understanding of their beliefs, worship, and culture. It will help us see the power of Paul's presentation to these people if we learn a little more about the context. Paul had been reasoning about the Gospel not only in the synagogue with Jews and God-fearers but also in the marketplace every day with anyone who happened to be present (v. 17). Paul got into a discussion with a group of Epicurean and Stoic philosophers, and because he was communicating some completely new ideas to them, they invited him to address a meeting of the Areopagus. The Council of the Areopagus had supreme authority in religious matters. It had the power to appoint public lecturers and had been for many generations, in fact from legendary times, the most respected Athenian court.

The message Paul gave in this setting was clearly very different from those he gave in the synagogues. Some have said that this sermon was so intellectual that Christians ought to refuse to regard it as a model for our communication today. This criticism is inaccurate as well as providing an unhelpful excuse for ignoring what God is teaching us in this passage through Paul's example. The words of Paul to the Areopagus assembly were certainly profound, as is any faithful presentation of the Gospel; but Paul's teaching here was also very clear and not, in fact, difficult to understand. What is striking is the knowledge Paul had about his hearers as revealed in his address.

It is immediately obvious that there are no quotations from the Old Testament, whereas Paul's synagogue sermons—for example, the one given in Pisidian Antioch, recorded in Acts 13—were full of Old Testament quotations and allusions. His hearers in Athens were completely unfamiliar with the Old Testament; so no purpose would have been served by assuming knowledge of it and quoting from it except to confuse them. Instead Paul quoted from two of the Athenians' own thinkers (v. 28).

The first quotation—"In him we live and move and have our being"—was taken from a solemn invocation to the father and greatest of the Greek gods, Zeus, spoken by Zeus' son Minos.

> *They fashioned a tomb for thee, O holy and high—*
> *the Cretans, always liars, evil beasts, slow bellies!*
> *But thou art not dead; thou art risen and alive for ever,*
> *for in thee we live and move and have our being.*

The poem Paul quoted was written by Epimenides from the island of Crete. (This passage is also quoted in Titus 1:12, where Paul calls Epimenides one of the "prophets" of Crete.)

The second quotation, "We are his offspring," is from Aratus, the Cilician poet, and his words are very similar to those in a famous "Hymn to Zeus," a poem that will help us see how Zeus was regarded by these writers (Stobaeus, Eclogae I.1.12):

> *Most glorious of immortals, Zeus*
> *The many-named, almighty evermore,*
> *Nature's great Sovereign, ruling all by law—*
> *Hail to thee! On thee 'tis meet and right*
> *That mortals everywhere should call.*
> *From thee was our begetting; ours alone*

Of all that live and move upon the earth
The lot to bear God's likeness.
Thee will I ever chant, thy power praise!

In addition to these two quotations Paul began his address by referring to the altar "TO AN UNKNOWN GOD" (v. 23). There is a fascinating legend about the origin of the altar to the unknown God, and it is quite probable that Paul was familiar with the story, for the legend involved Epimenides whom Paul quoted. If we assume that Paul knew the legend, we are helped in our appreciation of the force of his message.

We know from writers like Pausanias that there were such altars to unknown gods in Athens. Another author, Diogenes Laertes, describes the legend attached to these altars. He tells how in a time of uncontrollable pestilence the Athenians sent for Epimenides the Cretan to advise them, for he was known as a man of great wisdom. He recommended the sacrifice of sheep to unknown gods, as those they worshiped had not answered their prayers and had not come to their aid. He also recommended that they set up altars commemorating these gods. When they followed his advice the pestilence came to an end, and the altars to the unknown gods who had delivered them from trouble remained on Mars Hill as an expression of the people's gratitude.

The fact that Paul referred to the altar to an unknown God, and possibly to this legend, is disturbing to some Christians. Some fear that such a reference suggests that Paul was approving of pagan ignorance and worship. This was not Paul's intention. Paul, of course, knew that there is but one true God; but he also knew that every blessing we humans enjoy comes from His hand. Men and women, like the Athenians, may worship other gods (even nameless ones) and thank them for their supposed gifts; but Paul declared that every prayer that has been answered, every deliverance and good gift enjoyed, came from the Father above, the Creator of heaven and earth.

Paul made exactly the same point in his words to the pagans in the city of Lystra when the pagans wanted to make sacrifices to him and Barnabas because they had experienced the blessing of physical healing:

"Yet he ["the living God," v. 15] has not left himself without
testimony: He has shown kindness by giving you rain from

*heaven and crops in their seasons; he provides you with plenty
of food and fills your hearts with joy."*
—ACTS 14:17

God is gracious to all human beings, whether they worship Him or
not, and He is gracious even when they mistakenly worship other gods
who are not gods and thank them for the blessings that come only from
His hand.

In addition to the words from Epimenides, two other passages in
Paul's Mars Hill address may possibly be allusions to some words of
Plato. In verse 24, "The God who made the world and everything in
it" is very close to an expression of Plato's in the *Timaeus*. In verse
27 Paul's words "so that men would seek him [God] and perhaps
reach out for him and find him" also echo words and thoughts of
Plato's.

In verse 25 we find Paul showing his familiarity with the ideas of
the Epicureans and the Stoics, the two groups whom Luke tells us were
represented among Paul's hearers. As part of their beliefs, the Epicureans
believed that God needs nothing from humanity, and the Stoics regarded
God as the source of all that exists. We find Paul alluding to these views
when he says:

*"And he [God] is not served by human hands, as if he needed
anything, because he himself gives all men life and breath and
everything else."*

As we consider these examples of Paul's efforts to show his acquaintance with the ideas of the men and women who were listening to his
words, we have to conclude that Paul had done his homework. He
respected his hearers sufficiently and had a deep enough care for them
that he had worked at understanding their ideas and their religion. In
fact, as we have seen already, Paul tells us that this commitment governed all his communication and the way he lived every day:

*I have become all things to all men so that by all possible means
I might save some.*
—1 CORINTHIANS 9:22

Paul was able to enter the culture of others in order to reach them. His motivation was love for Christ and love for those he met.

A CHALLENGE FOR US TODAY

Sometimes our evangelism does not make the effort to understand what people believe or why they believe it. Consequently it fails to communicate. Either this need for understanding is considered unnecessary ("Don't bother with what people believe; just preach the Gospel"; or "You don't have to be concerned with what they think; conversion is only a matter of the will"; or "Ignore the mind and strike for the heart!"). Or it is assumed that everyone in our society is in the place of the Jew or of the God-fearer of the New Testament. If we think this is the case, we will take for granted that they are familiar with the Bible, that they will appreciate quotes from it, and that they will have no difficulty understanding a straight biblical message in biblical language. A third reason for the failure to do the hard work that is necessary to understand people is that sometimes we are plain lazy and cannot be troubled to rouse ourselves to make the effort to find out what other people think and believe.

Proclaiming the Gospel in the Former Soviet Union

Whatever the reason for our failure, some examples of the value of understanding might be helpful here. One of the outstanding works of God today has been the opening up of the former Soviet Union to the Gospel. God has filled the hearts of many Christians with the desire to take advantage of these open doors. One notable effort has been the Commission Project directed primarily at schoolteachers in the Commonwealth of Independent States, the former Soviet Union countries. At first it was assumed that those teaching at the various congresses that were arranged would be able to present the Gospel very directly, just as Paul did in the synagogue in Pisidian Antioch. It was very quickly observed that the Russians and others who came to the meetings were not responding and were not understanding; communication was not taking place. The organizers realized the necessity of having speakers with an understanding of Marxism and materialism, for the thinking of everyone present was deeply shaped by those worldviews.

Francis Schaeffer in Post-War Europe

Another example is the work of Francis Schaeffer. When he arrived in Europe, just a few years after the close of the Second World War, he discovered that much evangelism was missing the mark and was no longer communicating with people. The vast majority of Western Europeans had no knowledge of the Bible at all, for the culture was almost everywhere post-Christian. Consequently it was not possible to begin with the message, "You are a sinner; Jesus was the Messiah promised in the Old Testament; repent and believe in Him." This was a sermon Paul could preach in any synagogue. But it was not a talk he could deliver on the Areopagus in Athens or in any other pagan setting. Nor was it a message that Francis Schaeffer could preach to Europe's post-Christian people without first laying down some preliminary foundations. The message of Christ's death and resurrection needs to be communicated; but there are many settings where other aspects of the truth must be communicated first. That was the situation for Paul in Athens, and it was the situation for Francis Schaeffer in post-Christian Europe.

This is not because there is anything inadequate about the content of the message of Christ's death for our sins. That is of course the truth! But with the superstitious idol-worshipers of Lystra or the pagan philosophers of Athens or the secular and cynical post-Christian people of war-ravaged Europe or the great majority of Americans under fifty today, this Good News does not begin at the right point. In such settings the good news of Christianity begins with the existence of a living and personal God who has made heaven and earth. It begins with the reality of a moral order to the universe—a moral order rooted in God's character—and with the dignity of human persons who are made as the offspring of this one true God. The Good News climaxes with the work of Christ and salvation through faith; but that is not the only good news, and the Good News does not begin with faith in the death of Christ.

This recognition that it is necessary for a Christian to understand people in order to communicate with them has always been sensed by missionaries who have sought to be faithful to the New Testament and who have loved the people to whom they have been sent by the Lord.

William Carey, Apostle to India

William Carey, the founder of the modern missionary movement and an evangelist to India, saw this very clearly. He devoted himself not only to learning the languages of the people of India but also to the study of Hindu religion. He translated Hindu Scriptures into the language the people spoke, so they could read them for themselves. He did this both because he was genuinely interested in what Indians believed and also because he realized that it was essential for him to have a deep understanding of the Hindu mind if he wanted to communicate the Gospel faithfully and effectively to the Indian people. Just like Carey, we need to be able to read the culture in which we live, so that the Good News touches people where they are able to hear it. It is a remarkable and sad commentary on contemporary practice in evangelism that this need to understand one's hearers is so often ignored or even decried.

Sometimes it is presented as the mark of a faithful witness and almost as the height of spirituality to make as few adjustments as possible in one's presentation of the Gospel regardless of the person to whom one is speaking. "The less thinking I have to do, the more the Gospel is lifted up; the less effort I make, the more the work of the Holy spirit is magnified." Not so.

Certainly it is through the message of the Gospel that God saves people, not through the servant who makes the Gospel known. Assuredly it is the Holy Spirit who softens the hard heart and creates faith within. But these wonderful truths do not lessen our obligation to be faithful in our efforts to communicate the Gospel with grace, respect, gentleness, care, and wisdom. Consider these words of the apostle Paul:

> But by the grace of God I am what I am, and his grace to me was not without effect. No, I worked harder than all of them— yet not I, but the grace of God that was with me.

By the grace God has given me, I laid a foundation as an expert builder, and someone else is building on it. But each one should be careful how he builds.
                                        —1 CORINTHIANS 15:10; 3:10

These passages, and indeed all of Scripture, give us a beautiful balance of the supreme power of God and of His delight in calling us to be His fellow workers, required by Him to labor hard and to be faithful and careful in our task of making His Word known. There is no biblical justification for us to be sloppy, careless, or thoughtless as we seek to communicate the truth. What church will keep supporting a pastor who refuses to prepare his sermons, even if he claims that his lack of effort uplifts the Word and magnifies the Spirit? It simply is not honoring to God, nor is it obedient to His Word, nor does it show any respect for unbelievers if we refuse to make the effort to understand them.

32

REVEALING THE HEART'S
SECRETS I

In addition to understanding the religious ideas and worldviews that shape the thinking of people in any society, it is also important to understand each individual's heart. Jesus was a master at revealing the secrets of the heart; so we will now reflect on His meetings with individuals to see what our Lord has to teach us. We begin with an encounter with which many believers, and even unbelievers, are very familiar—Jesus' conversation with the expert in the Law (Luke 10:25-37), the passage we know as "The Parable of the Good Samaritan."

What does the Gospel writer mean by describing a person as "an expert in the law" (v. 25)? This man was a leading Bible scholar of his day. He had spent his life studying and teaching the Scriptures and was clearly confident of his knowledge. He came to Jesus with a question: "Teacher, what must I do to inherit eternal life?" What a great question to be asked! Wouldn't any Christian be pleased if someone, anyone, came with such a question? But as we read Jesus' response we see that He never answered this man's great question. Jesus did not tell the scholar how he could inherit eternal life! This is at first sight troubling and raises several questions for us: "How would you or I have replied?" "Why did Jesus not answer this question?" "Why didn't Jesus preach the Gospel to him?" "What are we being taught by the way Jesus replied?"

Luke helps our understanding by letting us know that the scholar's question was not sincere; rather, he was testing Jesus (v. 25). He was not coming to Jesus so that he might learn from Him. Rather, he was saying in effect, "Let's see if you know your Bible. Are you fit to teach the Law? Are you properly trained, like me?" Jesus saw his heart and responded, not with the answer to his question, but with a question of his own: "What is written in the Law? How do you read it?" By "the Law" the Jews of Jesus' time could refer to the Ten Commandments, all the laws of Moses, the five books of the Pentateuch, or the whole Old Testament—the Word of God. Here, Jesus means: "What does God's Word teach about this?" The scholar could have replied, "I asked first!" But he could not resist showing off his knowledge; so he gave his answer, demonstrating that he was not really interested in learning from Jesus.

The scholar's answer is a wonderful one. He displayed a deep knowledge of Scripture. He summarized the whole Law of God in his reply:

> *"'Love the Lord your God with all your heart and with all your soul and with all your strength and with all your mind'; and, 'Love your neighbor as yourself.'"*

In fact, his summary was the same as that which Jesus Himself gave on another occasion (Mark 12:28-34). If any of us were to keep these commandments of loving God with our whole being and loving our neighbor as ourselves, we would indeed inherit eternal life! So Jesus commended the teacher for his answer, but added, "Do this and you will live."

What should have been the expert's response at this point in his discussion with Jesus? He should have said, "I have tried to keep these laws, but I am unable. My heart is so often cold toward God; and I am afraid that I do not love my neighbor as I love myself." If he had answered in this way, we may be sure that Jesus would have answered his initial question. Instead the expert tried to justify himself (and perhaps gain some time, as Jesus words were not what he had expected and had clearly set him back a little). So he asked a question: "And who is my neighbor?"

Jesus answered by telling him a story, a story we know as "the Parable of the Good Samaritan," one of the best known stories in the world.

A Word about Parables

Jesus told stories that seem very simple and clear, but his stories are rarely as simple or as straightforward as they seem. Some (though not all) of them work on four levels. First, they are marvelous stories that capture the imagination of the reader or hearer. Second, they teach moral behavior, what it is to be a truly good person, the way of life that is pleasing to the Lord. Third, they teach about the kingdom of God, how God's kingdom is different from earthly kingdoms. Fourth, they teach us about Jesus Himself. What is this story teaching the Bible scholar and us?

Loving My Neighbor

What does it mean to love my neighbor, to keep the second great commandment? True love for my neighbor is the sacrifice of my time, money, energy, convenience, and even safety—of *myself*—for another. True love is spending on others the time, energy, etc. that I would spend on myself. It is easy enough to say, "Love your neighbor as you love yourself." It is quite different to put it into practice.

Who Is My Neighbor?

My neighbor (the one whom I am obligated to love) is not only my spouse, my children, my family, my close friends, people I love. My neighbor is *anyone* in need of my help, perhaps even an enemy. The Old Testament Law is clear about this (Exodus 23:4-5; Deuteronomy 22:1-4). For a Jew "my neighbor" might be a Samaritan, for a Samaritan a Jew. Like the expert in the Law, we all like to restrict the scope of God's commandments to make them more manageable. Jesus exposed this as self-justifying hypocrisy!

Knowing and Doing

People who know God's Word well are not necessarily obeying that Word. Even those who are called by God to be scholars and teachers of the Law may not be practicing what they preach. The priest and Levite (and by implication the "expert in the law" himself), examples of those God appointed to uphold and teach the Law, are not obedient to the

Law in Jesus' story. They pass by on the other side, and therefore they fail to love God or to love their neighbor. Expert knowledge does not necessarily lead to living the law of love.

A Surprising Twist

But maybe a Samaritan *is* fulfilling the Law! Jesus used the most difficult example possible for His story in order to make it scandalous for the scholar. The one obedient to God's Law is the one least expected to do so! To understand the power of Jesus' depicting a Samaritan as the one obedient to God's Law, we need to imagine a person or a representative of a group of people we would least like to have be the hero of this story.

Jesus finished the story with another question (v. 36):

> *"Which of these three was a neighbor to the man who fell into the hands of thieves?"*

The teacher could not bring himself to name the Samaritan, and so he replied, "The one who had mercy on him."

The encounter between the two came to an end, much to the scholar's relief, with Jesus' parting words: "Go and do likewise."

Jesus challenged him to bring his practice of truth up to the level of his knowledge. What lessons about making the Gospel known are we to draw from Jesus' conversation with this Bible scholar?

LESSONS IN EVANGELISM

Evangelism Is Often a Slow Process

Jesus was content on this occasion to send the expert away without the message of the Gospel, but instead with some issues to ponder in his heart. For us, the challenge is, do we believe that God is the one who saves? Do we trust God enough to send someone away without telling that person how to inherit eternal life? Do we recognize that many of those we meet are not yet ready to hear the Gospel, just as the expert in the Law was not ready?

Asking Questions

We need to learn to ask questions that will help us understand what is in a person's heart and mind. That is what Jesus did with this man, and we find Him taking this approach repeatedly in His discussions with people. Francis Schaeffer used to say that if he had only one hour with someone, he would spend fifty-five minutes asking questions and five minutes trying to say something that would speak to his or her situation, once he understood a little more about what was going on in his or her heart and mind. What is needed is genuine love and concern for the person we are meeting, a readiness to ask questions because we truly desire to know the person, and prayer for the discernment of the Holy Spirit about what to say. Jesus, we remember, spoke only the words the Father gave Him to say. If He felt it was important to pray for the Father's wisdom as to what questions were appropriate to ask each individual He met, then so should we!

Moving People to Self-Understanding

We need to try to help people understand themselves. This scholar clearly did not understand his own heart; he had little self-knowledge. Most people we meet are in a similar position, for the heart is deceitful, and none of us know ourselves very well! Jesus sought to help the expert in the Law look into his own heart and understand his motivations: "Why did I ask that question?" "What is my attitude to people in need of my help?" "Why could I not say 'the Samaritan'?" "How deep is my own obedience to the commandments I know so well?" The challenge for us is this: Can we help people move toward self-understanding like Jesus did?

Coming at an Angle

Jesus did not always confront people head-on. He did on some occasions (for example, in His encounter with Nicodemus, but Nicodemus was not far from the kingdom of God). Here, where the expert in the Law was further from the kingdom, Jesus did not come at him with a full frontal attack, for He knew very well that such a move can incite a person's pride and create antagonism in the heart. Much evangelism does this if the ground of the person's heart is unprepared. A direct approach can have the effect of raising barriers against the Gospel, giving people answers to questions they are not yet ready to ask. Such directness can burn the ground rather than helping to prepare it to become ready soil for the seed of the Word.

Instead of confronting head-on, Jesus often asked questions and told stories in order to say things that were difficult for a person to hear. Questions and stories may both be indirect. Penetrating questions resonate in the memory and in the heart. A good story can be subversive, engaging the imagination and emotions. A fine story, like that of the Good Samaritan, is hard to forget. It keeps working in the mind of the hearer long after it is told, seeking to turn the hearer's world upside-down. For example, in this case Jesus' story was intended to exercise the scholar's heart and mind: "Do I love my neighbor?" "Do I obey the commands I know so well?" "Will my knowledge of what is true and good qualify me for the kingdom of heaven?"

Questions and stories work in this way long after they are heard because they engage a person so fully and so subtly. Consider C. S. Lewis. He was perhaps the most effective apologist of this past century, partly because he was such a fine storyteller, and therefore he engages many people through their imaginations who are not, for whatever reason, ready to hear a direct presentation of the Gospel.

Law Before Gospel

Many people need to hear the Law before they are ready to hear the Gospel. This was true for this particular Bible scholar. It is true for many people we meet and indeed for many people in our churches. They think they are living decent lives. They feel that God could not possibly judge them. Many have little idea of what God's Law truly demands. There is often very little sense of sin. Such people need, like this scholar, to hear the Law clearly first and to be told to go and keep that Law, so that they might discover that they cannot keep it and come back humbled and prepared to hear the good news of the Gospel of forgiveness. This is in effect what Jesus said to the scholar: "Go and keep the Law you think you know so well, and then come back and tell Me you have tried and you have failed." But for this man there was no Gospel yet!

The Hidden Christ

Even though Jesus preached the Law to the expert rather than the Gospel, He did not leave the man without hope. I pointed out earlier how some of Jesus' stories tell us about Himself. This is the happiest aspect of the parable of the Good Samaritan. It points to Jesus by encouraging its hearer to ask the question, "Do I know anyone like this, anyone who truly loves his neighbor as he loves himself, who even loves his enemies with such self-sacrificing love?" The expert in the Law would have to ask himself, "Are there any good Samaritans out there?" As he learned more about Jesus, he ought to discover that, yes, there is one, One who loves His neighbor, and even His enemy, fully and self-sacrificially, One who loves God with all His heart and soul and mind and strength. Perhaps one day (we will find out someday if this was indeed the case) he would return to Jesus as his Good Samaritan. He would look to Jesus as the One to whom he could come in his need to be rescued from sin, from self-centeredness, and from the pride that chained his heart. He would bow his head and his heart before the Lord and ask for mercy, for self-knowledge, and for his heart to be changed to a heart of love. Perhaps one day he was able to say, "Lord, I need You every day to be my Good Samaritan, to love me in the way Your story has taught me about love, so that through You I might be healed and inherit eternal life."

This hidden presentation of Christ is one of the beauties of storytelling. It is possible to teach people about Jesus through stories, even when those people are not yet eager to know about him. Again, C. S. Lewis is a wonderful example of this. His Narnia stories about the lion, Aslan, have introduced many people to Jesus, people who would not normally go to church or read the Bible or attend an evangelistic meeting. People are entranced by Aslan and through loving him come to worship the Lion of Judah, Christ Himself.

33

REVEALING THE HEART'S
SECRETS II

The Bible scholar or "expert in the law" (Luke 10:25) came to Jesus not as an earnest inquirer but rather to question Jesus' right to teach. He did not want to know whether Jesus was the Messiah or a true prophet from God. Instead, once Jesus gave him the opportunity, he showed off his own training and knowledge. He did indeed know the Scriptures and summarized well the teaching of the Scriptures concerning "the whole duty of man" (see Ecclesiastes 12:13). Yet despite his knowledge of God's Word, he did not know himself. Jesus sent him away to reflect on his own obedience to the Law that he knew so well. Jesus, rather than having an argument with him that would have incited his pride and made him even more closed to the Gospel, told him a story, a story that reveals what it truly means to love one's neighbor as oneself.

Stories have the power to enlighten the imagination and to engage the mind and will in a way that a direct challenge might not. We all experience this when the Holy Spirit brings to our memory encounters we have had with people—encounters in which we failed to love our neighbor as ourselves. How our mind recalls the humiliating details! How our conscience pricks us! How we try, in vain, to justify ourselves!

In just this way the Bible scholar would remember his encounter with Jesus for the rest of his life. He would recall his insincere question, his eagerness to reveal his knowledge of the Law, and his attempt to justify himself with his second question. He would reflect on the story of a man who fully loved his neighbor, his own reluctance to utter the name "Samaritan," and Jesus' final direct words to him: "Go and do likewise." One day we will find out how these troubling memories worked away in his heart and whether they eventually brought him to the truth. Meanwhile, his encounter with Jesus can teach us the art of witness by conversation and can trouble us!

In this chapter we turn to the account of another man who asked Jesus the same question as the Bible scholar (Mark 10:17-22; Luke 18:18-30): "What must I do to inherit eternal life?"

Who is the questioner on this occasion? Luke describes him as "a certain ruler," and as the conversation with Jesus unfolds we also learn that he was wealthy. Matthew tells us that he was a "young man" (19:22). A "rich young ruler" is how we usually think of this man. By "ruler" Luke probably means us to understand that he was a ruler or elder of the synagogue. A similar word is used to describe Jairus (Luke 8:41). It is possible he was a young member of the Sanhedrin, but it is more likely that he was an elder of his local synagogue. In a church context today he would be an elder or deacon (depending on the denomination) in his local church. We can easily imagine this young man. We all know men like him—bright, successful, eager to learn and serve, earnest and well meaning; an upright, outstanding, good man; the kind of man we would be proud to have as a son, a son-in-law, or a friend.

It is clear that this man's question was sincere. He was genuine when he addressed Jesus as "Good teacher" (v. 18). Mark (10:17) adds for us the detail that he "ran up to Jesus and fell on his knees" at Jesus' feet to ask his question: "What must I do to inherit eternal life?"

This encounter again raises the question, Why does Jesus not answer him? Why does He not tell him how to inherit eternal life? Why does He say to sell all he had? We can understand why Jesus did not answer the Bible scholar, but why did He not preach the Gospel to *this* man? The ruler was sincere. He was eager to know. He genuinely respected Jesus. And Mark (10:21) tells us that "Jesus looked at him and loved him." What was going on? Was Jesus driving him away? Was Jesus teaching him salvation through good works? Was He telling him he could be saved by the act of giving up his wealth? Here was a man wanting to know the truth! To understand what Jesus was doing, we need to look carefully at this conversation.

A DIVINE STRATEGY

Jesus, as He did on so many occasions, responded to the young man with a question. The question (as with the expert in the Law) was meant to reveal the heart and mind of this young man and to help him understand his own heart and mind. In one sense it was an indirect question, for Jesus did not ask the young man, "Are you good?" or "Am I good?" Rather, Jesus replied, "Why do you call me good? No one is good—except God alone" (Luke 18:19).

What was Jesus asking with this question? There are perhaps four questions within Jesus' words.

1. What is true goodness? Do you understand what it means to describe someone as good?

2. What does it mean to recognize that only God is good? What does that mean for any ordinary human person who does not measure up to the goodness of God?

3. Why are you calling Me good? If you truly see Me as good, then who am I?

4. What about you? If you truly understand what goodness is, then are you good? And if you are not good, what are the consequences?

The young man missed all four of the points that Jesus wanted him to think about as Jesus asked His question, spoke of the goodness of God alone, and then summarized the second table of the Law for this youthful elder. The young man was, of course, thoroughly familiar with the second table of the Law with its outline of what it means to love our neighbor as ourselves. He not only knew this outline of the Law—he had spent his life being devoted to observing these commandments. So he responded, "All these I have kept since I was a boy" (v. 21).

He was clearly not aware of the vast gap between his own "goodness" and the true goodness of God. He had not yet understood the full meaning of these commandments that are so simple to learn and even simple to obey (externally). He did not yet see that the commandments demand purity of the heart. He did not yet realize that adultery is not just an outward act but lust of the eyes and mind; that murder is not only refraining from killing someone but is hate, scorn, and despising another in one's heart; that theft is not merely the stealing of someone's property but is covetousness toward property, reputation, ability, or anything else that belongs to another; that false testimony is not simply telling falsehoods in court to harm another but is any failure to tell the truth, the whole truth, and nothing but the truth about my neighbor. And it is the same with every other commandment.

The young elder of the church had not begun to reflect upon the extent of the righteousness that the Law requires, and so he was unaware that he was not a good man and that his true state was that he was in desperate need of the forgiveness of God. He believed himself to be a decent man. He missed entirely Jesus' statement, "No one is good—except God alone," for he claimed goodness for himself.

Instead of refuting the ruler's claim of goodness with the statement, "You are a sinner; you have not kept these commandments," Jesus tried once more to help the man see the true state of his heart. Jesus asked him to give up his wealth, give it to the poor, and then return to follow Him. Why did Jesus say this to him? The young man did not yet see that he did not understand the requirements of the second table of the Law. So Jesus brought him back to the first table of the Law, the commands to worship and serve God alone.

By challenging him to give up his wealth, Jesus was asking the young elder, "What has the place of priority in your heart? You think you are obeying the commandments and are therefore good! But what or whom do you worship? What do you live for?" The young man knew that the Law commanded him to love and serve God alone, and he thought that he did love and serve God alone. So what was Jesus telling him or seeking to help him understand?

Devotion to Wealth

Jesus desired to expose the young man's devotion to his wealth; to turn his eyes inward to his own heart where he would see not only love for God but the love for money hidden there.

True Righteousness

Jesus wanted this elder of the synagogue to realize that he lacked true righteousness toward God and toward his neighbor. Did he in fact love the poor as the Law of God commanded? Was it not rather the case that when he saw the poor he often closed his heart against their need of his help?

True Treasures

Was this man's treasure on earth, or was it in heaven? Was he genuinely seeking eternal life, the life of the heavenly kingdom, or was it his present comfort that was most important to him? What governed the choices that he made—life now or the life to come?

"Follow Me"

Jesus also claimed to be the One the young man should love and serve, saying in essence: "Forsake everything else in your life and follow Me. I am indeed good, as you say, and that means that I am God; and therefore you should forsake your riches and serve Me alone."

These were challenging words to this young leader of the church, as they are to everyone who hears and understands them, and so he went away sorrowful. Jesus had spoken to his heart at last. He began to understand that he was not, after all, a good man; but he was not yet ready to reveal the secrets of his heart to Jesus and to acknowledge his need: "I see now that I have not kept the commandments from my youth. In fact, I see that I have not kept them one single day of my life. There is nothing I can do that will qualify me for entrance into the kingdom of heaven. My heart is torn between devotion to God and to my wealth. I know that I am a selfish man who is sometimes kind to the poor, but so much more often I am kind only to myself. My treasures are mostly here on earth. How did You see into my heart? How were You able to tell me everything I ever did? Lord, help me! I want to follow You." That was what he needed to pray that day, but he did not.

It seems probable that the young elder of the synagogue came back to Jesus later, for the early church seems to have identified the rich man who provided a tomb for Jesus' body with the man of this encounter with Jesus. We will find out for sure one day, but it seems likely that Jesus' revealing the man's heart's secrets to him did begin to draw him back to the love that Jesus held for him. What was impossible for him was possible for Jesus!

LESSONS IN EVANGELISM

What are we to deduce for ourselves from this conversation? Some of the lessons about evangelism that we learned in our last chapter are affirmed by Jesus' words to this man.

Asking Questions

We need to learn to ask questions that will help us understand the heart and mind of each individual we meet. The fundamental issue here is one of love. Do we care enough for people that we want to get to know them, so that what we say to them will be an apple of gold in a setting of silver, a word fitly framed to touch the inner being of the unique person before us?

Opening the Heart

We need to learn how to help people understand themselves and see the motivations and passions of their own hearts. The rich young ruler was an earnest seeker, but he did not see himself with any clarity. Until a man or woman begins to know his or her own heart, he or she cannot begin to know God. True knowledge of ourselves, as Calvin says, leads us by the hand to the true knowledge of God.

The Value of an Indirect Word

We need to learn the wisdom of being indirect in our conversations when a person is not yet ready to hear a straightforward presentation of gospel basics. Even someone who is genuinely seeking, or at least thinks he or she is genuinely seeking to know God, may not be at the point where he or she can hear and understand a simple and direct account of what he or she must do to come to know God and inherit eternal life. This requires love on our part and the willingness to give time and energy to understand a person so that we can speak wisely and appropriately to him or her. Not only the words He said but even the manner in which He said them was taught to Jesus by the Father. You and I need to be taught by God when to be direct and when to be indirect, and He will gladly teach us if we are willing to learn from Him.

Law Before Gospel

We need to see the importance of the Law being understood before the Gospel is proclaimed. How can someone see the true significance of Jesus if he or she does not see his sin? As Jesus did with the Bible scholar, He sent this man away to learn that he was a sinner, so that he would return another day knowing his need: "God must do for me what I cannot! He must be my righteousness; and He must deal with my failure to be righteous."

Idols of the Heart

We need to learn that for many people the idols of their hearts must be exposed before they can understand their need of Christ. People may think they are good, may think they serve God, until the secret devotion of their heart is uncovered. It was Jesus' uncovering of his idol that spoke to this young man's heart. Can we learn to help people see what governs the choices and priorities of their lives? This is a difficult task and one for which we need to ask the help of the Holy Spirit. He sees the heart's secrets, and He can help us uncover them. But this work of wounding people must be done with love, just as Jesus loved this young man when He sent him away sorrowful.

34

SPEAKING THE RIGHT
LANGUAGE—PRINCIPLE IV

In these past several chapters we have been thinking about the beliefs of others and also about the secrets of their hearts. We saw how important it is to try to understand people so that our words are shaped for each individual hearer, rather than giving exactly the same message to everyone regardless of what is going on in each person's heart and mind. Evangelism that bypasses understanding runs the risk of offending people and turning them away from Christ. Such evangelism makes them feel treated without respect or discernment, just a number on the end of a sales pitch. Or they may sense they are being used to assuage our sense of guilt about not doing enough evangelism, or that we are doing some spiritual good work that will make God pleased with us but that shows no concern for them.

As we read the Gospels we find something very different. Jesus treated each person He met as a unique individual with particular beliefs, life experiences, and problems. Consider His words to Nicodemus (John 3), the Samaritan woman (John 4), the woman taken in adultery (John 8), the man born blind and the Pharisees who mistreated him (John 9), Mary and Martha (John 11), and the centurion (Luke 7). We could read through each of the Gospels and find dozens of examples like this. Jesus demonstrated a marvelous understanding of every person or group of people that He met (Pharisees, Sadducees, lawyers, tax collectors, lepers, a crowd at a funeral, etc.).

Of course Jesus had an advantage! He was (and is) God! He knew what was in people's hearts. However, as we learned in our last two chapters, much of what Jesus discovered, He brought into the open by asking questions. His example challenges us to seek understanding so that our efforts at evangelism may in some little way be like His and be pleasing to Him. Such knowledge of people can only be gained by faithful prayer for the Spirit's help in attaining discernment and by working hard at building relationships through spending time in conversation and reflection. Once we have such understanding, then we can, from a heart of true involvement in the person's life, readily and gladly find points of contact, discover ideas and concerns that we may commend, and choose the appropriate bridges for making the Gospel known.

This need to build our communication on a deep understanding of each person leads us to our next topic—using the right language. What language are we to use when we try to talk about God and the truth He has made known in Jesus Christ? Paul's ministry is again a model for us. As we read through Acts we find Paul shaping his language to his hearers, changing his very words to aid the understanding of those listening to him.

PAUL IN THE SYNAGOGUE IN PISIDIAN ANTIOCH (ACTS 13:16-41)

When Paul spoke in the setting of the synagogue, he expressed his message in language that we are all accustomed to hearing in sermons. Not only the details of the content, but almost every word was taken from the Greek translation of the Old Testament Scriptures. Those listening would have been very comfortable with the language Paul used, for the language was typical of the teaching they heard at every service they attended.

PAUL ON MARS HILL IN ATHENS (ACTS 17:22-31)

Among the Athenians and others gathered in the Areopagus Paul's language was very different, though the message Paul gave was thoroughly biblical in its content. We might describe his talk as taken from the teachings of the early chapters of Genesis. It was about the nature of God and the nature of human persons and about what is appropriate in the worship of God. However, the language was not from the Old Testament. Instead it was truly the language of the Greeks, and not just in the sense that Paul used Greek words. He had spoken in Greek in Pisidian Antioch, but in Athens he assumed that his hearers had no familiarity with the language of the Scriptures.

He spoke about God by using his hearers' expressions for God rather than those of the synagogue. In verse 23 Paul used a word in the neuter to speak about God, and also in verse 29. He used this expression—"the divine"—so that he could begin his message with their belief in God as an impersonal force or essence. Of course, Paul was not content to stop with such a view of God or such language for God, for from that beginning he proclaimed the personal God, Creator, Sustainer, and Judge of all.

Paul did not use the name Jesus *or* Christ, *for those names would have meant nothing to his hearers.* Instead he spoke about a "man" God had appointed (v. 31). Paul substituted the ordinary Greek word for *man* in place of the most common title used for Jesus in the Gospels, "Son of Man" (a different Greek term for man).

Paul's speech was also full of alliteration in the Greek, particularly with the letter p. The Greek word for *all*, which begins with *p*, is repeated frequently with other words in alliterative sequence (see vv. 24, 25, 26, 30, 31). In addition, assonance is used in verse 25. The consequence of Paul's employing alliteration, repetition, and assonance was that the style of his speech was formal and elevated, almost poetic, very appropriate for Mars Hill.

If we study the Greek of this message carefully, we find that local idioms were used and even some words and phrases in the Attic dialect, the dialect of Athens. Paul worked hard to adapt his usual manner of speaking to the context of this gathering of Athenians and other philosophers. Maybe he stayed up all night preparing his words, praying and working hard to commend the Gospel to these men and women! If any Christian today were asked to speak in such a setting, we could be quite sure that he or she would do a great deal of praying and sweating over his or her preparation. We should not imagine that Paul was any different.

We ought always to take our attempts to communicate God's Word as seriously as Paul did. This care is appropriate and necessary for those who get to speak to a group of highly educated philosophers—and it is appropriate and necessary in every other context too! Such care should arise out of a genuine love and respect for all people, whoever they are, and out of a longing to serve God faithfully.

PAUL IN THE COURTROOM

Yet another incidence of Paul's varying his language comes in the three trial scenes recorded in Acts 22, 24, and 26. In this setting Paul used language appropriate for the courtroom. He spoke of making his defense, testimony, witness, charges, punishment, jury decisions, arrest, and proof.

THE APOSTOLIC PATTERN

Throughout the New Testament we find many examples of this flexibility of language. Much of the language we think of as particularly Christian is actually the language of the Greco-Roman society to which the apostles ministered. Words like *adoption, redemption, eyewitness,* and many more are examples of this. They are not words (and sometimes not even the concepts behind those words) that are common in the Old Testament. For example, adoption was not widely practiced among the Jews but was common in Roman society. Yet this is one of the terms that Paul uses to describe a believer's new relationship with God. Imagine the encouragement of that word to the many slaves who heard Paul use it when he was proclaiming the Gospel.

Many of the terms used to describe the Christian life in the letters to Timothy and Titus are borrowed from the Stoics—*training, piety, decency, uprightness, serious, self-controlled, soundness of speech, disciplined, temperate, respectable.* This is true also of the house codes, the pattern of teaching for husbands and wives, parents and children, masters and servants that we find in Ephesians 5—6, Colossians 3—4, and in truncated form in several other epistles also. This form of giving moral instruction is adapted from a Stoic model.

To claim that Paul and the other apostles borrowed religious and ethical language and teaching patterns from the surrounding culture is troublesome to some Christians. However, this does not need to cause anxiety. The point is not that Paul was taking the content of Christian doctrine or morality from his culture. Not at all! Rather Paul, in his choice of language and teaching patterns, was being a good ambassador of the Gospel. In his own ministry Paul was practicing what he preached. He worked at being all things to all people. With the Jews he used the language of the Jews. With the Greeks he used the language of the Greeks. His message was the same true Gospel in both contexts. It was simply the means of delivery of the truth that varied.

In addition Paul, with his careful use of language, was concerned to help believers live in their culture in a way that brought credit to their faith. The Stoic non-Christians who lived alongside the believers in Asia Minor (the context of Paul's letters to Timothy) valued the ethical characteristics of modesty, decency, propriety, temperance, sobriety, etc. So Paul was helping the Christians to see that to model these qualities by the power of Christ would bring honor to Christ and to the Gospel. Of course Paul chose Stoic virtues that are indeed appropriate for a Christian. He would never have commended any values put forward by unbelievers if they were in contradiction to the Gospel of Christ. As well as helping them live in a way that brought glory to God, Paul also, by his choice of words, wanted to help believers communicate the Christian message to those around them in language that would be readily understandable.

THE MINISTRY OF JESUS

What was true of the missionary work of Paul and the other apostles was also true in the ministry of Jesus on earth. Consider the parables in which Jesus used the language and picturesque details of farming, fishing, and everyday scenes to communicate His message. Yet, when Jesus was with the Pharisees and teachers of the Law He was completely comfortable using the theological terminology with which they were familiar. If one reads the four Gospels paying attention to Jesus' choice of words, it becomes evident that He was a master at finding just the right language to reach into the hearts and minds of each of His hearers. Why would this surprise any Christian? Jesus is the Word made flesh. In His life and in His every word He was (and is) the embodiment of the truth about God and the embodiment of God's love for the world. His choice of words expressed that love perfectly, announcing that He came into the world not to condemn it but to save it.

THE CHALLENGE TO CHRISTIANS TODAY

So often we believers use what English Christians call "the language of Zion" without thinking about whether people comprehend it or not. We use this language because it is precious to us. We know and we love what this Christian terminology conveys, for we are familiar with it. It is like an old pair of slippers that are well-worn and comfortable to wear. But in truth much of the language we use in our churches today is no longer understood by many of our contemporaries. Words like *redemption, justification, sanctification, incarnation,* and even *sin* are not exactly words that are part of everyday speech in the early twenty-first century. Other words that are still part of everyday language, such as *faith*, have lost much of their biblical meaning. Consider the expression "leap of faith," which communicates something exactly opposite to New Testament usage.

The New Testament challenges us to express God's unchanging truth in the language of our time rather than in the language of the sixteenth or seventeenth centuries or even of the early part of the twentieth century. We ought not to become like the popular image of a computer nerd who speaks in words with which no one else has any familiarity. It is boring, unthinking, and ultimately disrespectful to unbelievers to use words that may be understood by us and are precious to us as if they were the only words that we could find to express the truth about Christ. Instead we ought to think of our language like the apostle Paul did. The language we choose should aid communication and help us in our bridge building. An example of this might be the word *freedom*, as it is such a commonly used word.

FREEDOM

How is the word *freedom* used in our culture? What do people around us mean when they talk about freedom? Political, economic, and religious freedoms are glories of American society. We value these freedoms and regard them as a birthright hard-won by our forebears and worth defending with our lives. We are grateful for freedom of the press, though we stress that it, along with other freedoms, cannot be separated from responsibility. In thinking about these freedoms a Christian will find common cause with unbelievers, and this shared cause is an excellent bridge builder. I have often spoken on freedom in meetings at which many non-Christians were present, because freedom is a subject that enables me to commend certain values in our culture and in the lives of those present.

Yet, freedom in our culture is our shame as well as our glory, and so freedom is a bridge for communication and also a starting place to confront people with the truth. Many of our contemporaries want freedom from control or from any constraint, freedom from the government interfering in their life in any way, freedom from church or other moral authorities telling them what to do, even freedom from God. They desire "freedom for myself, freedom to choose, freedom to do as I wish, freedom to make my life exactly what I want it to be."

Setting freedom out starkly like this demonstrates how problematic such a view is to the Christian. Yet, even a moment's reflection should be enough to enable us to see how all of us, believers too, are affected by it. This view of freedom is inescapable in our culture; it is the air we breathe. Yet it ought to be obvious to us that even though we are all influenced by this approach to life, such supposed freedom is in fact enslaving and destructive. Consider how miserable a spoiled boy is, one who is constantly demanding and getting his own way. Think of the consequences of the freedom to use addictive drugs, or the freedom to be sexually promiscuous, or the freedom to abort one's child in the womb.

If we contrast this ideal of freedom with the way that freedom is described in Scripture, we discover a radically different usage, and behind that usage a radically different understanding of human life. God promises us freedom from His judgment, freedom from guilt, and freedom from sin. He desires that we be set free from the problems that arise from doing what is right in our own eyes, free from the passions of our own flawed and self-centered natures. In Christ God offers us the freedom to acknowledge the truth that we are finite and sinful and do not know exactly how to live. He offers us freedom to serve Himself; freedom to let God be God and to acknowledge that we need His direction, His forgiveness, His wisdom, His help; freedom to serve one another in love.

The freedom that Scripture presents could hardly be more opposed to the freedom our culture treasures. The sober truth is that it is degrading and enslaving to live simply for oneself and for the fulfillment of one's own desires. All true and lasting fulfillment comes from loving and serving God and from loving and serving others.

> *"If you hold to my teaching, you are really my disciples. Then you will know the truth, and the truth will set you free. . . . So if the Son sets you free, you will be free indeed."*
> —JOHN 8:31-32, 36

> *You, my brothers, were called to be free. But do not use your freedom to indulge the sinful nature; rather, serve one another in love.*
> —GALATIANS 5:13

35

REASONED PERSUASION—
PRINCIPLE V

In our last chapter we considered the need to speak a language that our hearers understand. We saw how Paul and the other apostles learned the language of their time and so were able to communicate effectively whether their audience consisted of Jews who were familiar with the Bible or pagans who were not. The first eighteen verses of John's Gospel are a masterful example of this careful use of language. In this passage the apostle John used the Greek term *logos* (translated as *Word* in our English Bibles) to introduce Christ. It was a term with a long history in both Greek and Jewish thought and therefore would have "rung bells" in the minds of the readers.

Jews would have been reminded of the opening verses of Genesis 1: "In the beginning God created the heavens and the earth" and the repeated statement "And God said." In addition Jewish readers would have been reminded of all that the Old Testament has to say about the living and active "Word of the Lord," responsible for creation and revelation. Greek readers would have reflected on the tradition of thought that ascribed the orderly structure of the world to the "Word" and saw this same "Word" as the principle of rationality giving light to human life.

If we reflect on this thoughtful use of language by the apostles, it is evident that they were building a carefully reasoned presentation of the truth to their hearers. In chapter 1 of his Gospel John is seeking to persuade his readers that the Word, who is the Creator of the universe and the revealer of God to the human race, has been made flesh in the person of Jesus Christ. The human person Jesus of Nazareth is indeed the one true God, and John wants to convince his readers, both Jews and Gentiles, of this fact.

Toward the end of his Gospel John is explicit about this purpose in writing:

> *Jesus did many other miraculous signs in the presence of his disciples, which are not recorded in this book. But these are written that you may believe that Jesus is the Christ, the Son of God, and that by believing you may have life in his name.*
>
> —20:30-31

Later he adds, using language that conjures up a courtroom where eyewitness evidence is a necessity for the argument presented to the judge and jury:

> *This is the disciple who testifies to these things and who wrote them down. We know that his testimony is true.*
>
> —21:24

John is presenting evidence intended to convince his readers of the truth of his message. His words are reasoned and persuasive; he wants to prove his case about who Jesus is and the need to believe in Him. Many Christians become anxious when they hear talk about reason, persuasion, convincing proof, or a powerfully argued case. They wonder if faith and reason should be spoken of together in this manner. They fear that the truth of the Gospel might become dependent on clever arguments so that only brilliant Christians with the mind of a lawyer can be effective evangelists. These are important questions, and I will return to them later in the chapter. But first we will look again at Paul's presentation of the Gospel to see whether he made a reasoned appeal to his hearers.

PAUL IN THE SYNAGOGUE (ACTS 13:16-41)

If we examine this sermon to Jews and Gentile God-fearers, we find that it was a powerfully reasoned message aimed at persuading those present that Jesus is the Messiah promised in the Old Testament. To what did the apostle appeal?

- Paul argued from God's revelation of Himself in the Old Testament and His promises about the coming of the Messiah.
- He demonstrated how these prophecies were fulfilled in the life and death of Jesus of Nazareth.
- He appeals to the testimony of John the Baptist about Jesus.
- He spoke about those who were witnesses to Jesus' resurrection from the dead.

We may summarize Paul's approach by saying that he gave his hearers reasons to believe in Jesus. His appeal was primarily to evidence from special revelation—that is, from Scripture. This is not entirely so, for he also appealed to the evidence of John the Baptist's ministry (John was highly respected by the Jews) and to the living eyewitnesses of Christ's resurrection.

PAUL AMONG THE PAGANS (ACTS 14:15-17; 17:22-31)

With the pagans in Lystra and Athens Paul obviously could not appeal to the testimony of Scripture, of special revelation, as they were completely ignorant of it (though his message was thoroughly scriptural). Instead Paul appealed to general revelation—that is, to what God has made known about Himself through the created order.

- Paul reasoned from the knowledge of God, which is in the heart and mind of every person.
- He appealed to their understanding of the dependence of all life on the Creator. They knew that the universe and its creatures are not self-created or existing in their own power.
- He pointed to their daily experience of God's providential care (14:17): "He has not left himself without testimony: He has shown kindness by giving you rain from heaven and crops in their seasons; he provides you with plenty of food and fills your hearts with joy."
- He called them to reflect on God's compassionate rule over history and over the lives of nations, a rule that should lead people to seek God and worship Him.
- He argued from their recognition of the unique dignity of

human persons. They knew there is something "divine" about men and women; their own poets and thinkers acknowledged that "in him we live and move and have our being . . . we are his offspring" (17:28).

• He urged them to see the inadequacy of their worship and to be consistent with their own understanding that human temples cannot contain God, who they knew to be the Creator of heaven and earth.

• He insisted that idolatry is self-evidently foolish, because idols are made by people who themselves are the creation of God.

• He climaxed his argument by appealing to the "proof" of the resurrection of Christ (17:31), which all people may know about by looking at the testimony of witnesses.

We can summarize Paul's approach to these pagans in the following way: The message was aimed at giving his hearers compelling reasons as to why they should become worshipers of the one true God and why they should put their hope in His Son, Jesus Christ, the One whom God has appointed to be the universal judge.

OBJECTION: PAUL RENOUNCED REASON

There is a widely held view among Christians that Paul renounced the use of reason, and therefore so must we. Why is this view held, and to what Scriptures are believers appealing when they reason in this way? The primary passage used to support the rejection of reasoning in evangelism is a section in chapters 1 and 2 of 1 Corinthians. I excerpt here some of the verses at the heart of this debate:

> For Christ did not send me to baptize, but to preach the gospel—not with words of human wisdom, lest the cross of Christ be emptied of its power.

> For since in the wisdom of God the world through its wisdom did not know him, God was pleased through the foolishness of what was preached to save those who believe.

When I came to you brothers, I did not come with eloquence or superior wisdom as I proclaimed to you the testimony about God. For I was resolved to know nothing while I was with you except Jesus Christ and him crucified.

My message and my preaching were not with wise and persuasive words, but with a demonstration of the Spirit's power, so that your faith might not rest on men's wisdom, but on God's power.
—1:17, 21; 2:1-2, 4-5

Clearly, these are strong words. So we need to ask at least the following three questions arising from the appeal to them.

1. Are these words a denunciation of Paul's own practice of reasoning in the synagogue and in particular in Athens? In other words, did Paul repent of his message to the Athenians; did he regard it as a failure and a mistake? Some Bible teachers have taken this view and argue that after Athens Paul decided that he would literally speak only about "Jesus Christ and him crucified" in his preaching from that point onward. No more reasoning, no more talk about "the God who made the world" (Acts 17:24), no more talk about pagan worship and idolatry, but rather just proclaiming the ABC's of the Gospel in the future.

2. In the book of Acts how does Luke present the preaching of Paul before he went to Athens, while he was in Athens, and after his time in Athens when he spent several years in Corinth and Ephesus? What kind of language does the inspired writer, Luke, use to describe what he saw and heard in the ministry of the apostle? Does Luke present Paul as one who simply preached Christ and the cross? Or does Luke present Paul as one who reasoned about the truth of the Gospel, whether that truth concerned the nature of God and of true worship or whether that truth concerned the person and work of Jesus Christ?

3. What does Paul mean by his strong language about "men's wisdom" and "persuasive words"? What is Paul criticizing in 1 Corinthians 1 and 2? Is he attacking his own past ministry, or is he challenging some other problem? And if the latter, what is the other problem? In answering this question we need to think about the relationship between trust in the power of God to save people and our efforts to communicate the Gospel wisely and well.

36

ANSWERING THE OBJECTIONS TO REASONED PERSUASION

There are powerful objections to the use of reasoned persuasion in proclaiming the Gospel of Christ. In this chapter we will attempt to answer these objections, which in the last chapter were set out as three questions that must be considered as we face this issue.

WAS PAUL'S PREACHING IN ATHENS A FAILURE AND A MISTAKE?

We begin with the charge that Paul's preaching in Athens was, in fact, both a failure and a mistake and that Paul himself came to realize this and repented of his approach to the Athenians. To answer this charge we need to look at the way Luke presents Paul's time in Athens. If we read Acts 17 with care, we find no suggestion that Luke considered Paul's approach in Athens to be mistaken in any way. Even though Luke wrote his book of Acts many years after the events he describes, we know that he was a friend, fellow traveler, and co-laborer with Paul. It is evident that these two men were well acquainted and regarded each other with deep respect. If Paul had felt his work in Athens was unworthy of the Gospel, we may be sure that he would have made this known to Luke; but nowhere does Luke breathe any hint of this.

Furthermore, Luke's account of Paul's ministry in Athens is an account inspired by the Holy Spirit. It is part of Scripture and is therefore to be regarded as an authoritative account, binding on the readers. It is a dangerous way to approach Scripture to suggest that a speech of Paul is a mistake when it is clearly recorded by Luke as a part of the ministry of the apostle whom Christ had appointed to be his ambassador to the Gentiles. This is not an argument from silence. If Paul was mistaken in his approach, we may be sure Luke would have informed us of this. As it is, Luke presents Paul's work to us as something to be admired by us, his readers, and to be emulated by us. This is true in Athens, and it is true of Luke's record of Paul's ministry in other cities and to other people. We cannot and must not pick and choose between passages of Scripture as if we were the judges of which part of the sacred text meets our ideas of how evangelism is to be done! This would be an arrogant and dishonoring way of reading the Word of God.

Was Paul's ministry in Athens a failure? Again, to make such a suggestion, when Luke does not tell us that Paul's message was a failure, is a dangerous way to approach a text of Scripture. On this particular occasion Luke tells us, quite explicitly, that people were converted:

> *A few men became followers of Paul and believed. Among them was Dionysius, a member of the Areopagus, also a woman named Damaris, and a number of others.*
>
> —17:34

Some argue that not many were converted, so that proves Paul's ministry in Athens to have been inadequate in some way. But this does not read like failure! Given the pagan, and even more the intellectual context (a context that breeds arrogance in the human heart), it is a miracle that there was a response of faith in a few of the hearers. I have many times spoken in university contexts. How glad I would be to return from such a meeting and tell of the conversion of several faculty members! We should note, too, that when Luke gives us the names of individuals who are converted, in this case Dionysius and Damaris, it is usually an indication that these individuals became persons of particular significance in the life of the church in years to come. What is more, every individual is precious in the eyes of the Lord. He is prepared to leave the ninety-nine who are safely in his fold and go to extraordinary lengths to save just one (Luke 15:3-7). When I look at just one of the men or women who came into the kingdom during the thirty plus years of my ministry, I consider all the time, energy, and self-sacrifice to have been well-spent.

But if Luke had not told us explicitly of the "success" of Paul in Athens, would we then have reason to consider his ministry there a failure or a mistake? Certainly not! When we are not told of conversions in the Gospels after Jesus ministered to a group of people, are we to conclude that Jesus was a failure and that His ministry was inadequate or His approach mistaken in some way? There are many occasions in the Gospels when Jesus ministered and no one seemed to respond immediately. Yet Jesus, just as with you and I, often was sowing seeds in the human heart rather than reaping a harvest of converts.

For Jesus, much of the fruit of His ministry was not realized until after His resurrection and ascension. In the early chapters of Acts we read of huge numbers of people becoming Christians. One day we will find out just how many of these people had heard Jesus preaching and teaching in their towns and villages during His earthly ministry. For example, we read of many priests coming to faith (Acts 6:7). Who can doubt that the majority of these priests had heard Jesus teaching long before they put their hope in Him?

In the same way it would be wrong to conclude that Paul's communication of the Gospel in a particular setting was a failure and inadequate simply because Luke records only a few conversions. Should we decide, for example, that Paul was hopelessly wrong in the way he defended himself in court because Luke does not tell us of anyone coming to faith in Acts 22, 24, 25, and 26? This would be a cavalier and even sinful conclusion; indeed, one cannot imagine any Bible teacher putting forward such a proposal with any seriousness. The same applies to the suggestion that Paul failed and was wrong in his approach in Athens. The idea that 1 Corinthians 1 and 2 is a statement of repentance by Paul is an example of setting Scripture against Scripture in an indefensible manner.

How Does Luke Present the Preaching of Paul?

To answer this question we will look at a series of summary statements made by Luke as he describes Paul's ministry in different settings.

Shortly after his conversion on the road to Damascus Paul spent time with the believers in that city. Luke tells us (Acts 9:20-22): "At once he began to preach in the synagogues that Jesus is the Son of God. . . . Saul grew more and more powerful and baffled the Jews living in Damascus by proving that Jesus is the Christ." In this passage we see Luke summarizing Paul's communication with the word *preach* but includes within his account of that preaching language that shows Paul was committed to powerful argumentation—Paul "*baffled . . . by proving.*"

From Damascus Paul went to Jerusalem, where once again Luke presents Paul as becoming quickly involved in evangelism after he was introduced to the Christian community by Barnabas (Acts 9:27-29). Barnabas describes Paul as having "preached fearlessly in the name of Jesus" in Damascus. In Jerusalem, we are told, Saul was "speaking boldly in the name of the Lord. He talked and debated with the Grecian Jews." Again Luke uses both the language of *preaching* and the language of reasoning—Paul *debated*.

Many years later we find Paul on the first of his missionary journeys. Luke describes the ministry of Paul and Barnabas in the city of Iconium (Acts 14:1-3). In the synagogue they "spoke so effectively that a great number of Jews and Gentiles believed." They spent considerable time in Iconium "speaking boldly for the Lord" there. Here Luke's language is not specific; it could include both straight proclamation and reasoned persuasion and almost certainly did include both.

Next we turn to Luke's account of Paul's ministry on his second missionary journey. This time we find Paul in Thessalonica in northern Greece (Acts 17:1-4). In accordance with his regular custom, Paul went first to the synagogue. There "on three Sabbath days he reasoned with them from the Scriptures, explaining and proving that the Christ had to suffer and rise from the dead. 'This Jesus I am proclaiming to you is the Christ,' he said. Some of the Jews were persuaded and joined Paul and Silas, as did a large number of God-fearing Greeks and not a few prominent women." On this occasion we see Luke using the language of *reason*, *persuasion*, and *proof*, though Paul himself describes this reasoned presentation as *proclamation*.

Our next passage is from the account of Paul's ministry in Athens, before he was taken by some of his listeners to the Areopagus (Acts 17:16-18). In response to his distress at the idolatry of the Athenians, Paul "reasoned in the synagogue . . . as well as in the marketplace day by day with those who happened to be there." Some of those listening "began to dispute with him" and called him "a babbler," an accusation they made "because Paul was preaching the good news about Jesus and the resurrection." Here Paul evidently was reasoning and discussing with people, but once again this approach can be referred to as *preaching*.

From Athens Paul traveled to Corinth, where he met up with Priscilla and Aquila, the beginning of a friendship and a shared and mutually appreciated ministry that was to last for many years. Luke's description of Paul's ministry in Corinth will be quoted at length here, for it is clearly at the heart of this discussion of the value and importance of reasoned persuasion.

> *After this, Paul left Athens and went to Corinth. There he met a Jew named Aquila, a native of Pontus, who had recently left Italy with his wife Priscilla. . . . Paul went to see them, and because he was a tentmaker as they were, he stayed and worked with them. Every Sabbath he reasoned in the synagogue, trying to persuade Jews and Greeks. When Silas and Timothy came from Macedonia, Paul devoted himself exclusively to preaching, testifying to the Jews that Jesus was the Christ.*
>
> —ACTS 18:1-5

As he describes Paul's communication of the Gospel in Corinth— the very place where Paul is said to have renounced reason and persuasion—Luke tells us that Paul "reasoned . . . trying to persuade." However, despite this clear statement, some appeal to the following verse where Luke says that "Paul devoted himself exclusively to preaching." It is argued that these words describe the transition in Paul's ministry. From this point on he would reason and persuade no more. His words in 1 Corinthians 2:1-3 ("I did not come with eloquence or superior wisdom as I proclaimed to you . . . I resolved to know nothing while I was with you except Jesus Christ and him crucified. . . . My message and my preaching were not with wise and persuasive words") are claimed to reflect this radical change in Paul's approach—persuasion and reasoning in the past, but now only proclamation and preaching.

This appears to be a convincing argument, but is it? It would require us to believe that all the years of Paul's ministry up to this point were fundamentally displeasing to God. He had been reasoning when God only wanted him to preach. He had tried to use persuasive words when

God only wanted him to trust in the Spirit. He had tried to prove that Jesus was the Christ when God wanted him "to let go and let God." Yet Luke makes no mention of such deep repentance having taken place in Paul's life.

In addition it should be noted that Luke is not contrasting persuasion and preaching despite the claim that this is his intention in Acts 18:1-5. We have already seen that Luke can use the language of preaching and persuasion alongside each other with no sense of contrasting the two. Rather, in Acts 18 Luke is drawing attention to the amount of time Paul has to make the Gospel known. Before Silas and Timothy arrived from Macedonia, Paul was working as a tentmaker along with Aquila and Priscilla, in order to support himself in his ministry. Once Silas and Timothy were present, Paul was able to devote himself exclusively to preaching. He no longer had to work as a tentmaker.

Why? The answer to this question is given in Philippians 4:14 and 2 Corinthians 11:8-9. In these two passages Paul informs us that, during his ministry in Corinth and elsewhere, he preached for free. He was insistent that he did not want to be financially supported by the group of people to whom he was then proclaiming the Gospel. This was a principle of his ministry (see 1 Corinthians 9:18: "What then is my reward? Just this: that in preaching the gospel I may offer it free of charge"). Paul tells us that he either supported himself by being a tentmaker or he was supported by already established churches. The passages from Philippians and 2 Corinthians referred to above tell us that the Christians of Philippi were some of the first to support Paul and that in particular they supported Paul when he was ministering in Corinth. When Silas and Timothy arrived in Corinth, they brought with them a gift from the Philippians so that Paul no longer had to make tents to support himself. From that time on he was able to devote himself "exclusively to preaching."

In describing Paul's full-time ministry in Corinth, Luke tells us that Paul's preaching consisted of "testifying to the Jews that Jesus was the Christ." The word translated "testifying" here is a word from the courtroom, a word that signifies the use of evidence and the presentation of a persuasive and convincing case. Paul's preaching did not suddenly lose its carefully reasoned nature in Corinth. It continued to be the same as it always was, a thoughtful presentation of the Gospel given with the aim of persuading those listening. After a year and a half of ministry in Corinth, the Jews in the city charged Paul with just this offense: "This man is persuading people to worship God in ways contrary to the law" (Acts 18:13). Even Paul's enemies, long after this point in time when he is alleged to have changed his approach, recognized him to be a master of persuasion!

After about two years in Corinth, Paul moved on to the city of Ephesus. Luke describes for us his method of preaching the Gospel there: "He . . . went into the synagogue and reasoned with the Jews" (Acts 18:19). Paul's ministry continued to be the same as always. When Paul had to leave Ephesus, Apollos arrived there to join Priscilla and Aquila in the work of making the Gospel known. Apollos' preaching was encouraged and aided by these two who knew Paul and his methods so well. After being helped by them, Apollos was invited to join the team ministering in Corinth, and Luke tells how effective his preaching was: "On arriving, he was a great help to those who by grace had believed. For he vigorously refuted the Jews in public debate, proving from the Scriptures that Jesus was the Christ" (Acts 18:27-28).

Luke happily describes Apollos' ministry in Corinth as one of powerful reasoning. This would be impossible if Paul had indeed in Corinth renounced reason and debate. It is also clear from this passage that Luke sees no conflict between vigorous argument intended to convince people of the truth and the work of God's grace that draws the human heart and mind to faith.

Paul returned to the city of Ephesus to work there for almost three years. Luke, in now familiar language, writes about Paul's preaching in that city:

> *Paul entered the synagogue and spoke boldly there for three months, arguing persuasively about the kingdom of God. But some of them became obstinate; they refused to believe and publicly maligned the Way. So Paul left them. He took the disciples with him and had discussions daily in the lecture hall of Tyrannus. This went on for two years, so that all the Jews and Greeks who lived in the province of Asia heard the word of the Lord.*
>
> —ACTS 19:8-10

Long after his supposed change of heart, Paul was still committed to argument and persuasion. There simply is no evidence for the view that Paul renounced reason and merely proclaimed that Jesus was the Christ after supposedly experiencing a profound revolution in his ministry.

WHY DOES PAUL USE SUCH STRONG LANGUAGE ABOUT "MEN'S WISDOM" AND "PERSUASIVE WORDS"?

To answer thoroughly the misinterpretation of 1 Corinthians 1 and 2, it is necessary to understand why Paul spoke so passionately about persuasion and wisdom in this passage. If he reasoned wisely himself and used persuasive language, what was he attacking? To answer this question we should notice Paul's use of the following expressions: "the philosopher of this age," "the wisdom of the world" (1:20-21); "Jews demand miraculous signs and Greeks look for wisdom" (1:22); "man's wisdom," "men's wisdom" (1:25; 2:5); "eloquence or superior wisdom" (2:1); "the wisdom of this age," "the rulers of this age" (2:6, 8).

With these expressions Paul is drawing our attention to the fundamental problem of the Greek mind in his day. Each culture has its idols that stand between its people and the Lord. Just as the Jews were skeptical about Jesus because they had become proud of their own heritage as the people among whom God had worked His miraculous signs, so the Greeks were proud of their heritage of great wisdom. God's gift of wisdom and philosophy had become a snare to them. Instead of worshiping the Giver of wisdom, they worshiped their own brilliance of mind. They trusted in their own wisdom rather than in God.

Their wisdom announced to them that God could not intervene in human history. This world, they decided, is a closed system of cause and effect. For this reason they considered the good news that Jesus was the incarnate Son of God to be an impossible idea. For this reason in Athens they mocked Paul's teaching about the resurrection of Christ (Acts 17:18). For this reason they regarded the Gospel to be foolishness. Their wisdom was simply human wisdom that ruled out as unthinkable the true wisdom that comes from God and is made known in Jesus Christ. The message Paul proclaimed is not and never will be the philosophy of "this age" or "the wisdom of the world" or "man's wisdom." In every age and in every culture the prevailing wisdom is opposed to the basic doctrines of Christianity.

Paul, however, denounced their human wisdom as the true foolishness. The Greeks declared the Gospel to be foolish, but it was their own thinking that in the end was foolish. This was exactly the thrust of Paul's message on Mars Hill—that is, that the greatest minds of the Greeks had after all not come to a saving knowledge of the one true God; instead, their thinking had led them into the folly of idolatry. If we compare Paul's argument in Acts 17 in the Areopagus with his words in 1 Corinthians 1 and 2 and with his words in Romans 1:18-32, we will discover that in each of these three passages Paul's message was the same. People in their rebellion against God think they are being wise; but the truth is that it is their thinking that is foolish and God's Word that is wise.

In 1 Corinthians 1 and 2 Paul is also denouncing the Greeks' confidence in rhetorical skills rather than in truth. In Paul's day there were schools of Sophists who prided themselves on their rhetorical skills, on their ability to use "persuasive words" to win any discussion. They would hire themselves out for a fee to anyone who desired to win a case. They boasted that they could persuade any court by their ability to reason, whether the case they defended was true or false. This is not too different from some in the legal profession today who will for a fee hire themselves out to persuade juries of the guilt or innocence of a client, regardless of the merits of the case. Rhetoric and clever argumentation can win in our courts today, just as they did among the Greeks. Paul insisted that the message he presented to the Corinthians was different; it was God's truth, and it was God who convinced the hearts of the hearers, not simply some clever words.

Paul, however, was not renouncing a reasoned presentation of the Gospel or carefully chosen words or the appeal to evidence. The Gospel is the truth, and all the reasons in the world support its claim to be truth. Paul therefore sought to persuade people of that truth, and at the same time he prayed for the work of the Spirit to draw people to that truth and to truth Himself, Jesus Christ.

37

CLARIFYING THE GOOD NEWS—
PRINCIPLE VI

In these past chapters we have considered the first five principles of communicating the Gospel—respect, building bridges, understanding what others believe, using the right language, and persuasion. Some might ask, "What about the presentation of the truth itself? When are we getting to that? Haven't we spent enough time bending over backwards to accommodate ourselves to the people we meet?" I hope all will recognize that accommodating ourselves to our hearers is precisely what all faithful communication of the Gospel must be, for the Gospel itself—God becoming flesh for us—is the greatest imaginable accommodation to those who need to be saved! Especially when we think about how to present the content of this good news of God's accommodation, we are to conform to the requirement to be all things to all people. We always must commit ourselves to shape the message for the unbeliever. We never escape the obligation to imitate the Incarnation.

With this sixth principle, clarifying the Good News, we consider the need to tune the message of the Gospel itself to the ears and hearts of those listening. God requires us to clear away confusion in the minds of unbelievers, to speak His Word with clarity so that we define the Gospel carefully for those to whom we speak. He calls us to build bridges with our hearers—that is, to find points of contact, areas of agreement where we can commend the thinking of those to whom we come with the Gospel. But we must go a step further; our bridges are to be bridges for the communication of truth that is not yet known and not yet believed. We build a road or bridge to cross a chasm; in the same way, our bridges of understanding are built in order that we may cross the chasm of unbelief and ignorance with the truth of God's Word. We now turn once more to our examples from Paul's preaching in different settings.

PAUL IN THE SYNAGOGUE (ACTS 13:16-41)

How did Paul set about clarifying the message of the Gospel in the synagogue in Pisidian Antioch? He had built the bridges of his hearers' confidence in the Old Testament Scriptures, their expectation of the Messiah, and their honor for King David. Then he told them that all those Old Testament passages speak of Jesus. The prophecies point to Him as the Christ. Every detail of His birth, life, death, and resurrection demonstrate that He is indeed the Messiah about whom all the Scriptures are written. The people believed the words of David and honored him as their greatest king. David wrote of not decaying in the grave; yet he lay in his tomb to the very day on which Paul was speaking to them. However, Jesus, the one David was writing about, had come out from His tomb and was risen from the dead.

In the same way, Paul said, John the Baptist, a figure they respected greatly, focused all his words on Jesus. He did not proclaim himself to the people; rather he turned their attention to Jesus and declared that He was the One they should honor, just as he himself did by declaring that he was not worthy to untie Jesus' sandals. Paul declared to them that Jesus is the One to believe in, that forgiveness of sins and life everlasting can only be received through faith in Him.

Paul's every message in the synagogue might be summarized as follows: "You long for the Messiah. Good! I have even better news for you. *Jesus* is the Messiah! You believe the Scriptures. Good! The Scriptures speak of Jesus. Believe in Him! You honor John the Baptist. Good! John the Baptist tells you to honor Jesus!" Paul, we might say, in defining the truth they were to believe, always pushed those hearing him one step further. "So far, so good. But you need to move beyond that place to this one where you will find Jesus, and in Jesus you will find life."

PAUL AMONG THE PAGANS (ACTS 17:22-31)

In Athens Paul was faced with a very different group of people from the Jews and Gentiles he addressed in the synagogue. They had no knowledge of the Old Testament Scriptures; so his bridges could not be built on their confidence in the Scriptures or in the hope of the Messiah that the Scriptures convey. Instead, the bridges in Athens were their religious sense, their belief that there is divinity, and their understanding of the uniqueness of human persons. How did Paul clarify the message of the Gospel in this setting?

Where the Athenians had a sense of divinity so that they were prepared to build an altar to an unknown God, Paul declared with confidence that God exists, that He rules heaven and earth, and that He has made Himself known. Where even their greatest philosophers struggled to come to some knowledge of God and struggled even more to make God known to others, Paul insisted that God reveals Himself clearly through creation and through His providential rule over history, and in particular through the person of His Son, Jesus Christ. Where they recognized that human persons are God's offspring, Paul agreed and urged them to see how glorious and majestic God must be, for we, in our human and finite glory, are simply His creatures made to honor and glorify Him, the infinite and personal Lord.

Paul clarified the Gospel by telling the Athenians that their deepest longings were met in the truth of who God is. He declared that their wisest thinking was fulfilled and surpassed in the revelation God had given about Himself and that their most cherished ideas were transcended and completed in the message of Jesus, the man whom God appointed as His ambassador. Again we might summarize Paul's message to the pagans in the following way: "It is good that you have a longing to know God; it is better to come to know Him as one's own Lord and Savior. It is good that you seek after God to try to find Him; it is better to understand that God seeks after us and that despite our ignorance and willful twisting of the truth He has made Himself clearly known. It is good that you honor God as the one who gives us life; it is better to see Him in His true greatness as the Lord and Creator of everything in heaven and on earth and who cannot be contained in temples or appropriately honored by a statue."

People need to have the Gospel made clear to them. To every human person the message that must be communicated is that there is good news from God for us. The good news of the Gospel is, indeed, that Jesus is the Messiah promised by God in the writings of the Old Testament prophets. The good news is that Jesus is God's Son who died for our sins and who rose again from the dead for our justification. But the good news is also that there is a personal and infinite God who made heaven and earth and everything in them. The good news is that there is a God who is holy and just and whose character provides a moral order to this universe so that there is a distinction between good and evil. The good news is that human persons are special, for we are made in the image of the Trinitarian God who loves, who is good and kind, who thinks wise thoughts, who rules His creation, who has a marvelous imagination. The good news is that there will be a resolution to the problem of suffering, that every tear will be wiped away, that death will someday be no more for those who know Him, that righteousness and justice will one day fill the earth.

The Gospel fulfills every right longing of the human heart. It answers every honest question of the searching mind. It delights and surpasses every good impulse of the creative imagination. It meets and transcends the ache in every soul to come to know the living God. C. S. Lewis wrote concerning his own conversion that he was surprised by joy when the hopes and desires of his inner being were completely satisfied as he was humbled before God and as he put his trust in God's Son, Jesus Christ.

THE TEACHING OF JESUS

As we read through the Gospels and see Jesus' encounters with unbelievers, we find that His teaching always had a razor-sharp edge to it, clarifying a right understanding of God's Word, defining what people need to know, pressing His hearers toward a more accurate perception of the truth. Jesus was constantly trying to push people a step further toward a knowledge of God. Consider, for example, His conversation with a group of Pharisees, recorded for us in Matthew 22:41-46. Jesus began the discussion with a question: "What do you think about the Christ? Whose son is he?" The Pharisees knew the Scriptures, and so they replied, "The son of David." This answer was, of course, accurate.

The Old Testament teaches us in many places that the Messiah would be descended from David. However, Jesus desired those gathered around Him to come to a deeper understanding of the person of the Messiah. So he asked an additional and much more difficult question:

> "*How is it then that David, speaking by the Spirit, calls him 'Lord'? For he says, 'The Lord says to my Lord: "Sit at my right hand until I put your enemies under your feet."'*"

Jesus was quoting here from Psalm 110, a Psalm in which David calls the Messiah his Lord and in which he presents the Messiah as reigning at the right hand of God the Father. Jesus was eager for the Pharisees to recognize that the Scriptures acknowledge the divinity of the Christ as well as his humanity. They were aware of the good news that the Messiah was coming, and they knew He was to be descended from David; but their knowledge was incomplete. So Jesus urged them to think more deeply on the biblical texts they thought they understood so well.

On this occasion Jesus used questions to advance His hearers' understanding, and we see Him asking just such penetrating questions in many of his discussions with people. Every evangelist needs to learn from Jesus the art of asking good questions, questions that will help push people one step further toward the true knowledge of God. Evangelism is not only straight proclamation of the truth; it is also asking questions that will aid people on their journey toward faith in Jesus Christ. But whether we clarify the message of the Gospel by a bold declaration or by asking searching questions, the task is always the same—to give a wise word that will assist the understanding of non-Christians.

> *Let your conversation be always full of grace, seasoned with salt, so that you may know how to answer everyone.*
> —COLOSSIANS 4:6

38

CHALLENGING THE HEART AND MIND—PRINCIPLE VII

In this chapter we come to the final principle that is to govern our communication of the Gospel of Christ. Whenever the Gospel is proclaimed, it comes as a challenge to the heart and mind of its hearers. To come into a saving relationship with Jesus Christ, people have to "repent and believe" (Mark 1:14; etc.). They have to repent; that is, they have to turn away from their sin and from whatever they live for or put their trust in apart from Christ.

This is true if they are obvious sinners living in flagrant disobedience to God's commandments about truth-telling, about respect for other's property, or about sexual fidelity. It is also true if they are living in the service of some other god or believing some other philosophy of life. Whatever our life is like before meeting Christ, coming to Him will mean repentance, turning from something else, and turning to Jesus. This is so for everyone, for every person is a sinner, living in disobedience to God and living in rebellion against God.

Because of this reality of disobedience and rebellion, the Gospel will always be experienced as a challenge. It will challenge the mind, for it confronts false belief with the truth. It will challenge the will, for it cuts to the core of our insistence on turning away from God and going our own way. It will challenge the heart, for our hearts are devoted to many masters in place of the one true Lord. Any faithful communication of the Gospel must come with this challenge. In fact, it is appropriate to assert that if there is no challenge, there is no genuine presentation of the Gospel. Luther said that we can preach the Gospel with the loudest voice and in the clearest manner, but if we are not preaching the Gospel at the point where it is currently under attack, then we are not preaching it at all. Our apostolic examples make this point with sharp clarity.

PAUL IN THE SYNAGOGUE (ACTS 13:16-41)

How did Paul challenge his hearers in the synagogue? There were three primary areas of challenge in Paul's words to the Jews and to the Gentile God-fearers gathered to listen to his words in Pisidian Antioch. The first came in Paul's words about the unjust trial and death of Jesus in Jerusalem. It was God's people, Israel, and their rulers, appointed by the Lord to lead the people in the service of God, who had put the Messiah to death. This must have been experienced by those listening to Paul as a shocking and, for some of them, an outrageous charge. Paul did not accuse; he simply stated this as sober history and insisted that Jesus' trial was concluded without adequate evidence of crime deserving the death penalty. For those listening to Paul, accepting his words as true would mean a radical change in direction. The present rulers of the people had led them into the rejection of God's most important messenger. Jesus, crucified as a common criminal, was the Christ sent by God. This called for repentance indeed!

The second major area of challenge came in what Paul had to say about the Law of Moses. Paul, of course, recognized that the Law was indeed given to the people by God, but he argued that the Law of Moses could never provide justification for the people. They were right to devote their lives to obeying God's commandments, but no matter how hard they tried, they would never be able to keep the requirements of the Law in a manner that would satisfy God's perfect standards. Instead, Paul told them, only Jesus, in His death on the cross, was able to justify them, for through His death their sins would be forgiven if they believed in Him.

Again, this message must have come as a profound challenge to those listening. The Jews present would have been devoting their whole lives to keeping the Law. Many of them would have seen their obedience to the Law of Moses as the guarantor of their salvation. It is probable that many of the Gentiles at the service that day would have been attracted to the synagogue because of the high moral standards taught in the Law. For everyone present, Paul's words would have caused serious reevaluation of their views both of the Law and of their own obedience to it. They would have gone home reflecting on the difference between an outward conformity and inner devotion to the requirements of the Law, and newly aware of their failure to measure up to the Law's demands for love, purity, and total commitment to God.

The third major area of challenge came at the very end of Paul's message. He warned them that if they did not listen to his words with open hearts, they would be like the scoffers against God of whom the prophets wrote. Here Paul's challenge was very direct. In essence he said, "Do you want to fulfill God's warnings against those who have proud and scornful hearts?" Such a challenge was intended to make those listening question whether they were truly the people of God: "Is membership in the nation of Israel sufficient? Is it enough to attend synagogue weekly, to tithe, to fast, to pray? How do we become confident that we are known and received by God?" These words would have cut anyone with a tender conscience to the quick; and indeed we see Paul and Barnabas talking personally to several such people once the service was over.

These three challenges were directed to the heart of what it meant to be a faithful worshiper of God, both for the Israelites and for the Gentiles hearing Paul's words. The hope of the Messiah as the deliverer of the nation, devotion to the Law, ownership of God's Word, and the conviction of being God's people—these were the strengths and glories of Judaism at that time. These were their pride and security, their basis for confidence in a hostile world, their sense of identity, the measure of what made them a unique and special race. Because of these distinctive marks they thought of themselves as a superior people, morally and religiously, compared with the pagans surrounding them. Paul aimed to shatter these notions and bring the people to their knees before God so that they might see their dependence on His mercy demonstrated in the life, death, and resurrection of Jesus Christ.

PAUL AMONG THE PAGANS (ACTS 17:22-31)

The challenges Paul made to the Athenians were very different from those he presented in the synagogue. But again they focus on what is at the heart of their way of life and worship. His first major area of challenge was the idolatry everywhere apparent on Mars Hill. "You," he says in essence, "should know better than worshiping at these temples. God is the Creator of all; He inhabits heaven and earth, not stone and marble structures erected by human hands. How can you think it is fitting to worship God in the form of an idol adorned with gold, silver, and precious jewels? These statues are simply the products of human design, and you yourselves know that human persons are the result of God's design. This is ignorance and folly!"

It may seem obvious to us that the Athenians' idolatry ought to be challenged, but we should remember that the buildings on Mars Hill were some of the most beautiful artifacts ever conceived and created by human imagination and architectural skill. These structures and statues were wonders of the ancient world, and some of them are still wonders of the world today! Paul, however, called those people to repentance. "God," he says in summary, "has in His long-suffering overlooked such foolishness, but no longer! Now is the time to turn away from all this to worship the true and living God."

Paul's second area of challenge was closely related to the first. He commended the Athenians for their desire to worship. He quoted their own writers with approval, for they had reflected on the glory of what it means to be human. He expressed appreciation for the thinking of the Stoics and Epicureans. But he moved on to tell them that their schools of philosophy, their wisest thinkers, did not have sufficient wisdom to lead them to the true knowledge of God. In comparison to the clarity of God's revelation of Himself in Jesus Christ, all their wisdom was darkness and ignorance. This challenge must have shocked those present to the core of their being. The wise men of Athens and their schools of philosophy were famed all over the ancient world. And yet not these great men but Jesus, a Jew they had never heard of, was the One through whom God had decided to make Himself known to the human race.

Paul's third challenge touched their sense of being a people set apart. The Athenians believed they were a superior race, God's gift to humanity. They looked down on other peoples as ignorant children and slaves who needed to learn from their Athenian wisdom. Paul, in contrast, told them that the human race is one, that it has a common ancestry. In addition, he said, true wisdom comes not from Greece but from Israel, and it is not an Athenian but a despised Hebrew who is the One sent by God to be the Judge of the human race. Nobody likes to have their sense of superiority called into question, but this was exactly what Paul did.

Paul's fourth challenge had to do with the resurrection of Jesus from the dead. This was the issue that had already caused some of the Athenians to refer to Paul as a "babbler." Most Greek thinking of that time accepted the idea of an afterlife, but it was thought of as a state in which the spirit would finally be set free from its bondage to a physical body and to a material world. The physical was regarded as temporary and inferior, the spiritual as eternal and far better. Aeschylus, in his play *The Eumenides*, has the god Apollo say:

> *But once the dust drinks down a man's blood,*
> *he is gone, once for all. No rising back,*
> *[literally, there is no resurrection]*
> *no spell sung over the grave can sing him back—*
> *not even Father can [i.e., Zeus, the Father of the gods].*

In the play the occasion of these words is the inauguration of the Areopagus court by Athena, the goddess of Athens, for the judging of Orestes. But in direct contrast the apostle declared in effect, "There is resurrection!" God had given proof of this truth to all people by raising a man from the dead. That man was Jesus, and God had raised Him up that he might be the Judge of everyone (Athenians and philosophers included!). Paul confronted the notion of the worthlessness of the body head-on. God designed human beings as physical/spiritual persons, and He intends that this is who we will be eternally.

Just as with the Jews, Paul's challenges were spoken to the beliefs and convictions that were at the heart of what it meant to be Greek, and above all Athenian. These cherished notions were their glory and their pride. Paul's purpose was to bring them to a point where they would begin to question their most precious assumptions about themselves and to doubt what they had believed. Only when this happened would they be humbled before God, turn away from what had captured their devotion, and turn instead to Jesus as their sole hope and confidence before

God. Christ must be their wisdom, their source of boasting, the One who gives them a sense of identity, their secure anchor for eternity.

Reflecting on the challenges Paul made in these two different settings, we should notice that it was the most precious things in each culture that Paul confronted. Why was this? At the heart of all sin, unbelief, and rebellion against God is pride. This was true for the Israelites who were the recipients of God's special revelation and therefore possessed God's gifts of the Word, the Law, the land, the patriarchs, the temple, and the Messianic promises. It was also true for the Greeks who were the recipients of God's general revelation and who therefore possessed God's gifts of wisdom, philosophy, poetry, drama, architecture, and sculpture.

Any gift of God, even His most precious gifts to any culture or individual, can become an idol, the thing we worship in place of God. It is not that there is something inherently twisted or idolatrous about the gifts God gives us, whether his Word, wisdom, beautiful buildings, or artistic abilities. God forbid that we should reject or slander His most special and lovely gifts to us! The problem is in the human heart, not in the gifts of God. It is we, individually and collectively, who turn from God, the Giver, to the gifts and make them into idols. Whatever is our glory we turn to our shame. Whatever most demonstrates God's kindness to us we pervert into a means of refusing to bow before Him. Instead of worshiping Him we congratulate ourselves that we are special because we have this particular gift. Instead of being humbled by God's generosity we think we are better than others who lack what has been entrusted to us. We make God's goodness shown to us in His gifts into a barrier between Him and ourselves and a barrier between ourselves and others. We become proud before God, self-satisfied, and critical of our fellows.

This is the reason why Paul commended what is good and true in the heritage and thinking of those gathered in the synagogue and of those gathered in the Areopagus, and yet he challenged them at the very same points where he commended them. The pathways for the Gospel are at the same time the problems for the Gospel; the bridges for the Gospel are its barriers. When we communicate the Gospel to anyone, we have to deal with those things that stand between a person and God, even if they are the most treasured possessions of the heart. Unless we have the courage to do this, we will not proclaim the Gospel faithfully, and people will not come to a saving relationship with Christ.

What are some of the major areas that must be challenged in our American culture early in this new millennium? We can begin to answer this question by reflecting on the glories of our culture, for it is these glories that will also be our shame, these gifts of God that we will worship instead of worshiping Him. We are one of the wealthiest nations the world has ever seen. Many of us experience the riches of a comfortable life that would have been unimaginable just a few years ago. Yet it is obvious to any thoughtful observer that God's good and generous material gifts to us are a source of pride, self-satisfaction, and above all, idolatry. It is not popular to challenge the idol of materialism, but it is essential if the Gospel is to be clearly proclaimed today. This has to be done, not by declaring that it is wrong to enjoy good things, but by exposing the failure to worship God alone. Jesus put it very simply: "No one can serve two masters. . . . You cannot serve both God and Money" (Matthew 6:24).

A second area for challenge in our culture is the understanding of freedom. We spoke of this in an earlier chapter, but here it needs to be stressed that unless we confront the notion of complete freedom to do what one wills, it is impossible to call people to faith in Jesus Christ. One cannot serve Christ and at the same time bow to the idol of autonomous freedom. People cannot obey God and be a law unto themselves.

A third point for challenge is closely related to freedom; it is the emphasis on self-affirmation that is so prevalent in our society. One of the glories of our culture is the value placed on the individual; but it does not take much wisdom to see that the family and every other social institution suffers at the mercy of the individual's pursuit of self-satisfaction. The message of self-affirmation and self-fulfillment is a constant cry of pop psychology, New Age religion, and the media: "You have to live for yourself and nobody else."

Even many churches and television ministries preach this message, and indeed there is a fulfillment of the self that is promised to us in the Gospel. But at the same time, Jesus challenges us to deny ourselves, to take up our cross, and to follow Him. Paul calls us to imitate Christ by thinking more highly of others than we think of ourselves. The biblical message is this: We have been created and redeemed to love God first and to love others as ourselves. According to the Scriptures this is the only way to be fulfilled, and this is the message that needs to be proclaimed clearly to our culture and to our churches. Only if we lose ourselves will we find ourselves. This is not a popular message, but it is fundamental to the Gospel of Christ.

A fourth idol of our time is the idol of tolerance. We properly delight in the diversity of the society in which we live, a diversity of races, of peoples, of cultures and their varied and rich heritages. Yet this delight in diversity easily becomes a refusal to value what is eternally true and good. "Let everyone value what he or she wishes. Let no one claim to have truth or to know what is right and good for all." In the face of this mentality the exclusive claim of the Christian message is an offense. But the truth is that there is only one way of salvation, only one name under heaven by which we can come to know God. Unless this is stated forthrightly, no matter how troublesome an idea it is to our contemporaries, we cannot preach Christ.

One final word of warning needs to be made here. God requires us to challenge people with His truth. Unless we challenge the idols of our time, we will not honor Him, nor will people come to know Christ through us. However, we are to always remember that God's Word is a two-edged sword. One sharp edge is given to us to wound people and call them to repentance; the other sharp edge is given to us to heal people with the gracious message of the Gospel. When we challenge the idols of our time, we need to recall this other edge of the Spirit's sword and bear in mind some warnings for ourselves.

The first is that we must never challenge others from a position of superiority. We have worshiped, and we continue to worship, at the same altars that attract people around us. It is never our place to attack and condemn, for if we do we will be condemning ourselves. We are to challenge and wound in order that people might be healed, not that we might delight in pointing out their faults. We are to wound only as those who know we suffer with the same wound.

The second warning is that as those who have been healed of our wounds by the grace of Jesus Christ, we are to always communicate grace even as we challenge. We have received the grace of Jesus Christ; it ought to be our passion to extend that same graciousness to others.

No matter how penetrating our words exposing the idols of the heart, we are to be full of mercy in our attitude.

> *Always be prepared to give an answer . . . for the hope that you have. But do this with gentleness and respect.*
>
> —1 PETER 3:15-16

> *Let your conversation be always full of grace.*
>
> —COLOSSIANS 4:6

CONCLUSION

The principles of communication that have been set out in the last few chapters are not intended to be another "seven-step program" of evangelism. They are simply an attempt to draw out some lessons for us all from the examples of evangelism that we find described for us in the pages of Acts along with a few supplementary accounts from the Gospels.

In another book (on which I am already working) I would like to explore in much greater depth some of the many stories of Jesus' work of evangelism recorded for us in the four Gospels. Jesus is the Great Evangelist in every conceivable way! Without His work on the cross no one could be saved. Without His asking His Father to send the Spirit, no one would ever come to faith. In His earthly ministry we see Him putting into "evangelistic" practice the grace that sent Him to the cross to bear the just punishment due to us. Christ communicates the truth in a manner that is supportive and illustrative of His love in dying for us. His communication of the truth is the pattern par excellence of evangelism. Jesus lived the principles I have sought to express in these chapters.

And when we turn to Paul's own testimony. he tells us that the principles by which he operated reveal his attempt to be an imitator of Christ. We have already seen the words in which he describes his work of evangelism: "I have become all things to all men so that by all possible means I might save some" (1 Corinthians 9:22). Later in the same letter Paul adds: "I try to please everybody in every way. For I am not seeking my own good, but the good of many, so that they may be saved. Follow my example, as I follow the example of Christ" (1 Corinthians 10:33—11:1). Elsewhere he writes, "Whatever you have learned or received or heard from me, or seen in me—put it into practice. And the God of peace will be with you" (Philippians 4:9).

The seven principles set out in this book are an attempt to describe how Paul devoted himself to the imitation of Christ. In looking at Paul's life it has been my desire for myself and my prayer for you, the reader, that, whatever we have truly seen of Christ in our study of Paul, we would commit ourselves to put that into practice. It is my longing that you and I might, with Paul, be imitators of Christ. The God of peace be with you!

Scripture Index

GENERAL INDEX